AMERICAN EDUCATION

Its Men

Ideas

and

Institutions

The History
of Educational Legislation
in Ohio
From 1803 to 1850

Edward Alanson Miller

ARNO PRESS & THE NEW YORK TIMES
*New York * 1969*

Reprint edition 1969 by Arno Press, Inc.

*

Library of Congress Catalog Card No. 72-89204

*

Reprinted from a copy in Teachers College Library

*

Manufactured in the United States of America

Editorial Note

AMERICAN EDUCATION: *Its Men, Institutions and Ideas* presents selected works of thought and scholarship that have long been out of print or otherwise unavailable. Inevitably, such works will include particular ideas and doctrines that have been outmoded or superseded by more recent research. Nevertheless, all retain their place in the literature, having influenced educational thought and practice in their own time and having provided the basis for subsequent scholarship.

Lawrence A. Cremin
Teachers College

The History
of Educational Legislation
in Ohio
From 1803 to 1850

SUPPLEMENTARY EDUCATIONAL MONOGRAPHS

Published in conjunction with

THE SCHOOL REVIEW *and* THE ELEMENTARY SCHOOL JOURNAL

Vol. III

September, 1920

No. 2

Whole No. 13

The History of
Educational Legislation in Ohio
From 1803 to 1850

First printed in
Ohio Archaeological and Historical Quarterly
Volume XXVII, Nos. 1 and 2

The History of
Educational Legislation in Ohio
From 1803 to 1850

By

EDWARD ALANSON MILLER, Ph.D.

Professor of Education
Oberlin College

THE UNIVERSITY OF CHICAGO
CHICAGO, ILLINOIS

PREFACE

Ohio's educational history has been an especially interesting one. Many causes have combined to make it so. It was the first state admitted from the Northwest Territory, and as such carried on the earliest experiments with the great state-wide grant of school lands that has characterized our policy since that time in the admission of new states to the Union. It was settled with unexampled rapidity, changing from a wilderness frontier to a great and prosperous commonwealth in a single generation. The settlement was a singularly heterogeneous one, coming from the East, the Middle States, and the South, with a considerable influx directly from Europe. These early settlements were being established, too, while those democratic and individualistic tendencies that marked the first decades of the nineteenth century were in progress. During these years the district school idea was at its height in Massachusetts and the East, the private academy was displacing the town grammar school, and state control of public education was at low ebb.

These causes, with others more local in nature, were instrumental in shaping the educational activities of the state in the first fifty years of its history and have left their imprint on all the later development.

It is my purpose to give a careful study and interpretation of the educational legislation of the state from territorial days down to 1850. In this legislation one finds the truest expression of the constructive educational thought and activity of the period.

In such a study there must be included not merely the laws that bear on the development of a state system of public education, but the much larger number that are concerned with private educational ventures of various kinds. To these must be added those laws that bear on higher and professional education, all that touch upon supplementary agencies of any kind, and also any provisions made for the indigent, defective, and delinquent classes.

A study of this kind is needed as a background before any adequate state or national history of education is possible. Such a study also gives the general student of history a view of one of the most important phases in the social development of a state, and a closer acquaintance with the growth of some of the most important institutions that society has discovered to aid it in its progress.

I have attempted in the following pages to present the material in such a way that it will be of service to the general student, and also in the appendixes to furnish a guide for anyone desiring further information from the source material on any particular phase of the state's educational activities.

The plan of arrangement is as follows: A discussion and interpretation of the laws passed from 1803 to 1850; Appendix A, a classified list of the titles of the more important acts; Appendix B, a complete index, page and volume, to all the legislation that in any way touches upon education, in the session laws of Ohio from 1803 to 1850, including both the general and the local laws.

In many cases I have not given the exact titles in the appendixes, for the sake of both brevity and clearness; enough of titles and content to indicate the general meaning of the act is given. In Appendix A a brief abstract of the laws is also included where it seemed necessary to give more information than the title itself conveys.

This is especially the case in the acts of incorporation of that large number of secondary and higher institutions that were so abundant in the first fifty years of Ohio's history. A complete tabulation of these acts is here given, and, as it is the only complete list of these institutions that has been made, it seemed best to preserve in a few words the chief points of historical interest that appear in the laws.

I felt this to be particularly the case with the secondary schools. These have nearly all passed out of existence, and, as they mark one of the most important stages in the development of our secondary education, a somewhat more complete abstract is given than that dealing with most of the other subjects.

The public-school laws are more easily accessible and they are usually indicated by title only. There was an exceptionally large amount of legislation, especially of a local and special character, dealing with the school lands. The more important of these acts are included by title in the first appendix with a mere tabulation of those that had only local significance.

The laws in Appendix A are grouped under the following headings:

I.   The public-school system.
  1. General legislation.
    a) Acts to incorporate the original surveyed townships including provisions for districting, establishing schools, apportioning money, etc.
    b) General school laws.
    c) Special acts concerning public schools.
    d) Fines, fees, etc., applied to the support of public schools.
  2. City and town school charters.
    a) Laws concerning common schools in cities and towns.
    b) Acts concerning local school funds.
    c) Acts concerning schools for poor children.
II. Laws concerning school lands.
  1. General laws concerning school lands.
  2. Special acts concerning school lands.
III. Secondary and higher education.
  1. Acts incorporating secondary institutions.
  2. Acts incorporating school associations.
  3. Acts concerning higher institutions.
    a) Colleges, universities, and theological seminaries.
  4. Acts concerning professional education.
    a) Medical education.
    b) Legal education.
IV. Acts concerning the education of defectives, dependents, and delinquents.
  1. Education of defectives.
  2. Education of dependents.
  3. Education of delinquents.
V.   Acts concerning the education of teachers.
VI. Acts concerning supplementary educational agencies.

Appendix B furnishes a page and volume index to all laws, resolutions, and memorials that have any educational significance in either the general or the local laws from 1803 to 1850. The indexes in the volumes of the session laws themselves are sometimes defective, and they are, too, an unreliable guide, as many important items are found in laws the titles to which give no hint that they contain material that relates in any way to education.

The primary source material has been the session laws of the state of Ohio. The Revised Statutes for this period have also been consulted.

It was found necessary to examine all the laws of the period, special and general, as the titles and indexes were not dependable. A considerable quantity of material was also found in the resolutions and memorials.

The United States Statutes at Large were used to secure federal legislation concerning school lands in Ohio.   Nashee's A Compilation of Laws, Treaties and Ordinances Which Relate to Lands in the State of Ohio was relied upon especially for acts passed during the territorial period.

The earliest congressional legislation was secured from the *Journals of the American Congress*, reprinted by Way and Gideon, in 1823, under the title as given.

The chief secondary sources consulted are indicated in the bibliography.

CONTENTS

GENERAL INTRODUCTION

This monograph is the second of a series on the history of the educational legislation of various states, principally in the period 1776–1850. In the first monograph, "Educational Legislation and Administration in the State of New York from 1777 to 1850," by Elsie Garland Hobson, there will be found a general introduction to this series explaining its scope and purpose. Attention is called to the fact that these monographs represent an effort to vitalize American educational history by emphasizing its institutional aspects, heretofore greatly neglected. The tendency to consider educational theory and method as the chief subject-matter of our educational history has done much harm, for no great progress can be made toward a comprehensive understanding of the evolution of American education until we have an accurate knowledge of all the laws passed by each state, affecting either public or private education. That knowledge is not now available. It may be noted also that detailed studies of this sort are of great importance to students of the general history of the United States, or the individual states, as well as to those who are especially interested in our social, religious, economic, or political history. The lack of such studies is the reason for the inadequate and inaccurate account of American education in general and special histories of the types mentioned above. The present volume is of special interest because it shows how the first frontier state formed from the Northwest Territory reacted to the problem of education and how it dealt with the difficult problem of the management of the federal land grants for the endowment of public education. The experience of Ohio had great influence on the attitude of other western states toward this problem. Professor Miller has made available information from original sources, hitherto practically inaccessible, and has given in the appendixes the data which make it possible for one to investigate in still greater detail the relation of the state of Ohio to education to 1850, so far as it is expressed in the legislation.

MARCUS W. JERNEGAN

UNIVERSITY OF CHICAGO
March 24, 1919

CHAPTER I

THE SOURCES OF OHIO'S PUBLIC-SCHOOL SYSTEM

INTRODUCTORY

Ohio was admitted into the Union as a state February 19, 1803.[1] It was the first state admitted from the Northwest Territory and the first state to which the grant of Section 16 for school purposes was made. The legislation concerning school lands was intimately connected with the development of the public-school system, and in the method to be adopted to make this great grant productive of the desired results Ohio had no precedents or warnings for her guidance.[2]

The constitution adopted when Ohio became a state remained in force until 1851. It made no specific provisions for education, but stated that means of education[3] should be encouraged by legislative enactments; that all institutions of all grades, endowed in whole or in part from revenues derived from the donations of the United States, should be open without distinction to all scholars; and that associations of persons might receive letters of incorporation from the legislature to enable them to hold estates for the support of their schools, academies, colleges, and universities.

No provision for public schools was made by any general law during the first eighteen years after Ohio's admission, the first school law being passed in 1821.[4] From this period until 1850 eight general school codes were enacted with numerous amendments and supplementary acts and a mass of special legislation concerning particular districts or territories.

The traditions of Ohio were from the first against centralization.[5] The first constitution was formed soon after the bitter political struggle between Jefferson and Adams, and at a time when the arbitrary domination of the territorial governor, Arthur

[1] Statistical Abstract of U.S., 1910, p. 21.

[2] Land set aside for individual towns had been common in New England and elsewhere, but there was no precedent to direct action in the case of a state-wide grant intended for the use of the individual townships.

[3] O.L., I., Art. 8, Sec. 3; Art. 8, Sec. 25; Art. 8, Sec. 27.

[4] O.L., XIX, 51.

[5] Orth, *The Centralization of Administration in Ohio*, p. 11.

St. Clair, had prejudiced the people against centralized executive power. Nowhere is this prejudice against centralized administration better illustrated than in the various phases of educational legislation. The tendency throughout the period under discussion was to depend largely upon local initiative and control. The encouragement of education by legislative provision specified in the constitution was interpreted by the legislature to mean the passing of a larger number of local acts to meet the special needs or desires of particular districts, or even, in the case of school lands, the desires of individuals, while the general laws may be said to have pointed out methods of organization and control rather than to have devised any efficient system of supervision or penalties actually to bring about specific educational results.

The general laws are largely permissive in character, with the initiative left in many cases to the discretion of the local community. There are doubtless other reasons for this than the prejudice against the acts of Arthur St. Clair and the general political state of mind in the West during the early period of Ohio's history.

Ohio in its early statehood was a frontier community, settled by a class of people that in the very nature of the case were compelled largely to be self-reliant and to solve their own problems, educational as well as other. It was a heavily timbered area. Means of communication were difficult. It would have been a hard matter to establish any general system of control or supervision in the early period, and when means of communication had become simplified, through a system of state roads and canals,[1] the people had become habituated to attending to their own educational needs.

The settlers in Ohio, too, had no common educational background. They came from New England, from Virginia, Maryland, and Kentucky, and, in fact, from nearly all the older states.[2]

A glance at the map on page 55 shows that the state was divided into a number of separate districts such as the Western Reserve, the Ohio Company's Purchase, the Symmes Purchase, the Virginia Military Lands, and the United States Military Lands. The early settlements in these sections were usually made up of people who came into the wilderness together from one or another of the older states of the Union.

[1] A large part of the early legislation of Ohio is concerned with state roads, turnpike companies, plank roads, canals, etc.

[2] Atwater, *A History of the State of Ohio, Natural and Civil*, p. 351.

Each of these districts, in its customs and ideals, reflected the current thought and practice of that part of the country from which its settlers came, and in no field was this more evident than in that of education. The Ohio Company's Purchase and the Western Reserve were at first largely settled by colonists from New England. Marietta, dating from 1787, and Cleveland, from 1796, were the respective centers of influence in these two districts.

Three colonies were planted in the Symmes Purchase in 1788; the one at Losantiville, later rechristened Cincinnati by Governor St. Clair, was destined to be in many ways a leader for the entire state as well as for the Miami country. The early settlers here, as at Marietta, had many of them seen service in the Revolutionary War. They came from no single locality, but New Jersey men seemed most prominent in the early settlement, aided by the other Middle States.[1] Later there were many settlers from Virginia, Maryland, Pennsylvania, New York, and the New England states.

The Virginia Military Lands,[2] located between the Little Miami and the Scioto rivers, received its first settlers from Virginia and the South. General Nathaniel Massie and Duncan McArthur founded Chillicothe, on the Scioto River, in 1796, the first colony in this district.

On the eastern edge of the state, south of the Western Reserve, are the so-called Seven Ranges, the name given to the ranges of townships first surveyed in Ohio. While there was no such colonization here as in the districts already named, the first settlers were largely from Pennsylvania, and of German stock, with a considerable number of Irish, Scotch, and Scotch-Irish.

The United States Military Lands seem to have had no early homogeneous group, but drew settlers from all the older states.

There was also a considerable French settlement at Gallipolis and a sprinkling of French all along the Ohio River.

From 1830 on there was a very considerable German influence from the influx of German immigrants that began at that time.[3]

The population increased with astonishing rapidity after Ohio was admitted as a state, constant accessions from the older states were added to the early settlements, and in the years from 1810 to

[1] Charles Cist, *Cincinnati in 1841—Its Early Annals and Future Prospects*, p. 38; Hinsdale, *The Old Northwest*, pp. 288-89.

[2] *Ibid.*, p. 290; *Western Reserve Historical Society*, II, pp. 153-54.

[3] Orth, *The Centralization of Administration in Ohio*, p. 164; Chaddock, *Ohio Before 1850. A Study of the Early Influence of Pennsylvania and Southern Populations in Ohio*, p. 30.

1840 the transformation from a thickly wooded frontier to a settled farming community had largely taken place. The census figures from 1800 to 1850 give some idea of this transformation. At the beginning of the century the population was 45,365; fifty years later it had increased to 1,980,329. The record of increase by decades which follows gives an even better picture of the sudden changes that must have occurred:

1800.....................................	45,365
1810.....................................	230,760
1820.....................................	580,434
1830.....................................	937,903
1840.....................................	1,519,467
1850.....................................	1,980,329[1]

The census figures for the last decade of this period show a foreign-born population of 218,193. In 1850 there were almost as many people of foreign birth in the state as its entire population had amounted to only forty years earlier in 1810. These people of foreign birth were largely of German stock.

It was no easy problem to develop a system of education to meet the needs of this surprising growth, coming as it did from all the older states and from foreign shores.

There was in these early years no agreement as to the means of financing any general system of education, nor any real agreement as to the needs of such a system. The educational traditions were quite different in different portions of the state. Samuel Lewis in his second annual report in 1838 says: "The people have not heretofore followed any particular system. The directors of each district have done that which was right in their own eyes, and generally adopted, as far as they could, the particular system of the state from whence they came."[2] Those from the South brought traditions of the private school and parental responsibility for education. The New England settlers brought with them the idea of a public-school system, with taxation and public control, but unfortunately for Ohio's subsequent educational history the New England migration came at a period when the public-school sentiment in Massachusetts and the East was at a comparatively low ebb, and when the decentralizing tendency that gave Massachusetts the district-school legislation of 1789 was at its time of greatest influence.

[1] Statistical Abstract of U.S., Washington, 1911, p. 40.
[2] Ohio Documents, 1838, Doc. 32, p. 30.

From this time for nearly forty years the process of decentralization went on. Martin says the year 1827 is "the high-water mark of modern democracy and the low-water mark of the Massachusetts school system."[1] The New England influence in Ohio began with the Marietta colony in 1787. By 1830 the population of the state had reached nearly a million, and it was during just these years that the school sentiment in Massachusetts was lowest.

It was at this time, too, that the academy was supplanting the Latin grammar school of the colonial period as the typical secondary school.

The New England settlers favored the public-school idea, but it was the highly decentralized district system with which they were familiar. The academy idea was the common possession of settlers from all the states.

The common school as a district school, the secondary school as an academy, were two fundamental conceptions in the minds of all those who were active in securing Ohio's early school legislation. While many influences were thus instrumental in shaping Ohio's early educational history, her debt to New England for the men and ideas most significant in determining her early public-school system is so large that a brief sketch of a few of these men and of the forces that worked through them is a necessary prerequisite to an intelligent study of the development of that system.

The most important of these forces were, first, the school lands;[2] secondly, the conception of a state system of schools; and, thirdly, the idea of state-wide taxation for the benefit of such a system.

The use of public lands for the aid and support of schools had its origin in New England. The men most instrumental in urging Ohio's first law, giving a legal basis to the conception of a state system of schools, were born in New England. The men most active in legalizing the idea of state-wide taxation to support this system were also New England born, and the man who did most to make these ideas, incorporated into law, actually operative in the establishment of schools and to give a real organization to the system legally created was a man of New England birth.

When Ohio was admitted as a state, Section 16 in each township, or an equivalent amount of land in those districts not belong-

[1] Martin, *The Evolution of the Massachusetts School System: A Historical Sketch*, p. 92.

[2] A discussion of the school lands, with maps, methods of survey, etc., is given in chapter iii.

ing to the United States, was permanently set aside for the use of schools.

This grant gave for the use of schools an amount of land equal to one square mile, or 640 acres, for each surveyed township of 36 square miles.

The practice of using public lands for the support of schools had been from early colonial times a common New England device, and by 1647 certain towns had "assumed responsibility for the support of schools out of public property, partly through gifts of land to schoolmasters, partly by setting aside tracts of land as a permanent endowment."[1]

This New England practice first found state-wide expression when Ohio was admitted to the Union, and from that time on became an established policy in the admission of all later states. The Ordinance of 1785 "for ascertaining the mode of disposing of lands in the Western territory"[2] reserved Section 16 in each township "for the maintenance of public schools within the said township." This provision, according to Donaldson,[3] was the inception of the rule of the reservation of certain sections of land for school purposes. The first action in accord with this provision occurred within the next two years, when Manasseh Cutler, as agent for the Ohio Company, completed the bargain for the lands acquired by the company at the mouth of the Muskingum.[4] Not only did Mr. Cutler obtain a reaffirmation of the provision for the grant of Section 16 for school purposes, but a grant of Section 29 in each township for the support of religion, and also an added grant of two townships for the support of a university. It was this bargain of the Ohio Company, engineered by Manasseh Cutler, that put into actual operation the provisions of the Ordinance of 1785 concerning school lands. This was followed immediately by the Symmes Purchase, between the Miami rivers, and Sections 16 and 29 were similarly reserved.

With the admission of Ohio as a state the same provision for schools, Section 16 or its equivalent for each township, was extended to the remainder of the state except the portion still held by the Indian tribes. Ultimately the reservation was extended to all territory within the state.

[1] Jernegan, "The Beginnings of Public Education in New England," *School Review*, XXIII, 379.
[2] Laws of U.S., 1789–1815, Vol. I, chap. xxxii.
[3] T. Donaldson, *The Public Domain*, chap. xiii.
[4] Hinsdale, *The Old Northwest*, p. 268.

In this state-wide grant was found an interest that directed the attention of settlers in all parts of the state, and from all parts of the United States, to the purpose for which the grants were made, the schools. The first legislation concerning schools is found in efforts made to work out a method of handling the school lands, and they remain during Ohio's early statehood one of the persistent incentives to educational legislation and a constant suggestion of a state school system.

The first general school act for Ohio was passed January 22, 1821.[1] It is a significant fact that the four men most instrumental in putting on the statute books of Ohio laws providing for a tax-supported system of common schools were all born in Massachusetts. These men were Ephraim Cutler, Caleb Atwater, Nathan Guilford, and Samuel Lewis.

Ephraim Cutler, of Ames, Washington County, near Marietta, was the son of Manasseh Cutler, the inspired lobbyist of the Ohio Company. He was born in Edgartown, Massachusetts, but spent his boyhood in Killingly, Connecticut, with his grandparents and came to Ohio in his early manhood. He was one of the drafters of the state constitution, and it was due to his efforts that there were incorporated the clauses providing that "religion, morality and knowledge, as essentially necessary to good government," were to be supported by the General Assembly and "that schools and the means of instruction shall forever be encouraged by legislative provision."[2]

Judge Cutler in December, 1819, introduced a bill in the House of Representatives providing for a system of common schools. The bill as introduced was passed by the House, but was allowed to die without action in the Senate. It was this bill, however, that led to the law of 1821, a substitute measure that did little more than outline a method of school organization and in so doing recognized the state's responsibility of legislating for schools.

Caleb Atwater was born in North Adams, Massachusetts.[3] He was appointed one of a committee of seven, in December, 1821, to consider the subject of schools and school lands and report to the House of Representatives. As a result of the deliberations of this committee a commission of five was appointed, January, 1822,

[1] O.L., XIX, 21.
[2] Cutler, *Life and Times of Ephraim Cutler*, pp. 8, 114.
[3] *History of Franklin and Pickawy Counties, Ohio*, p. 98.

to report to the next General Assembly on a system of common schools.

This commission collected much valuable material, which was presented to the Assembly in 1823, but the friends of education were in a minority, and no legislative action was taken during that session. One of the members of this commission was Nathan Guilford, a book-dealer and publisher of Cincinnati, the editor of *The Freeman's Almanack*, a western counterpart of *Poor Richard*, popularly known as *Solomon Thrifty's Almanack*.

Mr. Guilford was born in Spencer, Massachusetts,[1] and was educated at Yale. He was a constant advocate of popular education and of taxation for schools in Ohio.

Samuel Lewis, Ohio's first and greatest state superintendent of schools, was born in Falmouth, Massachusetts,[2] but came to Ohio as a boy. He was the author of, and prime mover for, the school law of 1838, which gave to Ohio its first completely organized school system.

The act of 1821 had done little more than legalize means by which the settlers in the townships could move to lay off districts and establish schools. It made no provision for taxation and organized no definite system. It was, however, important as the first state recognition of a system of common schools. It was evident to friends of public education that the law of 1821 was inadequate and ineffective, and there began at once a campaign for a more effective law.

Nathan Guilford used the sayings of Solomon Thrifty to arouse the people of the state to the need of a free common school education. In 1824 he says: "The Legislatures of Ohio and Kentucky have taken the subject of free schools into consideration. It is hoped that their zealous endeavors to establish a system of common education will be crowned with success. Millions unborn would rise and bless them."[3]

Caleb Atwater and his committee, after careful study and much correspondence, had recommended a commission of seven to report on the subject of the school lands and a school system. This commission[4] consisted of Caleb Atwater, Rev. John Collins, Rev. James Hoge, Nathan Guilford, Ephraim Cutler, Josiah Barber, and

---

[1] Randall and Ryan, *History of Ohio*, III, 374.
[2] William G. W. Lewis, *Biography of Samuel Lewis*, p. 13.
[3] "Maxims and Advice of Solomon Thrifty," *The Freeman's Almanack*, 1824.
[4] Atwater, *A History of the State of Ohio, Natural and Civil*, p. 259.

James Bell. The number corresponded with the total number of different grants of school lands, and each man was to study and report upon the condition of the lands in the territory assigned him. Caleb Atwater was assigned the Congress Lands; John Collins, the Virginia Military Lands; James Hoge, the Refugee Lands; James Bell, the United States Military Lands; Ephraim Cutler, the Ohio Company Lands; Nathan Guilford, the Symmes Purchase Lands; and Josiah Barber, the Connecticut Western Reserve Lands.

It was evidently the original opinion of many of the settlers in Ohio, and perhaps the design of Congress, that these land grants, if properly managed, would support public schools without a tax upon the citizens. There was a growing belief, however, that this one source of income would continue to prove inadequate. Nathan Guilford, who strongly advocated taxation, did not serve upon the commission, evidently believing that he could aid the cause of education better as a free lance. He addressed a public letter to the chairman of the board arguing for a school tax upon property and insisting that an adequate school fund could not be raised from the school lands alone.

The commission had been directed to report upon three topics: the actual condition of the school lands; a bill proposing a system of school law; a report on the necessity and value of the system proposed. Pamphlets were issued on these topics and widely circulated, and they served to awaken an interest throughout the state in public education.

The system proposed was modeled on the New York state system.[1] It provided for an economical management of the school lands, but made no provision for taxation. The legislature of 1823 was, however, opposed to any liberal action for public education. Atwater says: "In this legislature were many influential men who were opposed to a school system, to a sale of school lands and to internal improvements. . . . . This session had a majority of both houses opposed to a school system and the sale of school lands, and all that was done by them was to quarrel about these subjects. They finally broke up in a row and went home."[2]

In the campaign for the state election of 1824 the subjects of internal improvements, the public-school system, and the taxation

[1] Lewis, *Biography of Samuel Lewis*, p. 101.
[2] Atwater, *A History of the State of Ohio, Natural and Civil*, p. 261.

system of the state were the main issues before the people. A majority favorable to the public schools and internal improvements was chosen, among them Nathan Guilford, elected to represent Cincinnati. When the legislature assembled, Governor Morrow presented the necessity for adequate legislation on all these questions. His message recognizes the difficulty of bringing people of divergent educational views, with no common educational inheritance, to united action for public schools. In discussing the subject he says:[1] "In this state there are causes, extensive in their nature, for difference of opinion on the subject. The population is composed principally of emigrants from the different States of the Union, with habits and modes of thinking on the subject, as different as are the regulations of the States from whence they came. . . . . The act of the 22nd of January, 1821," he declares, is ineffective because the establishment of schools and school districts was made optional for the voters in each township. "Was this act made positive, and in some respects modified, we should have a system in force—perhaps not perfect—for the regulation of common schools, which could be further improved, as experience under it should point out its defects." A joint committee[2] was at once appointed in the General Assembly to study the subject and report an adequate bill. Mr. Guilford was made chairman of this committee and drafted the report and bill, which finally passed both houses without amendment and became the law of 1825. There was a widespread feeling in the state against imposing a tax for general school purposes, but Mr. Guilford and Mr. Cutler stood firm for this measure, and, with the assistance of the supporters of the public-school idea, insured its passage by forming an active coalition with those legislators who were working in the interests of internal improvements, especially the advocates of state canals. In this work Mr. Guilford showed himself a skilled lobbyist and shrewd judge of men in his personal campaign among the members of both houses.[3]

While the vote was proceeding in the house Mr. Cutler stood beside Mr. Guilford as they anxiously awaited the outcome, and when the result was announced, and it was assured that taxation for education had prevailed, he turned to his companion and

---

[1] Taylor, *A Manual of the Ohio School System*, pp. 132, 133.
[2] *Ibid.*, p. 141.
[3] Lewis, *Biography of Samuel Lewis*, p. 103.

exclaimed: "Lord, now lettest thou thy servant depart in peace, according to thy word, for mine eyes have seen thy salvation." The great initial victory for public education had been won, and had been won primarily by New England ideas backed up by New England men.

It remained to give these ideas and this system effective organization. This was not accomplished until thirteen years later, in 1838, under the leadership of Samuel Lewis, when a wholly new school code was adopted. Following the act of 1825 there were numerous modifications and amendments of the law, but no essential change in the system of administration was made until 1838.

The law of 1825 had made no provision for centralized control, and had created no adequate machinery for uniting the various schools and districts established into a true state system. There was no state, county, or township supervision, and but little actual knowledge, and no control, of what various communities were doing educationally. While the law had established the fundamental principle of taxation for schools, the actual system remained a headless, disjointed, decentralized, and ineffective one.

The first suggestions for reform came from the friends of education in Cincinnati. A group of teachers and other earnest advocates of popular education had organized a voluntary association known as the College of Teachers or Western Academic Institute.[1] This body met annually for the discussion and study of educational topics and attracted to its meetings, not only Ohio teachers, but educational leaders from the other western states as well. Partly as a result of a demand for a better organization created through the discussions of this association,[2] a bill was introduced in 1837 to create the office of state superintendent of common schools. It met with determined opposition, but finally passed the House by a vote of 35 to 34, and became a law in March, of the same year, with a decisive vote in its favor in the Senate.

Samuel Lewis, of Cincinnati, was the first and only incumbent of the office, which he held for three years. The law of 1838 was a direct result of the work of his first year and of his study of the needs and conditions of schools as he saw them while touring the state visiting the schools and addressing meetings in an attempt to arouse people to an active interest in the need of better school

---

[1] O.L., XXX, 232.
[2] Lewis, *Biography of Samuel Lewis*, pp. 119, 120.

conditions. In this work he visited more than three hundred schools, traveling on horse-back over twelve hundred miles over the rough country roads, visiting schools by day, addressing public meetings by night, and everywhere preaching the gospel of a better school system and a free education for every Ohio boy and girl. He always found it hard, and often discouraging work. He writes from Cleveland in November, 1837:

> I arrived here today almost worn down; have rode on an average twenty-six miles a day this week. I generally spend three or four hours a day in conversation, answering questions, giving explanations, and making suggestions. It is harder than it would be to deliver an address every day an hour and a half long. . . . . I fear you overvalue my efforts. . . . . I shall, however, do my best. I leave here on Monday, if health permit, and shall get along as fast as I can to Columbus, visiting on my route, as I suppose, about sixteen counties. . . . . The task before me is so great, that with all my time and close attention, I shall hardly be able to get through.

In a later letter he writes:

> On Saturday last, I delivered an address at Canton, and after riding twenty-six miles on Monday, spoke in the evening to a large audience, and I believe I did good. . . . . I work hard day and night, and I find it a kind of up-hill business. If men would only do something, even in opposition, it would be better than it is. Almost every man agrees with me; thousands listen and applaud; and even candid men of sense declare they have never heard this subject treated with so much interest, and then leave it to go alone, or get on unaided by their efforts. Still I am not discouraged, but am determined to work on till my report is in, hoping at least for the final triumph of sound principles and practice.[1]

His report for the year 1837, based on his own observation and such statistics as he could gather from the county auditors, gave the first assembled information about the common schools of the state. The report found the legislature in a receptive mood, and the law of 1838 was passed with but little opposition. The essential feature of the new law, in comparison with those that had preceded, consisted in the fact that it gave organization and headship to the system.

The new code retained the state superintendent at the head of the schools; the act of 1837 had created the office, but had done nothing to change the rest of the law or the machinery of administration. In each county the new law made the county auditor also the county superintendent of schools, and, as such, responsible

[1] Lewis, *Biography of Samuel Lewis*, p. 123.

to the state superintendent in all educational affairs.   Similarly in each township the township clerk was made the township superintendent of schools, subordinate to the county superintendent.

An organization had been established by means of which an authorized state officer could reach out into the most remote district of the state, either to give help or information or to see that the law was obeyed.   If equipped with the proper men, Ohio, through this law, had the mechanism for effective educational administration.

The real strength of the system rested in the office of state superintendent.   Mr. Lewis filled the office for three years, and in those three years did the same kind of work for Ohio that Horace Mann was doing for Massachusetts.   Unfortunately for Ohio and her subsequent educational history, Mr. Lewis, because of failing health, gave up the office after three years of tireless service, and the legislature, because some opposition had developed, transferred the work to the office of the secretary of state.   This office was given four hundred dollars additional for clerk hire, and the work became the collection of statistics and making of reports, not the administration of a state-wide school system.

We have seen that the old New England idea of using lands for schools first found application in Ohio, and that New England men were chiefly instrumental in giving to the state the first law of 1821, the principle of taxation in 1825, and the organized system of 1838.   We may now turn to a more detailed study of the laws themselves.

Before doing this, however, we must say a few words about the schools from 1803 to 1821, the date of the first school law. The general type of common schools during this period was the pay or subscription school.[1]   The following agreements and advertisements give a picture of the practice, such that any added explanation is unnecessary.

An advertisement in the *Western Spy*, October 22, 1799, reads as follows:

ENGLISH SCHOOL.—The subscriber informs the inhabitants of this town that his school is this day removed, and is now next door to Mr. Thomas Williams, skin-dresser, Main Street.   Gentlemen who have not subscribed may send their

[1] *Historical Sketches of Public Schools in Cities, Villages, and Townships of the State of Ohio*, a Centennial publication; gives an account of the development of the school system in 47 cities and villages of the state. In 41 cases the writers mention some form of private school as preceding or paralleling the public school.

scholars on the same terms as subscribers, (commencing this day). He also intends to commence an evening school in the same house on the third day of November next, where writing and arithmetic, etc., will be taught four evenings in each week, from 6 to 9 o'clock, during the term of three months. The terms for each scholar will be two dollars, the scholars to find firewood and candles. He also furnishes deeds and indentures, etc., on reasonable terms.

JAMES WHITE[1]

This is given by Venable, together with the following, appearing in a Cincinnati paper in 1804:

NOTICE.—The public in general and my former subscribers in particular, are respectfully informed that I expect to commence school again on the 1st day of January, 1805. I shall teach reading, writing, arithmetic and English grammar, indiscriminately, for two dollars per quarter. The strictest care will be given to the school, as my circumstances will then admit of my constant presence with the school. Those who place confidence in my abilities and fidelity may be assured that both will be employed to please the parents who shall commit, and benefit the children who shall be committed to my care.

EZRA SPENCER[2]

The two agreements between teacher and parents which follow illustrate the common practice in the employment of a teacher and establishment of a school:

This article between the underscribed subscribers, of the one part, and Jabez P. Manning, of the other, Witnesseth: That said Manning doth on his part engage to teach a school at the school-house near the center of Youngstown for the term of one quarter, wherein he engages to teach reading, writing, arithmetic and English grammar; and furthermore, that the school shall be opened at 9 o'clock A.M. and close at 4 P.M., of each day of the week (Saturday and Sunday excepted), and on Saturday to be opened at 9 o'clock and close at 12 o'clock A.M., and we, the subscribers, on our part individually engage to pay unto the said Manning $1.75 for each and every scholar that we subscribe at the end of the term; and we, furthermore, engage to furnish the necessary expense of furniture, wood, and all other things necessary for the use of the school. Furthermore, we do engage that unless by the 6th of April of the present year the number of scholars subscribed amount to 35, that the said Manning is in no way obligated by this article. Furthermore, we allow the said Manning the privilege of receiving five scholars more than are here specified.

(*Signed*) J. P. MANNING[3]

YOUNGSTOWN, March 31, 1818.

We the subscribers, do hereby mutually agree to hire Miss Sally Rice to teach a school in the school-house near Mr. William Smith's, for the term of

[1] Venable, *Beginnings of Literary Culture in the Ohio Valley, Historical and Biographical Sketches,* pp. 185, 186.

[2] *Idem.*

[3] *Historical Sketches of Public Schools in Cities, Villages, and Townships of the State of Ohio.* Evans, 'Youngstown Public Schools.''

three months, to commence on the 9th day of June, instant.   She is to commence the school at the hour of 9 o'clock in the forenoon, and keep until 12; and at the hour of 1, and continue until 4 o'clock in the afternoon.   She is to teach reading, and to instruct the young Misses in the art of sewing; and to keep all necessary regulations as is usual in schools; for which we agree to give her the sum of one dollar and twenty-five cents per week during the said term, which sum shall be assessed in proportion to the number of scholars we have set to our names. Provided, also, that in case more are sent by any individual than he has sub- scribed for, or any persons send who do not subscribe, they shall be assessed in proportion to the number they send; the money to be assessed and collected by a committee to be appointed for that purpose.   And for the performance of the foregoing we hold ourselves bound.

Dated this 8th day of June, A.D., 1814.[1]

This last agreement was for a school taught in Warren, Wash- ington County, and was signed by 19 subscribers, guaranteeing 28½ pupils, Ephraim Cutler leading with four, while five sub- scribers sign for only one-half a pupil each.

[1] Cutler, *Life and Times of Ephraim Cutler*, p. 172.

CHAPTER II

THE DEVELOPMENT OF THE PUBLIC-SCHOOL SYSTEM

THE PUBLIC-SCHOOL SYSTEM, 1803–50

The general educational legislation of this period is concerned only with the district school. There was no general legislative enactment to establish secondary or higher institutions of learning as a part of the state system of education, and it was not until 1847 that there was any legislation to make provision for town and city schools and a graded system, other than that found in special town and city charters.

The chief legislative enactments that divide this period and mark especially important phases in the growth of the system of public schools are as follows:

1821[1]—The first school law. Recognition of state need and responsibility.
1825[2]—The second school law. The first tax for schools.
1838[3]—A state system organized. A definite school fund guaranteed and the schools,[4] in theory, made free.
1847-48[5]—The Akron Act passed. A system for town and city schools established.

These dates mark off periods that may be roughly characterized as follows:

1803–21—Subscription or pay schools.
1821–25—State recognition of the public-school idea.
1825–38—Property taxation to aid schools.
1838–50—Operation under a loose state organization.
1847–50—The development of town and city school systems.

Numerous school laws were passed from 1825 to 1838, but the changes were minor in character and developed no new principles.

A clearer view of the growth of the public-school system can be gained if the more important phases of that development are treated separately, showing the various stages that each of these phases passed through during the entire period.

[1] O.L., XIX, 51.
[2] O.L., XXIII, 36.
[3] O.L., XXXVI, 21.
[4] School rates were not definitely abolished from the public schools until after 1850 (Taylor, *A Manual of the Ohio School System*, Introduction, p. 4).
[5] O.L., XLV, local, 187.

For the purposes of this discussion the following topics have been selected, and are discussed in the order given below:

The Organization of the School System, 1803–50
Methods of Common-School Support
Control and Supervision of Schools
Certification of Teachers
School Studies
Length of School Year
School Officers
Schools for Colored Children
City and Village School Systems

THE ORGANIZATION OF THE SCHOOL SYSTEM, 1803–50

It may be said that the school system of the state had its beginning in the grant of one section in each township for the use of schools that Ohio received from the United States when she became a state.[1] This grant, wasted as it afterward was, served as one center of common educational interest and brought the topic of common schools constantly before legislators and people.

The unit of organization during the entire period was the district. The earliest legislation bearing in any way upon the organization of schools is found in an act of January 2, 1806,[2] establishing the method of incorporating townships.

This act provides:

That so soon as there are twenty qualified electors in any original surveyed township of six miles square, or fractional township within the state wherein there is the reserved section number 16, granted by the Congress of the United States for the special use of schools; they are hereby authorized under the provision hereafter provided, to elect three trustees and one treasurer for the purpose of taking into their care the section above mentioned, who shall be a body politic, capable of suing and being sued, pleading and being impleaded.

This early legislation precedes any specific school act, and is found in the laws concerning the organization of the township. It is the undoubted result of the grant of school lands and is an indication of the importance of this grant in keeping before the people the ideal of state-wide education.

All parts of the state had land set aside for school use. This was the one common fact in all attempts to meet local educational

---

[1] A description of this grant and the use made of it will be found in the discussion of the school lands in chapter iii.

[2] O.L., IV, 66.

needs. On this subject there had to be legislation general in nature. It was the one subject of common educational interest. This earlier legislation was concerned primarily in determining how the scant funds from this source might be legally used, either to support for short periods schools that depended solely on this source of income, or to supplement and assist private and subscription schools of various kinds.

The trustees chosen in compliance with this legislation of 1806 were given authority to divide the township into districts for the purpose of establishing schools, but were not directed to do so. They were, however, directed to divide the profits[1] arising from the school lands, among the districts that *were* established, in proportion to the inhabitants. In passing this act the legislature was evidently primarily interested in the management of Section 16, not in the establishment of schools. Those townships that wished to do it were given the right to organize districts and use the funds obtained from the school lands to support their schools. It is evident from subsequent legislation,[2] and from the reports of Superintendent Lewis,[3] that these funds were also used to pay or lessen the expense of subscription schools already under way in the community. In all laws touching on this subject, following the act of 1806, the township trustees are the officers charged with the duty of dividing the township into school districts, but the final decision as to whether such divisions are to be made does not legally rest with them, although in practice it is evident that it often did so.

In 1814,[4] in an act supplementary to the foregoing, it was made obligatory upon the trustees to lay the township off in districts upon the application of six householders of the township, but no penalties were imposed for a failure to do so. This same act directed that those establishing a school in a district should choose three (school) trustees, whose sole duties seemed to be to get from the teacher a certified list of the pupils who had attended the schools, and the length of time they had been taught, and present it to the township trustees as a basis for the distribution of the revenue from the school section.

---

[1] Legal provision had been made as early as 1803, the year Ohio was admitted, for renting the school lands. See chapter iii for a discussion of the legislation concerning the treatment of these lands.

[2] O.L., XXXIV, 19.

[3] Ohio Documents, 36th G.A., Doc. 17, pp. 9, 10.

[4] O.L., XIII, 295.

On January 22, 1821,[1] Ohio's first general school act was passed. By its provisions the method of organizing districts legalized in 1814 is evidently repealed though it is not so specified. The specific provisions of the act that concern organization are that the voters in each township should have the right to vote upon the question of districting the township. In case the vote was in favor of such districting, the trustees were directed to lay off the school districts in such a way as to have not less than twelve nor more than forty householders in one district. They were also directed in their districting to have regard to any school companies incorporated, so as to include the members within one district.

The householders in each district were to elect annually a school committee of three and a collector. The duty of the latter was evidently to collect rates for the support of the school from those who sent children to it, the tax for building a schoolhouse in case such a tax was levied, and any amount levied as necessary for paying the rates for the indigent children of the district. This law also required the directors to appoint a district clerk, whose duties were to keep a record of the meetings, make out the tax bills when a tax was levied, and keep such accounts as the school committee might direct.

The legislation up to this point has been chiefly concerned in providing an organization for two purposes: a fair and legal method for distributing the revenues that arose from the school lands, and a method by which local communities could legally lay out their districts and set up schools. There was nothing in this earliest legislation that in any way approached a state system or compelled any state-wide action concerning education.

It was the evident intention of the next general law, passed in 1825,[2] to establish a system that should be state-wide in its operation. Its great advance over preceding laws was, however, in its use of the principle of state-wide taxation rather than any significant change in the organization of schools. The establishment of districts and schools remained a local and decentralized activity, and no true state system was formed.

It was made the duty of the township trustees to lay off each incorporated township in the state into one or more school districts. Certain negative penalties were imposed in this law upon

[1] O.L., XIX, 21.
[2] O.L., XXIII, 36.

townships that were not divided into districts and upon districts that did not employ teachers, but any real compelling force that such a provision might have had was destroyed by the excessive liberality of the time limitation allowed for meeting the minimum requirements of the law.

No township was entitled to receive any portion of the moneys collected for school purposes, either from the school lands or from taxation, unless it was laid off into districts. (It might be laid off in one district six miles square and meet the legal requirement.) Furthermore, if it were not laid off into districts within five years, the money due it arising from the school tax was apportioned to the other townships of the county which had been so laid off. Similarly, any district which for a period of three years failed to hire a teacher and keep a school was penalized by having the money due it apportioned to the districts that obeyed the law.

This did not refer to the money from Section 16. By the terms of the original grant, this was set aside for the use of the schools of the township, and the funds from it could not be alienated to the use of another township.

The law of 1825 provided for a school tax, and the penalty for not districting the township consisted[1] in losing after a five-year period the township share in this tax. No provision was made other than this for the enforcement of the law. There were no penalties for the township trustees, and no officers whose duty it was to see that the law was carried into effect. It was the evident idea of the legislators that the incentive afforded by a share in the school tax would be sufficient to bring about the erection of school districts in all the townships of the state. That this was not the universal result is shown by the fact that throughout the period, even as late as 1849,[2] there reappear in general laws and in amendatory and supplementary acts constant directions to the township trustees to lay off the township into school districts. The later directions probably usually refer to the organization of new counties and townships in the more unsettled portions of the state. In general, the townships seem to have followed the mandates of the law and availed themselves of the opportunity to share in the money raised by the tax.

[1] O.L., XXIII, 36.
[2] O.L., XLVII, 52.

Mr. Lewis in his first report as state superintendent, in 1837,[1] showed that there were 7,748 organized school districts in the state. There were 1,129 townships in 71 of the 75 counties of the state, which would give an average of nearly seven school districts to the township, an indication that the law was quite generally obeyed. There was, however, no uniformity in the amount of territory included in the districts (an entire township might be organized as one district), and, as Mr. Lewis pointed out, the number in each township did vary from one or two to eighteen. The district lines were "frequently made on personal considerations, or to defeat some contemplated improvement. It is not uncommon to find districts so bounded as to exclude whole tracts of land from the operation of the law."[2] The report further indicates that there were individual townships even in the older counties that had not organized school districts at the date of the report, 1837, "and many more in the new counties that have just commenced operations."

The organization within the district was effected by the district meeting choosing three directors, who were to have direct control and management of the schools.

It should be kept clearly in mind in this and subsequent legislation that the directors are officers of the district, the trustees are officers of the township.

The only compulsory feature in the district organization was a fine of two dollars, which was provided for by an amendment in 1830,[3] imposed upon any person who was elected school director or treasurer and refused to serve. This provision was repeated in the general laws of 1832[4] and 1834.[5]

These amendments were evidently caused by frequent refusal to serve by those elected to the school offices in the local districts. That the work was a real burden and rested upon a small army of local school officers may be seen in another quotation from the state superintendent's first report:

There is no feature in the present law more burdensome than that of requiring so many officers to spend several days in every year in doing what would be better done by one-fifth the number. . . . . The amount of time now required,

[1] Ohio Documents, 36th G.A., Doc. 17, p. 45.
[2] *Ibid.*, p. 20.
[3] O.L., XXVIII, 57.
[4] O.L., XXIX, 414.
[5] O.L., XXXII, 25.

if the officers do their duty, will, if computed at the average price of day labor, amount to a heavier tax than is assessed in money for the support of schools. . . . . There are now 38,740 officers, enough certainly to break down any system however otherwise good.[1]

To summarize: On the side of local organization, the law of 1825 directed the township trustees throughout the state to lay off the townships into school districts, in which the electors might organize by choosing directors, the only compulsion for either township or district coming from a loss in the share of the school tax.

County contact with the township and district was first established in the law of 1825,[2] by which the county officials were made responsible for the collection and distribution of the school tax,[3] and through the appointment of a board of examiners by the Court of Common Pleas. This county relationship was concerned only with the distribution of school funds and the examination[4] of teachers, and had in it no direct element of control or supervision. The certification of teachers by a county authority, rather than a local authority, did, of course, introduce one element of control.

The next step in the direction of county organization was taken in the law of 1836,[5] which provided that the county auditor should open an account directly with each school district in the county, and made the further provision that each district school clerk should report annually to the county auditor. The county auditor became the intermediary officer in gathering information for the use of the state as to the general school conditions. It is evident that the legislature felt the need of information regarding school conditions throughout the state as a basis for legislative action. The directions are specific as to the information wanted and include the following items: the enumeration of white children from four to twenty-one years old in the district; the time the school had been kept in the district; the time the school had been supported by the school fund; the time the school had been supported by taxation; the time the school had been supported by voluntary subscription; the amount of money from each source; the number of children that had been taught; the whole amount

[1] Ohio Documents, 36th G.A., Doc. 17, p. 19.
[2] O.L., XXIII, 36.
[3] See p. 33 for full explanation of this tax.
[4] See p. 41.
[5] O.L., XXXIV, 19.

spent for teachers' wages; the amount paid for schoolhouses and repairs, giving as separate items the sum raised by taxation for this purpose and that raised by voluntary subscription.

Each county auditor was directed to make an abstract[1] of the information so gathered for his county, and to report the same annually to the General Assembly.

It will be seen that the law up to this point connected the state, county, and district in a loose organization through a system of reports and through certain financial contacts in the collection and distribution of the school tax.

The system lacked a supervising head with definite responsibility for following up the directions given by the law and for seeing that the information asked for was actually gathered and used. The legislature evidently realized this, and the following year,[2] 1837, passed a law creating the office of superintendent of common schools, with an annual salary of five hundred dollars.

The chief duties of the office so created were to collect and tabulate statistics, to investigate the conditions of the various school funds resulting from the sale of lands, and, in general, to study the school needs of the state and suggest plans for better regulation and control of educational affairs to the General Assembly. Samuel Lewis, of Cincinnati, was appointed to the office April 1, 1837.[3] Following his recommendations, the legislature enacted in 1838[4] an act for the support and better regulation of common schools and to create permanently the office of superintendent of common schools. Mr. Lewis had recommended legislation the preceding year, which had included:

school libraries; a state school fund of two hundred thousand dollars; township high schools; township Boards of Education; evening schools in towns and cities; county superintendents; a school journal to be distributed to school officers gratuitously; encouragement for the formation of Teachers' Institutes; authority

---

[1] It was largely from these abstracts that Mr. Lewis made up the statistical tables in his first report. He recognized the incompleteness and inaccuracy in them, but despite that gathered much valuable information. In commenting upon the laxness shown in the reports he says: "If all the districts had reported accurately, the result would be bad enough; but they have not. . . . . There are in the state 75 counties of which 62 have reported in whole or in part; some are extremely defective, not only on account of the work of the school officers, but also the extreme carelessness of some of the auditors. Most of the auditors, however, have done the best they could with the materials furnished." (Ohio Documents 36th G.A., Doc. 17, p. 45).

[2] O.L., XXXV, 82.

[3] O.L., XXXV, local, 560.

[4] O.L., XXXVI, 21.

for districts to borrow money to erect school-houses; the employment of women as teachers; and full reports from teachers and school officers.[1]

The resulting legislation was the most important and complete act bearing upon public education passed in Ohio from 1803 to 1850, and was the last school code passed during the period. Much of its effectiveness was destroyed by subsequent amendments that will be indicated, but the act in itself attempted to establish an organized system of common schools for the state, with state, county, township, and district officers. The state superintendent stood at the head of the system. In each county the county auditor was made superintendent of common schools for the county, and in each township the township clerk was made superintendent of common schools for the township. The district meeting elected three directors, as in the case of the preceding laws. The district clerk was directed to make an annual report to the district meeting and to file a copy of his report with the township clerk. This report was to contain full financial and educational statistics of the district for the year. The duties of the township clerk, acting as superintendent, were as follows: to take an enumeration of the youth of school age in each district of the township (for failure to do this a fine of $15 was imposed upon him); to fill vacancies that occurred in any board of directors in his township; to appoint directors in case the district meeting failed to elect them, or in case the directors failed to serve, and, if those who were appointed refused to serve, to perform the duties of the directors himself for the district in question. He was directed further to report annually to the county superintendent an abstract of the reports made by the district clerks, and it was made his duty to visit each common school in the township at least once a year to examine the teacher's record and the discipline and mode of instruction and to keep a journal of his observations. He was also directed by the law to estimate each year the additional amount necessary to be raised in the district to maintain six months' school for all children.

The chief duties of the auditor as county superintendent of schools consisted in transmitting an abstract of the reports from each township to the state superintendent, and in distributing blanks, circulars, and other information from the state superintendent to the proper township and district officers.

[1] Ohio Documents, 36th G.A., Doc. 17, pp. 11–34.

It will be seen that in its working the system was nominal rather than actual, so far as any control of the local unit, the district, was concerned. It was designed chiefly to afford convenience for the collection of data needed by the state superintendent, and the dissemination of information from the state superintendent's office. It did provide for district officers, and even the possible establishment of schools, where the district failed to act, by giving the township clerk power to exercise the authority of the directors, and it also made some pretense at supervision through the same officers. Aside from this, it was a loose and inefficient system, depending for its value upon the energy and ability of the state superintendent in arousing educational sentiment throughout the state and upon the thoroughness with which the township clerk performed the duties laid upon him. There was still no actual compulsion in the law.

The strong points of the system consisted in the definite relationship established through state, county, township, and district officers, and the possibility of dissemination and collection of educational information through these channels. Its real effectiveness depended upon the wise leadership of the state superintendent. The law pointed out the way to a school system, and the superintendent, as an authorized educational agent, could do much to arouse state-wide interest in the schools. In his *Third Annual Report*, in 1839, Mr. Lewis speaks of the law in the following words:

This law, though not perfect, was the best that could be passed; and with all its imperfections, I still think it is better adapted to our wants than any other school law that has come under my notice. It gives to the people the power to do their own business, whether in townships or districts, as the majority may think best. The widest possible latitude is given for popular action. The most that the law does is to prescribe certain general rules within which the people can act under the sanction of the law, and it gives to such popular action the aid of law to effect its purpose. An arbitrary law imposing duties binding upon the people without their assent could prescribe the forms and details of the work in a few words and with great simplicity. Such would do for despotic countries, but in a free country where the actors are a people whose action depends upon their own wills, there must be a wide scope given, allowing each district to accommodate its own peculiar views, requiring it only to keep within the general outlines (and they must be only outlines) laid down by the law.[1]

The effectiveness of the organization was destroyed by action of the legislature March 23, 1840,[2] when the office of state superin-

---

[1] *Third Annual Report of the Superintendent of the Common Schools*, made to the Thirty-eighth General Assembly of the State of Ohio, p. 4.
[2] O.L., XXXVIII, 130.

tendent was abolished and the work of tabulating and transmitting school statistics and other educational information was transferred to the office of the secretary of state.

The one other point at which the law had promise of effectiveness was in the creation of the township and county superintendents. The weakness, of course, was in attaching these offices as mere appendages to the duties of the county auditor and the township clerk.

The supervisory duties of the township clerk were made dependent upon the decision of the township trustees in 1839,[1] and the amount of pay for the supervision of any one school was limited to a maximum of one dollar for any one year. This made actual supervision practically impossible. The results of these two acts were to leave the system without effective leadership and largely to destroy any possibility of controlling the school work of the district through supervision. There were portions of the state where the organization was felt to be ineffective. Samuel Lewis had advocated county supervision, and the appointment of the county auditor to this position was felt by many not to meet educational needs. Voluntary associations of teachers[2] discussed the question of school organization in their conventions. In 1846 Henry D. Barnard, of Connecticut, came to Ohio and lectured in numerous towns and cities,[3] urging the cause of free public schools.

As one result of these discussions numerous petitions were circulated in the northern and central portions of the state, asking for a law that would give county supervision. In 1847[4] the legislature passed a weak permissive act applicable to twenty-five counties located largely in the Western Reserve and in the central portion of the state near Columbus. This act shows clearly the general legislative willingness to legalize educational procedure and the unwillingness to adopt means to enforce the measures given the sanction of law.

The twenty-five counties in question were allowed to have county superintendents. The initiative was left in the hands of the county commissioners, who were authorized to set aside such sum as they deemed proper for the payment of a county super-

---

[1] O.L., XXXVII, 61.
[2] See chapter vi, p. 106, for a brief account of some of these associations.
[3] Taylor, *A Manual of the Ohio School System*, p. 359.
[4] O.L., XLV, 32.

intendent. They were allowed to levy a tax for the purpose if they wished to do so. If a sum were set aside for the support of this office, the county superintendent was elected by the district clerks of the county. He became chairman of the county Board of Examiners, and was directed to visit annually each common school in the county as a supervising officer.

The provisions of this act were made applicable to all counties in the state the next year, 1848.[1] The act remained virtually a dead letter in the original twenty-five counties as well as in the rest of the state. It simply pointed out a way in which a county might legally appoint a county superintendent of schools if it really wished to do so, and it left the initiative in the hands of the county commissioners, who were likely to be guided in action by financial considerations more than by educational needs.[2]

The legislature in 1850[3] passed another act that created again the office of state superintendent, but in a quite different form. This law was not permissive in form, but never actually came into operation since the General Assembly, which was the appointing body, allowed it to lapse through its failure to appoint the officers provided for in the law. In brief, this law provided for a state board of public instruction to consist of five members, appointed by the General Assembly. The first members were to be appointed for one, two, three, four, and five years. After that one member was to be appointed each year. Each member, during the last year of his term, was styled the state superintendent of common schools and carried on the duties of that office. These duties were largely limited to the collection of statistics and the reporting of the results to the General Assembly. The state was to be divided into four districts by the board, and each of the other members was to serve as a district superintendent. In this service they co-operated with the county examiners, and their signatures were necessary to give validity to teachers' certificates. The state superintendent was to prepare questions for all teachers' examinations. Teachers were required to pay one dollar on the receipt of certificates. The payment of this dollar entitled each teacher to receive a state educational paper and to attend teachers' institutes.

[1] O.L., XLVI, 86.
[2] Two counties, Ashtabula and Sandusky, elected superintendents under this law (Taylor, *A Manual of the Ohio School System*, p. 360).
[3] O.L., XLVIII, 44.

All fees and subscriptions to the school paper were to be paid to the state treasurer, and out of the fund so created the salaries of the state board were to be paid. The salaries were one thousand dollars for each district superintendent, and twelve hundred dollars for the state superintendent. The law specifically provided that no money from any other source should be used in the payment of these salaries. This law represented the efforts of the teachers' associations and the friends of education throughout the state. They were successful in getting the law upon the statute books by placing the responsibility for financing it upon the teachers themselves. The law, however, as has been said, was never put in active operation.

Summary.—The district was the unit of school organization throughout this period. A state organization was formed in 1838 with county and township officers. The effectiveness of the county and township organizations was largely nullified by the fact that the duties of the school officials were attached to offices primarily created for other purposes. The greatest possibility of usefulness in the system rested in the state superintendent, and this office, after a three years' trial, was abolished, and its duties transferred to the office of the secretary of state, where it became largely a clerical function.

METHODS OF COMMON-SCHOOL SUPPORT

The subject of the support of common schools during this period is an involved one as there are many sources of revenue and frequent changes in legislation. These sources may be classified as follows: school rates paid by parents; the revenue from school lands; permanent funds; revenue from the United States surplus; a guaranteed state school fund; state taxation for school support; county taxation for school support; optional township taxation for school support; district taxation for school support; revenue from fines, penalties, and fees of various kinds; district taxation for school buildings; voluntary contributions for school buildings; contributions and bequests.

Rates paid by parents.—It has already been said that the earliest schools in Ohio were subscription or pay schools. The responsibility for the education of the child during the first twenty-two years of statehood rested on the parents, not upon society or the state, except as the money received from Section 16 might assist in maintaining the local school. The principle of school rates for at least a portion of the expense was recognized in the laws of 1821,[1] 1829,[2] 1831,[3] 1834,[4] and 1836.[5] In the three acts last cited it was provided that the parents should pay any additional amount needed, unless it were raised by voluntary subscription. Provision was also made for the exemption of indigent students. School rates, as a source of revenue, were not specifically recognized in the code of 1838,[6] but reappeared the following year in an amendment,[7] and remained until 1850 as a legal source of support.

The practical working of the law and its amendments is well shown by another quotation from Mr. Lewis' first report:

As it will be impossible to give a full history of my observations, an example of the several classes must suffice. In one town a free school is taught three months in the year, by one teacher, in a district where more than one hundred children desire to attend; they rush in and crowd the school so as to destroy all hope of usefulness; the wealthy and those in comfortable circumstances, seeing this, withdraw their children or never send them; the school thus receives the name of a school for the poor, and its usefulness is destroyed. This example is one that represents nearly all the free schools in the State, as well in the country as in the cities and towns.

Another and much larger number of the districts, adopt a practice of which the following is an example: The district has funds which would pay a teacher one quarter or less; but in order to keep up a school as long as possible, it is divided between two or more quarters; the teacher makes his estimate of the amount, besides public money, that must be paid by each scholar, and gets his subscription accordingly. Here none send but those who can pay the balance; of course, the children of the poor, the very intemperate and careless, with sometimes the inordinate lovers of money are left at home.

This mode, though it defeats the primary object of the law, really secures a greater aggregate amount of instruction than the other. Another class proceeds on the same plan, with the exception that the teacher is bound to take the very poor free, if they prove their total inability to pay. This is but little, if any, better than the last, since the poor woman must humble herself, and in effect take the benefit of the poor law, before she can get her children into school; . . . .

Another part of this class is, where the directors agree with the teacher at so much per month, and, after expending the school money, levy, under the statute,

[1] O.L., XIX, 51.
[2] O.L., XXVII, 73.
[3] O.L., XXIX, 414.
[4] O.L., XXXII, 25.
[5] O.L., XXXIV, 19.
[6] O.L., XXXVI, 21.
[7] O.L., XXXVII, 61.

a tax on the scholars for the residue, sometimes admitting the poor, and sometimes rejecting all that are unable to pay the difference.

In some towns all the teachers receive a portion of the public money at the rate of so much per scholar, which they deduct from the subscription price. In these cases the schools are all strictly private, and no provision whatever is made for the poor. The officers in one place where this practice prevails, said that "if the schools were free, they would be so crowded as to be useless, unless they had more funds, but by the mode they adopted, every man who sent to school got a part of the public money;" if he was not able to pay the balance he was punished by losing the whole; which is certainly a bad feature in the practice, and a gross violation of law. Another custom is not to draw the school money for several years, and then, say once in two or three years, they can keep a crowded free school from three to six months. In some places public schools have not been taught this two years.

These examples give the practice in all the school districts in the State; the second and third named prevail the most generally; but it is not uncommon to find all the examples adopted in different districts in the same township.[1]

Revenue from school lands.—The revenue from Section 16, or land given in lieu of Section 16,[2] was by the terms of the grant to be used for the education of the children of the township or district of country to which it belonged. The basis of distribution within the township finally came to be the number of white unmarried youth from four to twenty-one years. The different bases of distribution used before this were as follows:

1805[3]—So that all citizens in the township shall obtain equal advantages.
1810[4]—In proportion to the scholars and the time taught.
1825[5]—In proportion to the number of families in each district.
1834[6]—In proportion to the unmarried white youth from four to twenty-one.

In the Virginia Military District the basis for distribution by the act of February 9, 1829,[7] was made all children from the age of four to sixteen, instead of four to twenty-one. This was changed to children from the age of four to twenty-one in 1831,[8] and a five-hundred-dollar penalty was assessed upon county auditors if they failed to make triennially a report of the number of school youth

---

[1] Ohio Documents, 36th G.A., Doc. 17, pp. 8 ff.
[2] O.L., III, 47, Enabling Act, reprinted.
[3] O.L., III, 230.
[4] O.L., VIII, 100.
[5] O.L., XXIII, 36.
[6] O.L., XXXII, 25.
[7] O.L., XXVII, 51.
[8] O.L., XXIX, 229.

of this age in their respective counties.   In 1836[1] the proportionate amount of territory in each county was used as the basis of apportionment in this particular district.

Permanent funds.—Schools lands: In 1809[2] the school lands set aside for the Virginia Military District were offered for sale at a minimum price of two dollars per acre, and the funds were deposited with the state treasurer to be funded and the income used for the support of schools within this district.

The policy of selling the school lands in the rest of the state was adopted in 1827[3] and was followed immediately by another act[4] creating a permanent school fund.   The money from the sale of school land was to be paid into the state treasury and placed to the credit of the particular townships to which the land belonged. This was impossible in the case of such districts as the Western Reserve, the Virginia Military District, and the United States Military District, as the land had not been given to the townships, but to the districts as a whole.   In these cases the money was set aside for the use of schools in the territories named.   The amount so paid in constituted an irreducible fund upon which the state pledged its faith to pay an annual interest of 6 per cent for the use of schools in the township or district.[5]   The lands were to be sold at the appraised value with no minimum price attached.   This act also provided that the money from the sale of the salt lands, which had not been originally given for the use of schools, should become a permanent fund belonging in common to the people of the state for school use.   To this fund was to be added any donations, bequests, etc., that might be made to the state for the use of schools.   The moneys from the two last sources were to be funded until 1832, and thereafter interest was to be distributed to the counties of the state in proportion to the white male inhabitants over twenty-one years of age.   These funds were loaned to the state for the purpose of building canals in 1830,[6] and from this time on the principle was followed of using the funds for state purposes and pledging the faith of the state for the payment of annual interest on the debt so incurred.

[1] O.L., XXXIV, 469.
[2] O.L., VII, 109.
[3] O.L., XXV, 56.
[4] O.L., XXV, 78.
[5] The money paid into the treasury from the school lands was used by the state in its canal projects, and interest was paid upon the debt so incurred.
[6] O.L., XXVIII, 56.

The amount of funds derived from this source is shown for the years 1830, 1836, and 1846, as follows:[1]

	1830	1836	1846
Virginia Military School Lands....	$47,014.31	$117,884.64	$135,033.96
U.S. Military School Lands.......	27,895.50	101,256.71	119,871.09
Salt lands...................	10,004.20	24,788.22	
Section No. 16...............	82,626.31	563,578.63	999,963.24
Western Reserve School Lands....		147,027.01	158,659.01
Moravian Tract School Lands.....			1,049.82
Totals......................	$167,540.32	$954,535.21	$1,414,577.12

Surplus revenue.—In 1837[2] the surplus revenue received from the United States was apportioned among the counties, the net income from this source to be used for the support of common schools. The method used for deriving an income was as follows: each county was held responsible for the payment of 5 per cent interest annually on the amount apportioned to it.[3] This 5 per cent was paid annually to the state treasurer and redistributed throughout the state for the use of schools. Any amount of revenue that the county had derived from the fund above 5 per cent might be retained by it and used for internal improvements, for the support of common schools, or for the building of academies. The entire fund apportioned to Ohio from this source was $2,007,260.34.[4] This fund was used in this way for the support of schools until 1850, but was finally pledged by the state for the payment of debts incurred in the building of state canals, and passed from the school finances subsequent to this date.

State school fund.—The law of 1838[5] established for the first time a guaranteed state common-school fund of two hundred thousand dollars. This was to be derived from the interest on the surplus revenue,[6] the interest on the proceeds of salt lands, and the revenue[7] from banks, insurance, and bridge companies. The state was to supplement from other funds whatever amount was

---

[1] O.L., XXVIII, Auditor's reports; O.L., XXXV, Auditor's reports; O.L., XLV, Auditor's reports.

[2] O.L., XXXV, 97.

[3] The amount distributed to the Ohio counties in 1837 was $1,882,418.92.

[4] Ohio Documents, 36th G.A., Doc. 3, p. 8.

[5] O.L., XXXVI, 21.

[6] Ohio's share of the surplus revenue distributed to the several states by the United States amounted to $2,007,260.34.

[7] The revenue from the state tax on banks, insurance, and bridge companies is reported by the state treasurer in 1837 as $64,931.53. Ohio Documents, 36th G.A., Doc. 2, p. 3.

needed to bring the total annual revenue up to two hundred thousand dollars. The added amount, when necessary, was raised, in fact, by a state tax. The amount of this guaranteed fund was subsequently in 1842[1] reduced for one year to one hundred and fifty thousand dollars, and in the following year[2] the money arising from licenses on peddlers, from auction duties or licenses on auctioneers, and from taxes levied on lawyers and physicians was added to this fund, the effort evidently being to raise the amount of the fund without the necessity of taxation. The basis for distribution of this fund to the counties was made the number of white youth between the ages of four and twenty years, resident in the county.

Taxation.—The principle of taxation for the support of schools first appeared in the general school act of 1825,[3] by which the county commissioners in each county were directed to levy a tax of one-half mill on the taxable property of the county for the use of schools. This principle continued from this date, and was later supplemented by a state tax and an optional township or district tax. The provisions of the laws concerning taxation up to, and including, the general law of 1838 are summarized in Table I, page 34. (This includes only taxation for school support. The provisions for taxation for school building purposes are given separately.)

In 1839[4] the law was amended to allow the county commissioner to reduce the county tax to any sum not less than one mill, instead of maintaining a flat rate of two mills throughout the state as the act of 1838 had done, and in 1847,[5] the sentiment against taxation for school support was so strong in the General Assembly that the county commissioners were forbidden to levy more than two-fifths of a mill for the use of schools. This was the lowest point reached in taxation for school support after the law of 1825.

The following year, 1848, the privilege of levying a local tax for the support of schools was extended from the township to the district.[6] The district clerks were directed to make an estimate of the

[1] O.L., XL, 59.
[2] O.L., XLII, 38.
[3] O.L., XXIII, 36.
[4] O.L., XXXVII, 61.
[5] O.L., XLV, 60.
[6] O.L., XLVI, 83.

amount needed in addition to the funds provided under the laws in force to keep a school in session for six months. The district meeting was then allowed to decide by vote whether an additional tax should be levied for this purpose. In no case could this added district tax exceed one mill. The same year the county commissioners were authorized to raise the tax from two-fifths of a mill to 1 mill[1] but they were not directed to do so.

TABLE I

	Year	Amount	Remarks
County tax required[1]...	1825	½ mill	
County tax required[2]...	1829	¾ mill	
County tax required[3]...	1831	¾ mill	County commissioners may assess ¼ mill additional.
County tax required[4]...	1834	1 mill	County commissioners may assess ½ mill additional.
County tax required[5]...	1836	1½ mills	County commissioners may assess ½ mill additional.
County tax required[6]...	1838	2 mills	
Township tax[7]	1836	Optional	If the county commissioners failed to levy the additional ½-mill tax, the township might vote to raise an additional 1½-mill tax.
Township tax.........	1838	Optional	The township might vote an added amount necessary to maintain schools six months.[8] Not to exceed 2 mills additional.
State tax.............	1838	Variable	An amount necessary added to the revenue from the permanent fund to produce $200,000[9] annually.[10] One-half mill levied by the state in 1838.

[1] O.L., XXIII, 36.
[2] O.L., XXVII, 73.
[3] O.L., XXIX, 414.
[4] O.L., XXXII, 25.
[5] O.L., XXXIV, 19.
[6] O.L., XXXVI, 21.
[7] O.L., XXXIV, 19.
[8] O.L., XXXVII, 61.
[9] Reduced in 1842 to $150,000 (O.L., XL, 59).
[10] O.L., XXXVI, 85.

The status of taxation for the support of schools at the close of the period was as follows:

The state guaranteed a fixed school fund derived from various sources. When other sources failed to make up this sum, a state

[1] O.L., XLVI, 28.

tax was levied to do so. (The fund had been reduced from two hundred thousand dollars in 1838 to one hundred and fifty thousand dollars in 1842.)

The county commissioners were directed to levy a tax in each county. This had been two mills in 1838, but was reduced to two-fifths of a mill in 1847, and was left optional, but not over one mill, in 1848.

Each township might vote to raise an added two-mill tax for the support of schools in the township.

Each district might vote to raise an added one-mill tax for the support of schools in the district.

The progress that had been made by the law of 1838 with its state-wide county tax of two mills and state tax amounting to one-half mill had been largely lost by allowing the county commissioners to reduce the amount of the county tax and by the reduction of the guaranteed school fund to one hundred and fifty thousand dollars.

Taxation for school buildings.—The law of 1821[1] authorized the householders in any school district by a two-thirds vote to levy a tax to build a schoolhouse and to pay for the schooling of indigent pupils, and stipulated the tax should not exceed one-half the amount that might be levied for state and county taxes the same year. The next law, that of 1825,[2] simply said that the district meeting should provide means for building a schoolhouse and for furnishing fuel, but gave no further directions as to how money was to be raised. In 1827[3] a maximum of three hundred dollars for a schoolhouse was established, and the district meeting might, by a three-fifths vote, decide whether the district should be taxed for building purposes or not. If it was decided to raise the money by a tax and the amount falling on any householder was less than one dollar, a minimum sum of one dollar was charged against him. The tax might be commuted by labor on the schoolhouse or by the furnishing of material for it. This last law evidently aroused opposition on the part of non-resident taxpayers, and in 1830[4] an amendment to the school law provided that not more than fifty dollars might be levied in any one year for building purposes unless one-third of the property in the district was owned by residents.

[1] O.L., XIX, 51.
[2] O.L., XXIII, 36.
[3] O.L., XXV, 65.
[4] O.L., XXVIII, 57.

If one-third to one-half of the property was so owned, the amount raised might be one hundred dollars.   If one-third to two-thirds of the property was owned by residents, the sum was increased to two hundred dollars.   This method of raising the money for buildings remained with but slight changes until 1838.   The minimum tax for a resident taxpayer was reduced from one dollar to fifty cents in 1830,[1] and to twenty-five cents in 1836.[2]   In 1838[3] the decision as to a building tax for a schoolhouse was for the first time left to a majority vote of the district meeting, and the partial exemption for non-resident taxpayers and the minimum tax features disappeared.

Fines, penalties, licenses, fees, etc.—In 1827[4] the principle of using fines for the support of schools, assessed for various offences, first appears.   By the provisions of this act all fines imposed and collected by justices of the peace for offences committed were to be used for the support of schools in the district in which the offences were committed.   This was repeated in 1829,[5] and then disappeared from the school law, but the principle reappeared in a series of acts concerning various offences and remained as a definite method of school support to the end of the period.   These offences and fines are so numerous that they are given here only in tabulated form (Table II).

TABLE II

DATE OF LAW	OFFENSE	PENALTY		AREA TO WHICH FINES WERE DISTRIBUTED
		Min.	Max.	
1829*....	Selling liquor without license..	$10.00	$ 50.00	County
1829*....	Liquor-seller permitting rioting, drunkenness, or gambling	10.00	50.00	County
1830†....	Killing muskrats out of season.	1.00	each	Township
1831‡....	Sabbath-breaking...........	1.00	5.00	Township
1831‡....	Selling liquor on Sunday "to others than travelers"......		5.00	Township
1831‡....	Disturbing religious meetings.		20.00	Township
1831‡....	Profanity.................	.25	1.00	Township
1831‡....	Exciting disturbance in a tavern, etc..................	.50	5.00	Township
1831‡....	Playing bullets, running horses or shooting guns in town...	.50	5.00	Township
1831‡....	Liquor dealer keeping nine-pin alley....................	10.00	100.00	Township

---

[1] O.L., XXVIII, 57.
[2] O.L., XXXIV, 19.
[3] O.L., XXXVI, 21.
[4] O.L., XXV, 65.

[5] O.L., XXVII, 73.
*O.L., XXVII, 11.
†O.L., XXIX, 469.
‡O.L., XXIX, 161.

TABLE II—*Continued*

DATE OF LAW	OFFENSE	PENALTY		AREA TO WHICH FINES WERE DISTRIBUTED
		Min.	Max.	
1831‡....	Exhibiting a puppet show, juggling, etc..................		$ 10.00	Township
1831‡....	Tearing down public notices..		10.00	Township
1831‡....	Selling liquor within one mile of a religious gathering.....		20.00	Township
1831‡....	Bull-baiting, bear-baiting, etc.		100.00	Township
1831‡....	Cock-fighting..............		100.00	Township
1831‡....	Horse-racing on a public road.	$ 5.00		Township
1831‡....	Justice of peace failing to pay over fine collected........	Double the amount collected		Township
1831§....	Selling at auction without license..................		100.00	State, for literary purposes
1831§....	Failure to render account of auction sales..............		1000.00	
1831‖...	Peddling without license......	20.00	100.00	District
1831¶...	Exhibiting circus without permit....................		100.00	County
1831**...	Neglecting to have fish inspected..................		5.00	County
1831**...	Failure to bury offal.........	5.00	50.00	County
1831**...	Inspector demanding more than legal amount, or purchasing articles condemned.	50.00		County
1834††...	Selling salt without inspection.		1.00 per bbl.	County
1834‡‡...	Medical malpractice of various kinds..................	100.00	500.00	County
1834§§ ..	Obstructing navigation in Muskingum River.............		50.00	County
1838‖‖ ..	Officer or corporation disregarding court orders in quo warranto procedure........		10,000.00	County
1840¶¶..	Keeping breachy or unruly animals...................	.25	1.00	District
1840***..	Harboring intoxicated Indians.	5.00	25.00	District
1841†††..	Selling liquor within two miles of any religious society gathered in a field or woodland..	5.00	50.00	Township
1844‡‡‡..	Allowing Canada thistles to mature...................		10.00	Township
	Knowingly selling seed which contains Canada thistle seed		20.00	Township
1845§§§..	Firing cannon on the public street..................	5.00	50.00	Township
1846‖‖‖.	Gambling or keeping a gambling-house................		500.00	County

‡O.L., XXIX, 161.
§O.L., XXIX, 304.
‖O.L., XXIX, 313.
¶ O.L., XXIX, 446.
**O.L., XXIX, 477.
††O.L., XXXII, 47.
‡‡O.L., XXXII, 20.
§§O.L., XXXII, 38.

‖ ‖O.L., XXXVI, 68.
¶¶O.L., XXXVIII, 4.
***O.L., XXXVIII, 57.
†††O.L., XXXIX, 34.
‡‡‡O.L., XLII, 37.
§§§O.L., XLIII, 17.
‖ ‖ ‖O.L., XLIV, 10.

In addition to the fines listed, the fees received from licenses for liquor selling,[1] for peddling,[2] and for auctioneering[3] were applied for the use of schools. There were also a number of local acts of this character applying to particular towns or counties.[4]

In 1830,[5] in the act incorporating the town of Steubenville, it is provided that for every license granted to "all groceries, porter, ale, and other houses of entertainment" there shall be paid into the county treasury "the sum of five dollars for the use of the common schools of the county." A similar provision is found in the act incorporating the city of Chillicothe,[6] in 1838, except that the money is to be paid to the district of the city. Acts of the same general nature occur, applying to Medina, Huron, and Erie counties,[7] and to the towns of Cuyahoga Falls,[8] Fulton,[9] and Akron,[10] and in 1845 an act was passed authorizing the towns of Painesville and Norwalk[11] to levy an annual tax "on all dogs six months old and upwards" for the use of common schools.

CONTROL AND SUPERVISION OF SCHOOLS

Ohio was especially weak in developing any plan of control or supervision. The law of 1825[12] and succeeding laws said that the county examiners might visit and inspect schools, but there was no compulsion placed upon them, no pay for the duty if performed, and no authority given to them in case they decided to make such inspection. In 1838[13] the establishment of the offices of state, county, and township superintendents would seem, at first view, to give the machinery for efficient control and supervision, but an inspection of the law will show that the actual control exercised was weak and ineffective. The only man in the entire system who was primarily engaged in school work was the state superintendent, and at the end of three years the office was abolished,[14] and the work

[1] O.L., XXVII, 11.
[2] O.L., XXIX, 313; O.L., XLVI, 36.
[3] O.L., XXIX, 304.
[4] O.L., XXVIII, 165; O.L., XLV, 131.
[5] O.L., XXVIII, 165.
[6] O.L., XXXVI, 274.
[7] O.L., XLV, 131.
[8] O.L., XLVI, 269.
[9] O.I., XXXII, 116.
[10] O.L., XXXIV, 433.
[11] O.L., XLIII, 379.
[12] O.L., XXIII, 36.
[13] O.L., XXXVI, 21.
[14] O.L., XXXVIII, 130.

transferred to the secretary of state, who was allowed four hundred dollars a year for the extra clerical work thus placed-upon him.

Samuel Lewis[1] in the three years he served as state superintendent accomplished much, but it was through arousing sentiment in favor of common schools and in collecting and presenting educational facts to the General Assembly and to the state at large, and not through the working of the system, except as it aided him in the collection of the desired facts and as he educated school officers in their duties through manuals, reports, and other educational material.[2]

With the transfer of the office to the secretary of state it became, naturally, largely clerical in character, as the secretary of state was devoted primarily to other duties. Similarly, the office of county superintendent was simply added to the duties of the county auditor, and that of the township superintendent to the duties of the township clerk. These men, too, were primarily chosen for work of a different nature, and the school duties were in many instances an unwelcome addition.

It is true that the law gave the township superintendent certain control over the district, investing him with powers to appoint directors if the district failed to elect them, or to perform in person the duties of the directors if those he appointed failed to serve. There was no machinery, however, to compel the township superintendent to act in the matter. He was also required by law to visit the schools in each district once in each year, but in 1839[3] it was made optional with the township trustees to excuse him from this duty, and his total pay for supervision in any one school was fixed at a maximum of one dollar for the year. On the whole the township clerks seem to have accepted the responsibility and to have acted for the best interests of the schools.

Mr. Lewis in his second report speaks of the working of the law at this point as follows:

Elections have very generally been held in the districts in September, 1838, and where they have been omitted the township clerks have, in most cases, made proper appointments, so that there are now school officers in nearly all the school districts and they are making the arrangements for schools. . . . . The power

[1] Taylor, *A Manual of the Ohio School System*, p. 335.
[2] O.L., XXXVI, local, 402, 410.
[3] O.L., XXXVII, 61.

of township clerks, to appoint district officers, is sometimes complained of, but without this provision or some other effecting the same object, organization could not take place.

There will be this winter at least one thousand schools that but for this provision would not have existed. Township clerks only act where the district has forgotten or neglected to act, and it would be unpardonable to suffer fifty thousand youth to go without instruction for want of officers to regulate the schools. . . . . I am satisfied that most of the township clerks desire most heartily to promote the interest of the schools, pay or no pay, but they are generally poor and cannot afford to spend much time without compensation.   Letters every day coming to my hands satisfy me that no money will be better laid out than that which secures the services of patriotic and public spirited township superintendents.[1]

While these quotations show the general attitude of these newly appointed officers as favorable to the schools, there were many individual instances where, through laxity or ignorance, the work was not done. One of the county auditors writing to Mr. Lewis says: "Great difficulties are found in school matters by the negligence of school district officers and township clerks, not that they are opposed to the common school system, but they complain of having so much to do without compensation, consequently they will not bother themselves with the matter."[2]

Another says: "I can assign no reason for the neglect of the township clerks in this matter . . . . but from want of attention merely. . . . . " "The township clerks have not generally made accurate returns."[3] "The carelessness of district officers has given township clerks an excuse, and my report is very deficient," are among other comments from auditor's letters cited by Mr. Lewis.

The only effective measures to compel the districts to establish schools were through the retention of the district's share of money from the school fund, and the moneys collected by taxation, in case of failure to keep school. The law of 1825[4] said that no district might receive its share of the money so collected except for the wages of a teacher duly employed and certified. There was no specification as to the length of time the teacher must be employed. If the district failed for a period of three years to hire a teacher and keep a school, the money due it was to be appropriated

[1] Ohio Documents, 38th G.A., Doc. 17, p. 51.
[2] Ohio Documents, 37th G.A., Doc. 32, p. 67.
[3] *Ibid.*, p. 70.
[4] O. L., XXIII, 36.

to the districts that did so.   In 1829[1] the provisions were repeated, and a minimum term of three months was established as a condition of receiving the district's proportion of school tax due.

There was a fine of two dollars assessed on any person elected as a director or clerk and refusing to serve,[2] and also fines on the district officers responsible for making returns of the enumeration of school youth[3] in case of failure to report.   It was found necessary in 1848[4] to pass a special act for the purpose of securing school statistics from the districts and townships.   This forbade the township treasurers to pay any teacher a salary unless there was presented with the order an abstract of the teacher's record of attendance.   The township treasurer was fined ten dollars unless he settled annually with the auditor of the county, and the possession of these abstracts was a necessary preliminary to the settlement. Other than this the state devised no means for controlling the educational procedure of the district.

CERTIFICATION OF TEACHERS

In 1821[5] the district school committee was authorized to employ competent teachers, and no mention was made of certification. In 1825[6] the principle of county certification appeared and with the exception of a two-year period, 1836 to 1838, remained until 1850.   The law of 1825 provided for the appointment of three examiners of common schools in each county by the Court of Common Pleas, who should examine and certificate teachers and, as previously noted, might visit and examine schools.   No teacher could legally recover any part of the pay due from public funds unless a certificate had been granted to such teacher.

In 1827[7] the Court of Common Pleas was allowed to appoint such number of examiners as they might deem expedient, not to exceed one for each organized township in the county.   It was the evident intent of this law to allow single examiners, for the sake of convenience, to examine within the township.

[1] O.L., XXVII, 73.
[2] O.L., XXVIII, 57.
[3] O.L., XXXIV, 19.
[4] O.L., XLVI, 28
[5] O.L., XIX, 51.
[6] O.L., XXIII, 36.
[7] O.L., XXV, 65.

In 1829[1] the Court of Common Pleas was directed to appoint not less than five examiners nor more than the number of organized townships in the county, and any two examiners might grant certificates.

In 1831[2] the examiners were directed to give the certificate in the branches in which the teacher was found qualified to teach, and no certificate was to be granted unless the candidate was qualified to teach reading, writing, and arithmetic.

The examiners might require the examination to be public and could determine upon uniform forms of certification.

This law was evidently deemed a little too rigorous and was amended at the following session in December, 1831,[3] to permit a district that wished to do so to employ a female teacher to teach reading, writing, and spelling only, and the examiners were authorized, on the presentation of a written request from the directors, to grant a certificate in these subjects.

In 1834[4] the court was directed to appoint five examiners, and the examination was to be given publicly each month at the county seat, with the provision that the examiners might appoint one examiner in each township to examine female teachers only. Reading, writing, and arithmetic were required for all certificates.

In 1836[5] the township became the unit for certification, and the method of choosing examiners changed. Each township was to elect annually three examiners, but with the code of 1838[6] the county became definitely the unit for certification, and the mode of appointment was again by the selection of the Court of Common Pleas. The number of examiners was fixed at three. Examinations were to be held quarterly by the board. Each teacher must be qualified to teach reading, writing, and arithmetic, and the certificate stated what other branches the teacher was qualified to teach. No teacher in any common school was allowed to teach a study not named in the certificate. In 1849[7] English and geography were added to the requirements for certification.

[1] O.L., XXVII, 73.
[2] O.L., XXIX, 414.
[3] O.L., XXX, 4.
[4] O.L., XXXII, 25.
[5] O.L., XXXIV, 19.
[6] O.L., XXXVI, 21.
[7] O.L., XLVII, 43.

SCHOOL STUDIES

No mention was made of the subjects to be taught in the common schools until 1834,[1] when reading, writing, and arithmetic and "other necessary branches" were specified. The state insisted on nothing more than these subjects, but in 1838[2] allowed other studies to be taught at the option of the directors, and allowed any other language beside English to be taught, but the three R's must be taught in English. This was amended in 1839[3] as a concession to German settlers[4] to allow each school district to have its school taught in whatever language it might prefer. In 1849[5] on application of three householders the directors were instructed to add English and geography to the subjects taught.

LENGTH OF SCHOOL YEAR

The minimum length of the school year was first fixed at three months in 1829[6] for any school receiving an appropriation of the money raised by taxation, and as much longer than three months as the appropriation paid the wages of the teacher. Nothing was done to extend the time until 1838,[7] when the township superintendent was directed to estimate for the township the amount it would be necessary to raise by taxation in addition to the funds already provided to furnish six months good schooling to all the white youth of the township.   The decision as to raising the amount needed to maintain the schools six months was decided by the voters at the township election, who voted "school tax" or "no school tax."   A six months' school remained the ideal held up by the law for district schools until 1850.

That this modest ideal of a six months' school was not commonly reached is shown in Mr. Lewis' first report, in which he gave the total number of children of school age in the state as 468,812; the number attending more than two months and less than four as 84,296, and those attending over four months as 62,144.[8] These figures show that 322,372 children of school age

---

[1] O.L., XXXII, 25.
[2] O.L., XXXVI, 21.
[3] O.L., XXXVII, 61.
[4] Taylor, *A Manual of the Ohio School System*, p. 170.
[5] O.L., XLVII, 43.
[6] O.L., XXVII, 73.
[7] O.L., XXXVI, 21.
[8] Ohio Documents, 36th G.A., Doc. 17, p. 44.

either attended school less than two months in the year or that they did not attend at all.   In his last report, three years later, for 1839, he gives the total number of schools (public) as 13,049— partly estimated—and the average length of the term as four months; the total number of pupils in attendance as 455,427, an increase of over 300,000.[1]   These figures are a significant indication of the changed attitude toward public schools that the law of 1838 had wrought under the leadership of a capable and devoted state superintendent.

SCHOOL OFFICERS

The township trustees were throughout the period given the power of establishing districts.   District officers were as follows:

1814—Three district trustees.[2]

1821—Three district trustees and a collector.[3]

1825—Three directors.[4]

1827—Three directors and a treasurer to be appointed by the directors.[5]

1829—Three directors, a clerk, and a treasurer.[6]

1838—Three directors, the directors appointing one of their own number as clerk and treasurer.[7]   The law of 1838 also created the offices of state, county, and township superintendents, the two latter being *ex officio* attached to the offices of county auditor and township clerk.

1840—The office of state superintendent was abolished, and its clerical functions transferred to the office of the secretary of state.[8]

1848—Counties were given the right on their own initiative to elect county superintendents of schools.[9]

SCHOOLS FOR COLORED CHILDREN

The first provision found in the general laws for the education of colored children occurs in 1848,[10] when a department of common schools for black and mulatto children was created.   Prior to this time the property of colored people had been exempt from taxation for school purposes.   This law provided that their property should be taxed the same as property of white people, and the

---

[1] Ohio Documents, 38th G.A., Doc. 17, p. 44.

[2] O.L., XIII, 295.

[3] O.L., XIX, 51.

[4] O.L., XXIII, 36.

[5] O.L., XXV, 65.

[6] O.L., XXVII, 73.

[7] O.L., XXXVI, 21.

[8] O.L., XXXVIII, 130.

[9] O.L., XLVI, 86.

[10] O.L., XLVI, 81.

money used to support colored schools wherever they were established, but added to the common school funds in those districts in which colored children were allowed to attend the common schools.

Any city, town, village, or township containing twenty colored children was created a district for the purpose of establishing a colored school, and the colored citizens were given authority to organize by the election of directors, in accord with the general school law.   If there were less than twenty colored children in the areas enumerated, they were allowed to attend the common schools unless there was a written protest filed by someone having a child in the school.   In the latter case they were not allowed to attend, and the property of colored people was not taxed.   At the next session of the legislature, in 1849,[1] the law was changed, and the authorities in towns, cities, villages, and townships were required to create one or more districts for colored children if they were not admitted to common schools.   The colored citizens then organized with their own officers and supported the schools by taxation upon their own property.

CITY AND VILLAGE SCHOOLS

Ohio's growth in population in the early decades of the nineteenth century was a phenomenal one.   In 1800, three years before statehood, her rank in population was eighteenth.   In 1820 she stood fifth in the sisterhood of states, and in the next ten years the numbers within her borders again almost doubled, jumping from 581,434 in 1820 to 937,903 in 1830.[2]

This growth in the early years was almost wholly a rural one. In 1820 there were only two towns in the state with a population of 1,000 or over: Cincinnati with 9,640, and Dayton, estimated to have 1,000.   Ten years later Cincinnati had grown to a city of 24,830, Dayton and Columbus were approaching 3,000 each—2,950 and 2,435, respectively—while three other towns, Cleveland, Springfield, and Canton, had just passed the 1,000 mark.

In the years from 1830 to 1850 the growth of towns and cities was a rapid one.   Cincinnati had increased to 46,340; Dayton, Columbus, and Cleveland had each passed 6,000, and there were eight other towns in the state with a population of over 2,000 each according to the census reports of 1840; while by 1850 Cincinnati

[1] O.L., XLVII, 17.
[2] Statistical Abstract of U.S., Washington, 1911, p. 34.

was a thriving metropolis of 115,435, Columbus and Cleveland were vigorous young cities of 17,000 each, Dayton had something over 10,000 inhabitants, and Zanesville and Chillicothe were rapidly approaching this number, while fifteen other centers had attained a population of 3,000 to 6,000 each.[1]

The school legislation of the first thirty years of Ohio's statehood recognized only the district school in the general school laws that were passed. This was partly a reflection of the rural character of the state in these early years, and partly a result of the decentralizing tendency in school affairs that the early settlers had brought with them. It was not until the law of 1838 was passed that any recognition was given to the fact that the educational needs of cities and towns were not the same as those of the country districts.

Samuel Lewis speaking to the legislature at this period said:

> In towns and large villages, the common schools are poorer than in the country. In the latter, neighborhoods depend more upon them, and, of course, take a deeper interest in their control, while in the former there is too frequently but little attention paid to these schools by persons able to provide other means of instruction.[2]

A few cities and towns had early felt the inadequacy of the general laws in providing any suitable system of schools, and had asked and received special charters from the state. By 1840 a number of municipalities had organized their schools under special charters, and in the years from 1840 to 1850 there was a general awakening in the urban communities to the need of better provision for public schools.

This aroused interest was shown in the school charters of Cincinnati, Toledo, Cleveland, Portsmouth, Zanesville, Dayton, Columbus, Mt. Vernon, and, finally, Akron, and the generalization of the "Akron Act" in such form that all municipalities in the state—of 200 or more inhabitants—could make use of it.

There was much that was progressive and enlightened for the period in the legislation for Ohio's cities and towns from about 1830 to 1850. The one great lack—found in all Ohio's school legislation prior to 1850, and for a half-century after that—was the lack of any form of compulsion. The general applications of the laws for municipalities were wholly permissive in character. They

---

[1] U.S. Census Reports, 1830, 1840, 1850.
[2] Ohio Documents, 36th G.A., Doc. 17, p. 10.

simply pointed out ways in which the schools could be legally established and organized, but, however excellent and needed these ways might be, no municipality was under the slightest compulsion to follow them.

The earliest special legislation for towns is found in the case of Marietta.[1] The legislature in 1825 granted her the right to vote in town meeting a sum for the support of schools. There was no further legislation for Marietta until 1841,[2] when an act was passed dividing the town, which had been united into one district by the law of 1838, into separate districts again, with three directors for each, and the ordinary rural district system.

Cincinnati.—Cincinnati was the leader in all the early efforts for better educational conditions. In 1829[3] she set an example to the rest of the state by securing a school charter that gave the city an organized, tax-supported, free system of common schools.

This charter divided the city into ten districts, two for each ward, and provided for the building in each district of a two-story building of brick or stone.

The city council was required to provide at the expense of the city for the support of common schools, and to levy a tax of one mill on all the property of the city as long as needed to defray the expense of acquiring sites and erecting buildings, and an additional tax of one mill for the support of schools.

The voters in each ward elected annually a trustee and visitor of common schools. The persons so elected constituted the Board of Trustees and Visitors of Common Schools, and had general supervision of school affairs. They were authorized to employ teachers and to visit schools as often as once a month. They also were to appoint six examiners and inspectors, whose duty it was to examine and certify teachers, and to visit and inspect schools. Once a year a public examination of the schools was to be given under the direction of the mayor, the Board of Trustees and Visitors, and the Board of Examiners. The schools were to be open at least six months of each year, and to be free to all white children. Black and mulatto children were specifically excluded. Reading, writing, spelling, and arithmetic made up the curriculum.

[1] O.L., XXIII, local, 65.
[2] O.L., XXXIX, local, 22.
[3] O.L., XXVII, 33.

While numerous amendments occur, there are few significant changes before 1850. In 1840[1] German schools were established, and evening schools provided for "such male youth over twelve years of age as are prevented by their daily avocation from attending day schools." The latter schools were to be open in the months of November, December, January, and February.

In 1845[2] the trustees were authorized to divide the city into suitable districts without reference to ward boundaries, and in 1846[3] they were given power to establish such other grade of schools as might seem necessary and have such other studies taught therein as they might prescribe. In 1850[4] provision was made for the annual election by the qualified voters of a "Superintendent of Common Schools, whose duty it shall be to visit and superintend all the common schools in said city, to establish courses of study, and perform such other duties as the Board may prescribe."

City of Ohio and Toledo.—In 1836[5] and 1837[6] the city councils in these two cities were given general superintendence over the common schools, with power to divide the city into districts, to erect school buildings, and to make provision for the government and instruction of children therein. It was left wholly optional to the city council as to what should be done.

Cleveland.—Provision for the government of the Cleveland schools was included in the city charter, adopted in 1836.[7] The provisions were quite similar to the Cincinnati plan. The council appointed one person from each ward instead of the voters electing as in Cincinnati. The people so appointed constituted the Board of Managers of Common Schools.

In 1848[8] the Board of Managers was made five for the entire city instead of one from each ward, and the council was authorized to establish a high school, for which purpose the city was to constitute one high-school district.

Portsmouth and Zanesville.—In 1838[9] the city charter of Portsmouth was amended to include most of the provisions of the Cin-

[1] O.L., XXXVIII, local, 157.
[2] O.L., XLIII, local, 413.
[3] O.L., XLIV, local, 91.
[4] O.L., XLVIII, local, 662.
[5] O.L., XXXIV, local, 226.
[6] O.L., XXXV, local, 32.
[7] O.L., XXXIV, local, 271.
[8] O.L., XLVI, local, 150.
[9] O.L., XXXVI, local, 329.

cinnati plan, and in the following year[1] the city of Zanesville secured a charter for the support of schools that had many similar features. The Zanesville charter provided for the election of six directors to be known as the Board of Education. The schools were to be kept in constant operation except for "reasonable vacations," and any deficiency in funds sufficient to keep the schools in constant operation was raised by a levy upon the parents. The board was allowed to exempt indigent students from payment of school fees.

General law for cities and towns before the Akron Act.—The general law of 1838[2] made each incorporated city, town, or borough, not specially regulated by charter, a separate school district. The voters in such a district elected three directors, who were given corporate authority and power to increase the number of directors so that there might be one for each subdistrict. They were authorized to divide the territory for which they were responsible and to establish schools of different grades therein. The question of an additional tax to furnish a school at least six months each year was to be decided by the vote of the community. The general law, as was so usual in Ohio legislation, merely pointed the way, but did not attempt to enforce the organization of city and town schools. The one compulsory feature that appears occurred the next year, 1839,[3] and stated that in towns, cities, and boroughs it was the duty of the directors to provide a sufficient number of night schools for the male youth over twelve years of age whose "daily avocation" kept them from attending day schools. While this law was compulsory in form, there was no machinery devised for its enforcement.

Dayton, Columbus, and Mt. Vernon.—In 1841[4] and 1845[5] the cities of Dayton, Columbus, and Mt. Vernon were granted special charters for the government of their schools. Dayton and Columbus each continued the principle of school rates in addition to taxation. The schools were to be kept in constant operation except for vacations, and any deficiency made up by a levy on the parents. The general features of control were similar to the Cincinnati plan.

The Mt. Vernon charter retained the district system and made each council member a special school director for his ward. Build-

[1] O.L., XXXVII, local, 194.
[2] O.L., XXXVI, 21.
[3] O.L., XXXVII, 61.
[4] O.L., XXXIX, local, 135.
[5] O.L., XLIII, local, 57; O.L., XLIII, local, 150.

ing taxes were to be collected from the subdistricts in which the buildings were erected, and were not assessed on the property of the city in general.

Akron.—In 1847[1] Akron secured school legislation that was especially significant, as the legislature the following year[2] allowed cities, towns, and villages to adopt the provisions of the act and its amendments on petition of two-thirds of the voters, and in 1849[3] enacted most of its provisions into a general law. By this means the Akron law became the plan usually followed in the establishment of graded schools in Ohio. This legislation is of sufficient importance to merit a brief description of the steps that were taken in securing it, and the school conditions in Akron preceding its enactment. The description, with some omissions, is the one given by Judge Bryan in an "Historical Sketch of the Akron Public Schools."

In 1846 there were within the incorporated limits of the village of Akron six hundred and ninety children between the ages of four and sixteen. Of this number there was an average attendance at the public and other schools the year through of not more than three hundred and seventy-five. During the summer of 1846 one of the district schools was taught in the back-room of a dwelling house. Another was taught in an uncouth, inconvenient and uncomfortable building gratuitously furnished by Captain Howe for the use of the district. There were private schools, but these were taught in rooms temporarily hired and unsuited for the purpose in many respects. . . . . It was, in view of this state of things, that Reverend I. Jennings, then a young man and pastor of the Congregational Church of Akron, self-moved, set himself to reorganize the common schools of Akron. There were many friends of a better education in the place who co-operated with Mr. Jennings, and on the 16th day of May, 1846, at a public meeting of the citizens, a committee was appointed of which he was chairman "to take into consideration our present educational provisions and the improvement, if any, which may be made therein."[4]

As a result of this interest, a committee of three was appointed to draw up plans and secure necessary legislation. The plan of the committee was as follows:

1. Let the whole village be incorporated into one school district.

2. Let there be established six primary schools in different parts of the village so as best to accommodate the whole.

[1] O.L., XLV, local, 187.
[2] O.L., XLVI, 48.
[3] O.L., XLVII, 22.
[4] *Historical Sketches of Public Schools in Cities, Villages, and Townships of the State of Ohio.* Bryan, "Historical Sketch of the Akron Public Schools," pp. 1-28.

3. Let there be one grammar school centrally located where instruction may be given in the various studies and parts of studies not provided for in the primary schools and yet requisite to a respectable English education.

4. Let there be gratuitous admission to each school in the system for the children of residents, with the following restrictions, viz.: No pupil shall be admitted to the grammar schools who fails to sustain a thorough examination in the primary school, and the teachers shall have power with the advice of the superintendents to exclude for misconduct in extreme cases, and to classify the pupils as the best good of the schools may seem to require.

5. The expense of establishing and sustaining this system of schools shall be provided for: first, by appropriating all the school money the inhabitants of the village are entitled to, and whatever funds or property may be at the disposal of the board for this purpose; secondly, by a tax to be levied by the Common Council upon the taxable property of this village for the balance.

6. Let six superintendents be chosen by the Common Council, who shall be charged with perfecting the system thus generally defined, the bringing of it into operation, and the control of it when brought into operation. Let the six superintendents be so chosen that the term of office of two of them shall expire each year.

The essential provisions of the plan adopted by this committee were incorporated in the law enacted February 8, 1847.[1] The more important features of this law may be summarized as follows:

1. The election of a board of education of six members, which should have full control of school property and school funds.

2. The incorporation of the city into one school district.

3. Provision for six or more primary schools and one central grammar school to teach "subjects requisite to a respectable English Education."

4. Free admission to all schools.

5. Examinations for promotion, and teachers given the power to classify pupils.

6. Assessment as a tax by the city council of the amount estimated by the board for erecting schoolhouses and for conducting the schools.

[1] O.L., XLV, local, 187.

7.   All school property vested in the city council.

8.   Three examiners appointed by the council.

9.   Annual public examinations.

In the original law there was no limit placed on the amount that might be estimated as necessary for school expense by the Board of Education, and the law directed the council to levy the estimate as a tax.   In 1848,[1] in order to make a concession that would meet the objection of the property-owners who opposed this feature, the maximum tax that might be raised in any one year for current expense was placed at four mills.   The power of making the levy was taken from the council and placed in the hands of the Board of Education, which reported its estimate direct to the county auditor, who was directed to assess the amount in the same manner as other taxes.

On February 14, 1848,[2] the act was extended to any incorporated town, city, or borough in the state upon petition of two-thirds of the qualified voters.   This required too large a majority to allow the act to be adopted in localities where there was not an overwhelming sentiment in favor of better school conditions, and in the following year[3] a general act was passed for cities and towns which might be adopted by a majority vote.   The main provisions of this act were similar to the Akron laws, as may be seen by inspection of its chief features:

1.   Any incorporated city, town, or village including within its limits and the territory attached, for school purposes, two hundred inhabitants might organize into a single school district.

2.   The question of adopting the law to be decided by a majority vote of the community.

3.   A board of education of six members elected by the voters.

4.   Building expenses and purchase of sites to be decided by popular vote.   When so decided and reported to the county auditor, the amount to be levied as a tax upon the property of the community.

5.   Primary and graded schools provided for.   No language other than English or German to be taught.

6.   Schools to be free to all children in the district.

[1] O.L., XLVI, local, 40.
[2] O.L., XLVI, 48.
[3] O.L., XLVII, 22.

7. Schools to be kept in operation not less than thirty-six nor more than forty-four weeks each year.

8. Board of education to estimate the amount needed for running expenses not to exceed a four-mill tax annually. Auditor to·levy the amount estimated as a tax.

9. If the amount raised is insufficient to keep the schools open thirty-six weeks, the balance to be raised by school rates on the parents. Indigent pupils exempt from such rates.

10. A board of three examiners to be appointed by the school board.

In 1850[1] the provisions of this act were extended to townships and to special districts, provided such township or district had five hundred inhabitants. The question of the adoption of the law was left, as in the case of towns, to the majority vote of the territory interested.

By far the most interesting and significant feature in the educational legislation of Ohio in the years just preceding 1850 are these laws passed for towns and cities. They indicate an awakening in the urban districts to the need of universal free education. Cincinnati had pointed the way to the other cities of the state since 1829, and had been followed by a considerable number of municipalities. The law passed for the benefit of Akron came when the social consciousness of towns and cities was ready for it, and the legislature responded to this sentiment by allowing communities to adopt its provisions, at first by a majority of two-thirds, but within a year by a simple majority.[2] The state made possible a town or city system that, on the whole, was an excellent system for the period, but the question of organizing under the system was left wholly to the educational interests or municipal pride of the individual communities.

[1] O.L., XLVIII, 40.

[2] Not all towns that adopted it were satisfied. Between 1847 and 1850 three special acts were passed repealing the provisions of the Akron law in the case of three towns that adopted it. Seven other special acts for schools in towns and cities were passed in these three years to meet the desires of municipalities that wished certain different features.

CHAPTER III

THE PUBLIC-SCHOOL LANDS

An enormous mass of legislation was passed by the General Assembly of Ohio, between the years 1803 and 1850, concerning the state school lands. Many of these laws were general in character, many applied to large individual tracts such as the Western Reserve, the Virginia Military Reserve, the United States Military Lands, and the Ohio Company and Symmes Purchases, and in addition to these there were approximately five hundred that were wholly local or special in their application.

A brief description of the more important of these reserves and purchases, some explanation of the various systems of survey used in Ohio, an account of the varying nature of the school grant in these different divisions, and a study of the accompanying maps and diagrams are an almost necessary prerequisite to any clear understanding of this legislation.

The most important of these grants, with their total acreage, including the school lands, are as follows:[1]

	Acres
The Virginia Military Reserve..............	4,204,800
The Western Reserve.....................	3,840,000
The United States Military Lands..........	2,560,000
The Ohio Company's Purchase.............	1,227,168
The Symmes Purchase....................	311,682

In addition to these there were a number of smaller tracts, but the names of only two of them appear in the discussion of the school land legislation. These two were the Refuge Tract, 138,240 acres, and the Moravian Tract,[2] 12,000 acres.

Over 12,000,000 acres were included in these various special districts. The remaining portions of the state were known as Congress Lands, and belonged to the federal government.[3] That portion of the government land which lay on the eastern border of the state, just south of the Western Reserve, was the first to be

---

[1] A. A. Graham, "The Land and Township System of Ohio," *Annual Report of the Secretary of State to the Governor of the State of Ohio for the Year 1885*, pp. 22, 23, 25, 29.

[2] F. H. Swift, *A History of Public Permanent Common School Funds in the United States, 1795–1905*, p. 370.

[3] The Indians still had title to lands in the state. Most of these titles were vested in the government by 1817, but the last titles were not stilled until 1842 (A. A. Graham, "The Land and Township System of Ohio," *Annual Report of the Secretary of State to the Governor of the State of Ohio for the Year 1885*, p. 28).

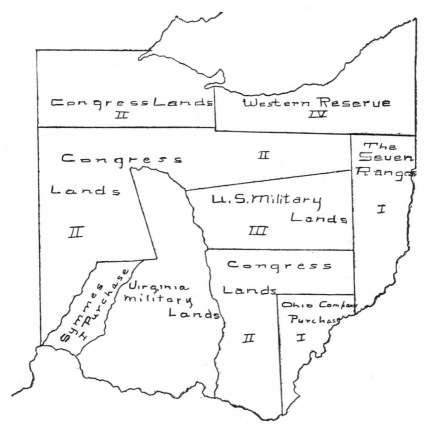

Fig. 1.—Land grants and Congress lands in Ohio

I

36	30	24	18	12	6
35	29	23	17	11	5
34	28	22	16	10	4
33	27	21	15	9	3
32	26	20	14	8	2
31	25	19	13	7	1

II

6	5	4	3	2	1
7	8	9	10	11	12
18	17	16	15	14	13
19	20	21	22	23	24
30	29	28	27	26	25
31	32	33	34	35	36

III

2	1
3	4

IV

3	2
4	1

Fig. 2.—Methods of surveying Ohio lands

surveyed into townships, and was commonly spoken of as the Seven Ranges, because seven ranges of townships west from the Pennsylvania line were included in this first survey.[1]

It has already been pointed out that a state-wide grant of land for school purposes began with Ohio's admission as a state, and that the precedent thus established has been followed in admitting all the later states.[2] It is also true that the rectangular method of laying out townships with meridian lines, sections, towns, and ranges was first practiced in the Ohio surveys,[3] and the method here established became, too, the universal practice in all subsequent government surveys.

Two great American inventions were thus first tried in Ohio— the state-wide grant of school lands, and the rectangular method of survey into six-mile square townships, with thirty-six sections, of one mile square, in each. Ohio was not only the first state to receive Section 16[4] as a school grant; it was the first state to *have* any Section 16.

The surveys in Ohio, however, were not all uniform in the method of laying out and subdividing the townships. The Seven Ranges, as has been said, were first surveyed. The townships here were laid out six miles square, and divided into thirty-six sections, each one mile square, but the numbering of the sections differs from that in the later surveys. The numbering was that shown on page 56, Fig. I. Section 1 is located in the lower southeast corner of the township, and the sections are numbered upward, in tiers of six, from the base line of the township. This method of laying out townships and numbering sections was also used in the Ohio Company and Symmes Purchases.

In the Western Reserve and the United States Military Lands the townships were laid out in five-mile squares instead of six, and at first were not surveyed into sections, but simply divided into four 20,000-acre blocks in each township and these numbered as shown in the diagram on page 56, Fig. IV.

The Virginia Military District is the only part of Ohio in which the rectangular system of survey was not employed. The early

[1] A. A. Graham, "The Land and Township System of Ohio," *Annual Report of the Secretary of State to the Governor of the State of Ohio for the Year 1885*, p. 20.

[2] See page 6.

[3] *Western Reserve Historical Society Tracts*, II, 188.

[4] Section 16 was the section reserved for school purposes in each township in the "Congress Lands" of Ohio and in the Ohio Company and Symmes Purchases. The precedent established has been followed in all the later states, and Section 16 has regularly been the school section. Since 1848, with the admission of Oregon, Section 36 has been added to the school grant.

settlers here chose each "for himself his lands, locating them by any natural boundary, however irregular it might be, taking care only to get the full amount of land demanded by the warrants."[1] "This led to no regular survey, and, as a consequence, an irregularity in township and county lines followed, which were generally based on the boundaries of the warrants."

The rest of the state was made up of Congress Lands, and in all of these the method of survey was that of the six-mile square township, and the division into sections. The manner of numbering the sections was changed from that in the Seven Ranges and in the Ohio Company and Symmes Purchases.

Section 1 in these lands is located in the upper right-hand corner—the northeast corner—of the township, and the sections are numbered to the west and east alternately, Section 6 lying in the northwest corner of the township, and Section 7 located just beneath Section 6 and numbering back to the east again, as shown in the diagram on page 56, Fig. II.

This method of numbering was settled by federal legislation in 1799[2] and has remained the same since that time.

The Land Ordinance of 1785[3] "for ascertaining the mode of disposing of lands in the Western Territory," provided that "there shall be reserved the lot No. 16 of every township for the maintenance of public schools within said township."

In accordance with this provision, as has been seen, Section 16 was reserved for schools in both the Ohio Company and Symmes Purchases. In these two tracts there is also found a reservation for religion as well as for education, a thing not true elsewhere in the state. As a part of the bargain in the purchase of these lands Section 29 in each township was granted by the government to the purchasers for religious purposes, and these sections have ever since been known as the Ministerial Lands.

When Ohio was admitted to the Union the provisions of the Ordinance of 1785, concerning school lands, were carried out as fully as possible in the rest of the state. In all of the Congress Lands Section 16 in each township was permanently reserved for

[1] *Annual Report of the Secretary of State to the Governor of the State of Ohio for the Year 1885*, p. 25. The statements concerning the surveys in Ohio are in the main based on A. A. Graham's article on "The Land and Township System of Ohio," *Annual Report of the Secretary of State to the Governor of the State of Ohio for the Year 1885*, pp. 18–29, and Col. Charles Whittlesey's discussions on "Surveys of Public Land in Ohio," *Western Reserve Historical Society Tracts*, II, 187–91 and 281–86.

[2] *Western Reserve Historical Society Tracts*, II, 282.

[3] T. Donaldson, *The Public Domain*, chap. xiii.

the schools of the township. It was not in the power of Congress to grant Section 16 in such tracts as the Western Reserve, the Virginia Military Reserve, and the United States Military Lands. These lands either did not belong to the federal government or there were prior claims and unsatisfied land warrants that stood in the way of any such granting of specific sections. The United States did not own the land on the Western Reserve, and in the case of the so-called Military Lands the private ownership of much of the land, through the taking up of land scrip or bounties by the soldiers of the Revolution, in the service of the federal government and Virginia, might conflict in any township.

For this reason the assigning of school land in these portions of the state could not take the form of reserving Section 16 in each township. Some other method of setting aside one thirty-sixth part of the land for the use of the schools in these regions had to be devised.

The land originally reserved for schools in the Virginia Military Lands was, in amount, one thirty-sixth of the entire tract, to be selected by the legislature of Ohio from the unlocated lands, after the warrants issued by the state of Virginia had been satisfied.[1]

In 1807[2] Congress, in response to a petition from the state legislature,[3] appropriated eighteen quarter-townships and three sections in lieu of the original grant. These new lands, however, were not located within the Reserve itself, but to the northeast, between the Western Reserve and the United States Military Reserve. This territory was in Congress Lands, title to which had been purchased from the Indians.

In two very significant ways a grant of this kind differed from the grant of Section 16 in each township. In the first place, an assignment of this character could not be made for the township individually, but had to be for the schools of the Virginia Military Reserve as a whole. Secondly, the school lands were at a distance, and not something immediately at hand and under the observation of all as in the case of Section 16 in each township. Something of this same sort was true in the case of each of the other large reserves, and this was bound to be reflected in some differences in legislation concerning these various grants.

---

[1] U.S. Statutes at Large, Vol. II, 225.

[2] Nashee, *A Compilation of Laws, Treaties and Ordinances Which Relate to Lands in the State of Ohio*, p. 157.

[3] O.L., V, 132.

The land reserved for the United States Military Tract[1] was similarly assigned by quarter-townships, but the reservation was made within the United States Military Lands themselves. The amount of the grant in this case was fourteen quarter-townships. It must be remembered in comparing this grant or that of the Western Reserve with those of other parts of the state that the townships in these two regions contain only twenty-five square miles, as compared with thirty-six elsewhere.

The school lands first selected for the Western Reserve consisted of fourteen quarter-townships, not located in the Reserve itself, but in the United States Military Lands. To this was added by the act of Congress in 1834[2] land that amounted to 37,758 acres, to be selected from the unlocated lands of the United States within the state, by sections, half-sections, and quarter-sections. This additional grant of 1834 was in lieu of one thirty-sixth part of that land in the Western Reserve, which belonged to the Indian tribes when Ohio was admitted, but the Indian title to which had been extinguished in 1805.

The Moravian Tract, mentioned once or twice in the legislation, was a comparatively small reserve of 12,000 acres in Tuscarawas County, originally granted by Congress to the Society of United Brethren, in trust for Christian Indians. These lands reverted to the United States in 1824, and in the same year Congress[3] set aside one thirty-sixth part of the tract for the use of schools.

The location of the more important of these various tracts can be most easily gained by consulting the map on page 55.

The Western Reserve is a strip of land on the northern boundary of the state approximately thirty-five miles wide and one hundred and twenty miles long, extending west from the Pennsylvania border. It was this land, which Connecticut claimed and to which she refused to cede her interests when the other states were yielding their claims in the Northwest Territory to the United States, that was known as the Connecticut Western Reserve, or, more generally, simply as the Western Reserve.

The Virginia Military District is located between the Scioto and Little Miami rivers, projecting to the northward considerably past the middle of the state. It takes its name from the fact that

[1] U. S. Statutes at Large, Vol. II, 225.
[2] Ibid., Vol. IV, 679.
[3] Ibid., 56.

this portion of the state was "reserved by Virginia from her cession of the territory northwest of the Ohio River, for the satisfaction of land bounties issued to her troops upon Continental establishment."[1]

The United States had also set aside a large tract of land to be used in paying the claims of her soldiers in the Revolutionary War. This reservation was known as the United States Military Lands, and is located just a little to the east and north of the center of the state.

It is a section of the state fifty miles in width on its eastern border, beginning at the northern line of the original Seven Ranges of townships first surveyed, and following the western boundary of the Seven Ranges fifty miles south. Its southern boundary extends from this point directly west to the Scioto River, while on the west the Scioto itself is the natural barrier; on the north it is bounded by the Greenville Treaty Line (the old Indian boundary line), running from the Scioto back to the Seven Ranges.[2]

In all these grants the purpose and intent of Congress was that the land should be for the use of schools in the particular township in which Section 16 was located, or where it was impossible to grant Section 16, that the lands should be for the use of the particular area for which the grant was made.

The care of the lands was vested in the legislature of the state, for the use of the particular townships and districts interested.[3] Some explanation of the excessive amount of legislation concerning these lands is found if one keeps clearly in mind the terms of the original grant and the ever-present tendency of the Ohio legislature to allow communities, so far as it could legally be done, to conduct their own affairs.

In all the school-land legislation passed in Ohio during this period, the legislature, formally at least, guarded against any diversion of the money received from these lands, but largely followed the desire of the local township or territory as to the handling of the lands, after setting up the formal legal guards. The lands were not regarded, and were not intended, as a grant to the state at large, and it is perhaps only natural that an attempt should have been made to carry out the desires of the townships and

[1] Taylor, *A Manual of the Ohio School System*, p. 83.
[2] *Ibid.*, p. 85.
[3] Nashee, *A Compilation of Laws, Treaties and Ordinances Which Relate to Lands in the State of Ohio*, pp. 154, 155.

districts to which the lands were felt to belong. Added to this there was the disposition to be lenient with the early settlers on the lands. No doubt, justice was not done to the cause of education, but it must be remembered that the schools had no advocate, while the petitioner asking special privileges or terms in regard to the sale or lease of lands was a concrete fact with concrete desires and needs, and the legislature doubtless felt that it had done its whole duty if the terms of the grant were formally protected.

Certain general policies of handling the lands may be outlined before the legislation is discussed in greater detail. These are: the policy of temporary leasing, 1803 to 1817; the policy of permanent leasing, 1817 to 1823; preparation for selling the lands, with temporary leasing, 1823 to 1827; the policy of selling the lands outright, 1827 to 1850.

The evident intent of the first acts concerning school lands was to devise a means of making them productive and valuable and to keep the lands themselves as a permanent source of revenue.

On April 15, 1803,[1] the legislature passed an act that provided for leasing Section 16 for a term that was not to exceed seven years, and the lands in the United States Military Tract, which included both the grants to that tract and to the Western Reserve, for a period not to exceed fifteen years.

The rent was to be paid by certain specified improvements. On each quarter-section (160 acres) fifteen acres were to be cleared and fenced in separate fields, five acres were to be sowed in timothy or red clover, three acres to be planted with one hundred thrifty and growing apple trees, and the remaining seven acres prepared for plow land. The leasing was to be carried on by agents in the several counties or districts appointed by the governor, and the leases were to be granted to those who guaranteed to make the required improvements in the shortest period of time.

The intention was to attract settlers who were unable to buy land or pay rent, and have them by their labor turn the school land into an attractive and productive piece of property, which would command a definite revenue. The difficulty with the plan from the lessees' standpoint was that, just at the time the land became productive, he must either move or begin to pay rent for improvements which he himself had made. With land cheap and

[1] O.L., I, 61.

abundant on every hand and terms easy, the ambitious and desirable settlers were not attracted by a proposition that did not allow them to keep the land on which they settled and the improvements which they had themselves made.

The results were evidently not satisfactory, for on February 20, 1805,[1] an act was passed giving the township trustees authority to lease the lands in their respective townships for a term not to exceed fifteen years to those who made the most "advantageous proposals." This was followed in 1806[2] by an act which allowed any surveyed township in which there were twenty electors to incorporate and choose trustees for the special management of Section 16. The section was to be laid off in lots of eighty to two hundred acres, and not more than one lot could be leased by any one person. It was made the duty of the trustees to guard against waste and to see that the terms of the lease were complied with. The provisions of these acts left the management of the lands and the terms of leasing wholly in the hands of the township, except for the fact that a fifteen-year term could not be exceeded and not more nor less than a specified amount leased to any one person.

None of the acts so far had made any provision for the land granted to the Virginia Military Tract for the use of schools. It will be remembered that this consisted of some eighteen townships lying outside the district and not located so that it could be locally managed.

By an act passed in 1809[3] these lands were offered for sale to the highest bidder at a minimum price of two dollars per acre, the purchaser receiving a ninety-nine year lease, renewable forever, with no provision for revaluation. It was the evident design to sell these lands out at once and create a fund the proceeds from which might be available for school purposes when needed.[4] The act provided that the lands were to be advertised in four newspapers within the state, and newspapers at Pittsburgh and Brownsville, Pennsylvania, and Wheeling, Virginia.

The purchaser was to pay down the sum charged against each quarter section for the expense of surveying and offering the land for sale, and on the purchase price yearly interest of 6 per cent for-

---

[1] O.L., III, 230.
[2] O.L., IV, 66.
[3] O.L., VII, 109.
[4] The money received was to be paid into the state treasury subject to appropriation by the state until it should be appropriated for the use of schools in the district (O.L., XIII, 307).

ever. Succeeding legislatures were given the right to make such commutations as they might deem expedient. This clause was evidently intended to leave the way open for legislation that would permit a cash payment in lieu of the 6 per cent annual rental.

The terms were made still easier for the purchaser by the act of 1810,[1] which provided that the amount paid down on each quarter section should be ten dollars (to pay for surveying, advertising, etc.), and that the 6 per cent interest should not begin until five years from the date of sale. The postponement of interest money for five years was doubtless made to meet the competition of United States land offered for sale within the state on easy terms and with taxes deferred for the first five years after purchase. Each purchaser was required by this act to build a cabin and clear three acres of land within three years.

In the same year[2] an act was passed allowing the township trustees to receive either money or produce as rent from Section 16, and requiring the lessee to make such improvements as the trustees thought proper, and in 1814[3] it was made illegal for any lessee of school lands to act as township trustee or treasurer.

This covers the main features of the land policy during the period of temporary leasing. Beginning with 1816[4] in the Virginia Military Tract, and 1817[5] in the rest of the state, the policy was inaugurated of granting permanent leases with a revaluation of the lands at stated periods.

The policy of selling the Virginia Military Lands was changed for the lands that were still unsold. The governor was to appoint "three disinterested persons to appraise them" and a register under a bond of ten thousand dollars was appointed to lease them. The leases ran for ninety-nine years, renewable forever, but the law provided that they were to be revalued in 1835 and each twenty years after that date, the rental to be 6 per cent on the appraised value, payable annually.

This principle, with certain changes in details, was adopted the following year, 1817, for the rest of the state,[6] with the exception of the Western Reserve school lands. Those who held school lands

---

[1] O.L., VIII, 253.
[2] O.L., VIII, 100.
[3] O.L., XIII, 295.
[4] O.L., XIV, 418.
[5] O.L., XV, 202.
[6] *Idem.*

under temporary leases were allowed to obtain permanent leases by making application to the county commissioners in the following manner: they must present, first, a certificate signed by the township trustees that they had complied with their present lease, and, secondly, the consent in writing of the trustees of the organized township and of a majority of the citizens in unorganized townships to the granting of a permanent lease in the place of a temporary one. The land was then appraised by three appraisers appointed by the county commissioners, and the value of all improvements was made a part of the appraised estimate (improvements under temporary leases were a part of the rental paid). The township trustees were then authorized to grant leases for ninety-nine years, renewable forever, at the rate of 6 per cent annually, and with a revaluation each thirty-three years. The same method was followed in the case of unoccupied lands, excepting the provision concerning compliance with the former lease.

In unorganized townships the county commissioners had charge of the leasing, and in the United States Military District the Court of Common Pleas. When land was revalued, it was to be appraised at the rate of unimproved land of the same quality in the vicinity. The appraiser was to consider only the general advance in land prices and not the value that had been added by the labor of the lessee.

Another act passed in 1821[1] directed that land in the United States Military Tract appraised at less than one dollar an acre should not be leased, and confirmed the principle of permanent leasing with minor changes in details of administration. Improvements made by settlers in this district were included in the valuation at the *first* appraisal after this date, being considered as a part of the rental on the temporary leases held by such settlers. These laws for permanent leasing at no time applied to the school lands belonging to the Western Reserve.

While the general policy of ninety-nine-year leases with a revaluation at stated periods began in the years 1816 and 1817, there had been many individual leases of this type legalized by special legislative action. It was not, therefore, a totally new departure. Prior to 1817 twenty-five local acts had been passed by the legislature legalizing permanent leases for portions of the school land in various localities, and in the leasing of the Ministerial

[1] O.L., XIX, 161.

Lands, Section 29, in the Symmes and Ohio Company Purchases, this plan had been adopted as early as 1806.[1]

The first school land to be so leased was the section belonging to the town of Marietta in 1808.[2]   From this time until it became a general policy, the wishes or needs of various communities were met by these special legislative actions.   It is interesting to note that in ten of the twenty-five acts so passed the reason assigned is the establishment of a flour mill, sawmill, or similar industry.   In these cases Section 16 evidently furnished desirable mill sites and water power, but lessees were unwilling to erect mills, so essential to newly settled communities, without some guaranty of permanence.

In general, the policy of permanent leasing was found undesirable.   From the present standpoint it can be seen that if it had been persisted in, and the leasing and revaluation had been carefully managed, it would have preserved to the state a school property of enormous value, which would eventually have produced an income far in excess of the method of selling the lands and funding the proceeds.   From the standpoint of the men of that time it was found undesirable because it did not succeed in producing any adequate revenue *then* for the schools.   Land was abundant and cheap.   Money for the support of schools was scarce.   The state was rapidly filling up,[3] but desirable settlers preferred to obtain land in fee simple.   It doubtless appeared to those most friendly toward schools and education that it would be more desirable to take advantage of the opportunity to sell, getting the best terms possible and assuring to the schools some definite support from the grant that had been made.   Up to this time the actual revenue derived from the lands had been very small.[4]

Caleb Atwater, of Cincinnati, a warm friend of the schools, as chairman of a committee in the Lower House, said in a report to the Assembly in 1822:

From all the committee have been able to learn it would seem[5] that more money has been expended by the state in legislating concerning these lands than they have yet or ever will produce, unless some other method of managing them

[1] O.L., IV, 38.

[2] O.L., VI, 96.

[3] See p. 4.

[4] Atwater, speaking of the first eighteen years of the state's history, said: "Scarcely a dollar was ever paid over to the people for whose benefit the land had been given" (Atwater, *A History of the State of Ohio, Natural and Civil*, p. 253).

[5] *Ibid.*, p. 258.

be devised than any hitherto pursued. . . . . The committee are impressed with the belief that unless these lands are soon sold . . . . no good and much evil will accrue to the state from the grant of these lands by Congress.

He was not alone in his opinion. A memorial addressed to Congress by the General Assembly in the same year,[1] speaking of school lands in general in the West, said that these lands had as yet been very unproductive, and while the legislatures of the states in which they are situated are restricted by the conditions attached to these grants they must ever be so. Indeed, it may well be doubted whether more money has not been spent than the whole amount derived from the lands.

The legislature at this session was evidently impressed by Atwater's report and convinced that the policy of leasing under any of the plans tried was a failure. The lands belonging to the Western Reserve were still being leased on temporary leases with a maximum of fifteen years' duration. Throughout the rest of the state the policy of permanent leasing was the authorized method.

The unleased lands belonging to the Western Reserve were first withdrawn from leasing. This act, passed January 21, 1822,[2] forbade any further leasing of unoccupied lands, and allowed occupied lands to be released not longer than to April 1, 1826. The following year, January 27, 1823,[3] the legislature authorized the surrender of leases for school lands throughout the entire state, and forbade the granting of any new leases for a period of one year. The intent of this law was evidently not to compel a surrender of leases, but to provide a way in which they might be legally terminated at the desire of the lessee, with a prospect of sale in fee simple at some future time.

This same act directed the various county auditors and the register of school lands in the United States Military District to make a complete report to the auditor of state showing "the whole amount of school lands in each county, what proportion is leased, what is vacant, how the lands are divided, distinguishing each tract by the number of acres, range, township, section and quarter, showing what parts are leased, what rent is reserved on each tract leased, how long the lease is to run, whether renewable, and if so, whether subject to reappraisement."

[1] O.L., XX, 64.
[2] O.L., XX, 34.
[3] O.L., XXI, 33.

It is evident that neither the legislature nor any state officer knew just what the situation was in regard to school lands throughout the state. This lack of information was the natural result of the various policies adopted for handling the lands. In organized townships the township trustees were in charge of the leasing and in unorganized townships, the county commissioners. In the United States Military District the Court of Common Pleas supervised the leasing of both the lands reserved for that district and those belonging to the Western Reserve, while in the Virginia Military District a land officer, appointed by the General Assembly, was in charge. There was no central office or body which had general supervision except the legislature itself. This body now felt the necessity of a general change of policy, but found that it lacked information as to what had already been done.

The cessation of leasing and the acquiring of the information desired prepared the way for this general change in policy. It was felt that more advantageous results could be obtained by selling the lands outright, but there was doubt in the minds of the legislators as to the authority of the state to permit the lands to be disposed of in this way. By the terms of the original grant, the lands had been set aside for the use of schools in the particular townships and districts forever. While the general management of the trust was vested in the legislature, it seemed doubtful if actual alienation of the lands was originally contemplated, even though the funds should be permanently invested for the use of schools.

In 1824,[1] a carefully phrased memorial was submitted to Congress, asking, first, for an additional grant of land for the use of schools in the Western Reserve,[2] and, secondly, that Congress confirm the right of the state of Ohio to sell the school lands. As an indication of the sentiment of the time it is an interesting document. It shows, first, that the general attitude of the state toward the grant from the United States was that the lands had been ceded by the United States in return for certain concessions made by Ohio, and, secondly, the difficulties that inhered in the attempt to derive a revenue from the lands themselves. The memorial argues

---

[1] O.L., XXII, local, 153.

[2] When the original grant was made for the Western Reserve, no lands were set aside for the use of schools in the lands then held by the Indian tribes within the Reserve. When the Indian title was extinguished, Ohio immediately asked for an additional grant equal to one thirty-sixth part of the land so held. This grant was finally made by Congress in 1834. (U.S. Statutes at Large, Vol. IV, 679.)

that the original grants were in the nature of a compact made with the state and were "granted upon full consideration arising from the increased value of the remaining lands belonging to the United States and also from the relinquishment, on the part of the state of Ohio, of the right to tax the lands of the United States within the state of Ohio until five years after the sale thereof"; "that it was the intention of the parties to the compact aforesaid that one thirty-sixth part of all the lands within the state of Ohio should be granted to the people thereof for the use of common schools, and should be placed under the control of the legislature," and that the state is of right entitled to the additional grant for the Western Reserve.

The memorial goes on to say that, in relation to the lands already appropriated, the legislature has "resorted to various methods of rendering them productive, and, in particular, that of leasing them to such individuals as have applied therefor; that experience has fully demonstrated that this fund will be wholly unavailing in their hands in its present shape"; that to accomplish the objects contemplated "the legislature should possess unlimited control over the lands" with the power of disposing of them in fee.

"The objections which are urged against the present mode of administering that fund are in the first place that by reason of the facilities which the state of Ohio affords for acquiring property in real estate, a necessity exists of leasing the lands to persons almost destitute of pecuniary means whereby the avails of these lands are rendered, at least, uncertain. In consequence also, that as these lands are detached over the whole of the state of Ohio, the expense which must necessarily be incurred by creating a superintendence over them renders them less productive than your memorialists conceive they might be rendered if the lands were sold and the proceeds concentrated in one fund."

"The fact, also, before adverted to, that these lands must necessarily be entrusted to the possession of those of the lowest class of the community, and who possess no permanent interest in the soil, has produced a waste upon these lands of their timber and otherwise, equal perhaps to the whole revenue which may have been derived from them."

The memorial recites further that the method of leasing "will invite and retain a population within her boundaries of a character not to be desired and in amount so great as to create an evil which can only be conceived of in a country where every individual possessing a very moderate portion of industry and economy may, within a single year, appropriate to himself in fee a quantity of land sufficient to furnish means of support for an ordinary family."

The memorial continues by saying "that these evils arise wholly from the system of granting leases and are such as cannot be remedied by legislative action, if, as some have supposed, the state have not the power, under the terms of the original grant, of disposing of these lands in fee." The memorialists believe that the state has the right, but "they are of the opinion that an act of the Congress of the United States declaratory of the extent of the grant aforesaid will be productive of much benefit in case the legislature of the state should hereafter determine to dispose of the same; that it will have the full effect of removing the doubt in the minds of the purchasers and thereby enhance the price which will be obtained for the same."

They therefore asked Congress to grant them the right to dispose of the lands in fee, the proceeds to be invested in a permanent fund, the income of which should be applied for the use of common schools in the townships or districts to which the lands were originally granted, provided that Section 16 should not be sold without the consent of the inhabitants of the township to which the land belonged.

Congress passed the desired legislation February 1, 1826,[1] and on January 27, 1827,[2] the legislature passed an act directing each township in the state possessing school land to vote upon the question of its sale, and also authorizing the inhabitants of the United States Military District[3] and the Virginia Military District[4] to decide the same question. Legislation authorizing a vote on the Western Reserve[5] was not passed until the following year.

In the meantime the policy of special legislation to meet local needs had continued. From 1817 to 1823,[6] the period of permanent leasing, twenty-one local acts had been passed making special provisions for leasing or extending the time for making payments

---

[1] U.S. Statutes at Large, Vol. IV, 138.
[2] O.L., XXV, 56.
[3] O.L., XXV, 103.
[4] O.L., XXV, local, 45.
[5] O.L., XXVI, local, 135.
[6] O.L., XIX, 35, 72, 75 are examples.

on leases, and from 1823 to 1827 eleven more acts were passed authorizing the revaluation of lands leased, changing the conditions for lessees, or authorizing short-time leases, etc.

The general policy inaugurated by the legislation of 1827 and 1828 remained the policy of the state until 1850, though certain changes were made correcting some of the more undesirable features.

The legislation of 1827 provided that the townships or districts interested should decide upon the sale of their school lands and described the method by which the sale was to be made in case the vote was favorable. It did not actually authorize the sale. This was to be done after the vote was taken by additional acts of the legislature, or in the case of the United States Military District by proclamation of the governor. The provisions governing the sale were as follows: Land that was unoccupied was to be appraised by the county assessor. The land was then advertised and offered for sale to the highest bidder by the county auditor. No bid could be received for less than appraised value. Payments were made to the county treasurer, and the money received by him was deposited with the state treasurer to the credit of the township or district to which it had belonged. When the money was all paid, the purchaser received a deed from the state.

It was in the legislation concerning the occupied lands that the greatest loss occurred to the state. Holders of permanent leases were allowed to surrender their leases, and by the payment of the appraised value upon which it had been originally leased receive a deed in fee simple. The terms of payment were easy, running over periods of seven to ten years, and by subsequent legislation further extended in many cases.

The following year, 1828,[1] the legislature authorized sales to be made in thirty-nine counties in which the vote had been favorable. From this time until 1850 there was a constant succession of local acts authorizing sales in various townships and counties; making provisions for leasing lands where the assent was not given to the sale; authorizing revaluation of lands where lessees thought the original valuation was too high, or the townships considered it too low; giving additional time in which to make the payments due; and in general enacting various laws that had only local application. Between 1827 and 1850 approximately four hundred such acts were

[1] O.L., XXVI, local, 4.

passed.   In 1828[1] those townships that had not voted to sell their school lands were authorized to lease it for periods of not less than three years for improved lands nor seven years for unimproved lands.   In case the consent of the townships had been given and the lands remained unsold, they might be leased from year to year on the best terms obtainable.   The entire arrangement and responsibility were placed in the hands of the township trustees.   In 1838,[2] largely through the influence of Samuel Lewis, the state superintendent of schools, the practice of allowing the holders of permanent leases to surrender their leases, and, by payment of the first appraised value, receive a deed in fee simple, was stopped, and by an act of 1843[3] such surrender was authorized only upon the land being reappraised and the amount of its new valuation paid.   From 1839[4] on it was a common practice to include a minimum price below which the land could not be sold, and in 1845[5] a general act was passed forbidding the sale of any school land in the state for less than five dollars an acre.   This act of 1845 is the last important school land legislation during the period 1803–1850.

SUMMARY

The first attempt of the legislature was to preserve the lands and make them productive through a system of short-term leases which provided for the payment of rents through improvements made upon the lands.   This system was followed until 1817 with the exception of the land belonging to the Virginia Military District.

The system of temporary leasing was found unsatisfactory, and in 1817 the state embarked on the policy of authorizing permanent leases with a revaluation of lands at periods of thirty to thirty-five years.   This system also proved unsatisfactory in practice.

From 1827 on the state legalized the sale of school lands in fee simple, but allowed the local community to decide whether the lands should be sold, and in case they were not, the management was left in the hands of the township trustees, with certain limitations as to the length of time for which leases might be granted. The money from lands sold was paid through the county treasurer's

[1] O.L., XXVI, 80.
[2] O.L., XXXVI, 63.
[3] O.L., XLI, 20.
[4] O.L., XXXVII, local, 88.
[5] O.L., XLIII, 58.

office into the office of the state treasurer and placed at the disposal of the state, the state pledging itself to pay a 6 per cent annual interest upon the moneys so deposited for the use of the schools of the township or territory to which the land had belonged. The revenue from leased land was handled directly by the township trustees and apportioned among the school districts of the townships. The basis of apportionment in each case was the number of white unmarried youth between the ages of four and twenty-one. During the whole period the legislature heeded local needs and wishes through local and special legislation.

The results of the system, or lack of system, entailed great loss. This loss was not due primarily to the leasing of the lands or the selling of them, but to the fact that the state had no central office whose business it was to oversee the lands and know exactly what the conditions were in regard to them, and to see that the laws in force were obeyed. The legislature was a changing body. It lacked necessary information for intelligent action in many cases, and it attempted to meet local conditions without complete knowledge of the facts.

The chief specific points in the general policy that resulted in loss were:

First, that of allowing permanent lessees whose lands had been appraised during the period from 1817 to 1823[1] to surrender their leases and obtain deeds by paying the original appraisal value. This policy was followed until 1838.

Secondly,[2] the policy of local appraisal. This might or might not work well. It depended wholly on the appraisers chosen. It was found necessary to forbid by law any appraiser purchasing land.

Thirdly, that no minimum price was placed upon the school lands until 1845.[3]

Fourthly, the policy of local control in leasing and of special or local legislation. Where the school sentiment was high this

---

[1] "Cases have come to my knowledge where land has been taken at six dollars per acre worth at the time fifty dollars. . . . . The tenants to be sure make their fortunes, but the schools are sacrificed" (Ohio Documents, 36th G. A., Doc. 17, p. 41).

[2] "In one very aggravated case the assessor was a lessee on the land" (ibid., Doc. 17, p. 41).

[3] "It is not uncommon to find land sold for fifty, forty, thirty, twenty, ten, and in one case, as low as five cents per acre. Men have become the purchasers of whole sections for a mere trifle, and that sometimes where it only required a few years to have realized five, ten, fifteen or twenty dollars per acre" (Third Annual Report of the Superintendent of the Common Schools, made to the Thirty-eighth General Assembly of the State of Ohio, p. 58).

might work well, but where it was low the results were likely to be disastrous.

The state lacked any settled, clearly defined policy, and it lacked administrative machinery to oversee the policies that were initiated. The legislators, in general, were doubtless honest in their efforts, but they were in session but a few weeks each year and then were engaged on all classes of legislation. It was only as one had opportunity to study the question in detail and in its bearing upon the state as a whole, and to carry on this work for a period of years, that a basis could be afforded for intelligent action. Samuel Lewis was enabled to give a portion of his time to this work in the three years from 1837 to 1840, and the legislation resulting saved thousands of dollars for the schools.

A quotation from the report of John Brough, auditor of state in 1839 and 1840, furnishes a fitting conclusion to this summary. Mr. Brough had previously been a member of the legislature and as a member was evidently satisfied that the general policy followed by the legislature was desirable. The quotation shows the change in his opinion when, as auditor of state, he gave the question careful study.

One of the most important items of state policy, and one which it is feared has been least investigated and understood, is the prudent management and judicious disposition of our school lands. Through the indefatigable labor of the state superintendent, public attention has been fully aroused to the waste that has been committed in this property, and a determination instilled to place additional guards upon the future. That determination cannot be too carefully cherished or rigidly adhered to. The investigations imposed by the ordinary discharge of public duty have thrown a light and sealed a conviction upon my own mind, at variance with my former opinions, which had been conceived upon a superficial knowledge of the subject;—and such will be the effect upon the mind of every one who will seek the records and gather the melancholy information they contain. Our school fund this year, arising from interest on sales of lands, and subject to distribution among the counties, is $73,618.78; and to accumulate this, we have sacrificed lands, which, if they had been judiciously held and managed, would have now given us at least ten times that amount and constituted a revenue sufficient to educate every child in the state.[1]

[1] O.L., XXXVIII, Auditor's Report, 32–33.

CHAPTER IV

SECONDARY AND HIGHER EDUCATION

SECONDARY EDUCATION

The legislation concerning secondary education in Ohio prior to 1850 deals wholly with the incorporation of private secondary institutions, except in the case of a few city or town charters in the last few years of this period, which make provision for schools of "a higher grade" or for high schools.

The state did not concern itself with secondary schools except to indicate the manner in which they might be incorporated and in placing certain limits upon their activities and upon the amount of property they might hold. Here again the principle was that of local initiative with the state willing to encourage local effort by legally recognizing the school established, but taking no responsibility or initiative for establishing, supporting, or controlling such schools.

The constitution declared that every association of persons having given themselves a name might, on application to the legislature, be entitled to receive letters of incorporation to enable them to hold estates for the support of their schools, academies, colleges, universities, and for other purposes.[1] When the legislature had granted the act of incorporation provided for, it considered its whole duty in the matter at an end. The idea of a free system of common schools gradually developed during the period and the conception of state-wide taxation for at least their partial support appears as early as 1825, but at no time prior to 1850 does the legislation show any conception of a state system of education embracing elementary, secondary, and higher education. Secondary education was for those communities that wanted and could afford to pay for it.

Mr. Lewis in his second report in 1838 had clearly in mind the beginnings of a state secondary system. He did not, however, advocate legislation that would in any way compel the state to take a part in the establishment of secondary schools, but rather a

---

[1] O.L., I, 3, Art. 8, Sec. 27.

law that would allow individual townships to establish such schools and support them from public funds, with the method of establishment and support warranted by the law of the state.

His advice to the legislature on the subject was as follows:

> There are some townships that have the means and the desire of establishing central township schools or academies, and in most of our townships the youth over twelve years of age could with convenience attend such a school. The number of townships now prepared for this measure is small, but will be increasing. I recommend, therefore, a provision giving the whole number of directors in the township authority to establish such a school, and assess upon the township such sum of money as may be required for that purpose, and to this end they should from their own number appoint a board of five, who should for the time being control such central school.
>
> The mere passage of the law could do no harm to those townships who would refuse to avail themselves of its provisions, and would give to those desiring the privilege, the right to exercise it.[1]

No action was taken upon this recommendation, and no general legislation concerning secondary education was enacted prior to 1850. Some city charters made provision for schools above the elementary, but the state did not concern itself with secondary education as a recognized part of the public-school system.

The usual type of secondary institution receiving letters of incorporation was an academy supported by a stock company, with shares selling for from five to fifty dollars each. A community that wished an education for its children beyond the three R's of the common school subscribed stock for the purpose of building and equipping a school of higher grade. The management was ordinarily in the hands of a board of trustees elected by the stockholders. In most cases the articles of incorporation do not mention tuition or rates, but in some cases it is specifically stated[2] that the running expense of the school shall be assessed upon the parents in proportion to the number of children attending, and doubtless in all cases tuition was charged. Occasionally the trustees are authorized to set apart a fund for the education of poor children.[3] A school of this type was usually called an academy; less frequently the terms "institute" and "seminary" appeared. The names "seminary" and "institute" are not used, with one or two exceptions, until after 1830. The name "high school" appears at this

---

[1] Ohio Documents, 37th G.A., Doc. 32, p. 28.
[2] O.L., XVI, 157. Towns of Harpersfield and Madison, 1818.
[3] O.L., IX, 57. Gallia Academy, 1811.

same period and is used occasionally to designate a school of this same general type of organization, supported by an association of subscribers, who formed a stock company to raise the funds for the establishment or support of the school. The first high school chartered in Ohio was The High School of Elyria, February 22, 1830,[1] followed the next year by the Woodward High School of Cincinnati.[2] The latter institution had been incorporated as the "Free Grammar School" as early as 1827,[3] but its earlier function was declared to be the "better instruction of the poor children" "in the rudiments of an English education." By the terms of the incorporation the trustees were directed to confine instruction to "the common and necessary branches of an English education" and not to extend it to the higher branches of such an education until the funds were sufficient to provide for all the poor children in the city.

The total number of secondary schools incorporated from 1803 to 1850 was 172, classed as follows:

Academies—	1803–10	4	
	1811–20	8	
	1821–30	10	
	1831–40	44	
	1841–50	27	
		—	
			93
Seminaries—	1803–10	1	
	1811–20	1	
	1821–30	0	
	1831–40	20	
	1841–50	10	
		—	
			32
Institutes—	1803–30	0	
	1831–40	13	
	1841–50	17	
		—	
			30
High schools—	1803–20	0	
	1821–30	1	
	1831–40	8	
	1841–50	5	
		—	
			14

[1] O.L., XXVIII, local, 116.
[2] O.L., XXIX, local, 43.
[3] O.L., XXV, local, 62.

Boarding school.................................   1
Universal school...............................   1
Independent school............................   1
                                                  ___
                                                    3
                                                  ___
Total..................................,....   172

The names of these schools and the dates of their incorporation arranged in chronological order are shown on pages 78-83 and their location is shown on the map that accompanies this list. The Erie Literary Society, located at Burton, on the Western Reserve, leads the list in 1803, followed by academies in Dayton, Worthington, and Chillicothe in 1808.

The Western Reserve far outstrips any other section of the state in the number of these institutions, having more than three times as many as any other section. The map shows, however, that with the exception of the western portion of the state, where the settlements were much later, these schools were fairly abundant in all parts of Ohio.

The ambitious boy or girl had before him the incentive to a higher education than the common schools afforded and the possibility of attaining it without going to any great distance. The omnipresence of the Ohio man later in our country's history may be in no small part accounted for by the omnipresence of the Ohio academy and college.

The list given and the institutions located on the map by no means give all schools of this type founded before 1850. Only those that received articles of incorporation from the state legislature are here shown.

Secondary Institutions in Order of Chartering, 1803–50

1. Erie Literary Society, Burton................................   1803
2. Dayton Academy...   1808
3. Worthington Academy......................................   1808
4. Chillicothe Academy..   1808
5. New Lisbon Academy..   1810
6. Steubenville Academy.......................................   1811
7. Gallia Academy, Gallipolis...................................   1811
8. Cincinnati Lancaster Seminary..............................   1815
9. Montgomery Academy..   1816
10. Tallmadge Academy...   1816
11. Florence Academy..   1818
12. Cadiz Academy...   1819

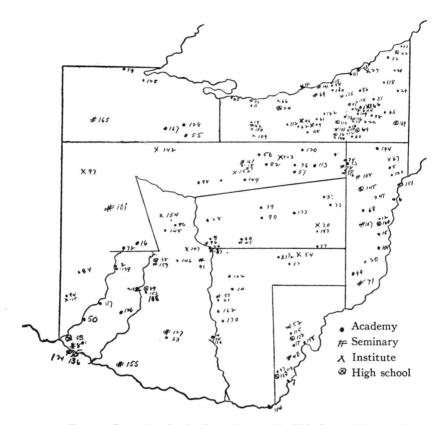

FIG. 3.—Secondary institutions chartered in Ohio from 1803 to 1850

60. Granville Academy... 1836
61. Sharon Academy.. 1836
62. Medina Academy... 1836
63. Cleves Independent School................................. 1836
64. Middleburg High School.................................... 1836
65. Warren Academy... 1837
66. Sheffield Manual Labor Institute......................... 1837
67. Neville Institute, Columbiana County..................... 1837
68. New Hagerstown Academy.................................... 1837
69. Berea Seminary... 1837
70. Philomathean Literary Institute, Antrim................. 1837
71. Monroe Seminary, Monroe County........................... 1837
72. Troy Academy... 1837
73. New Philadelphia Academy.................................. 1837
74. Massillon Academy.. 1837
75. Cleveland Female Seminary................................. 1837
76. Akron High School.. 1838
77. Cambridge Academy, Guernsey County....................... 1838
78. Massillon Female Seminary................................. 1838
79. Western Reserve Wesleyan Seminary, Streetsborough........ 1838
80. Edinburgh Academy.. 1838
81. Wayne Academy.. 1838
82. Norwalk Female Seminary.................................... 1838
83. Chester Academy, Geauga County............................ 1838
84. Eaton Academy.. 1838
85. Sandusky Academy... 1838
86. Union Academy, Union County............................... 1838
87. Dover Academy, Tuscarawas County.......................... 1838
88. Marion Academy, Marion County............................. 1838
89. Bigelow High School, Xenia................................. 1839
90. Martinsburg Academy, Knox County.......................... 1839
91. Blendon Young Men's Seminary.............................. 1839
92. Ashland Academy, Richland County.......................... 1839
93. Western Reserve Teachers' Seminary, Kirtland............. 1839
94. Oxford Female Academy...................................... 1839
95. Asbury Seminary, Chagrin Falls............................ 1839
96. Worthington Female Seminary............................... 1839
97. Universalist Institute, Ohio City......................... 1839
98. Parkman Academy, Geauga County............................ 1839
99. Barnesville Male Academy.................................. 1839
100. Brooklyn Centre Academy................................... 1839
101. Auglaize Seminary, Wapakoneta............................. 1839
102. Lithopolis Academy.. 1839
103. Meigs County High School and Teachers' Institute........ 1839
104. Mt. Pleasant Boarding School.............................. 1839
105. Cuyahoga Falls Institute.................................. 1839
106. Ravenna Female Seminary................................... 1839
107. New Hagerstown Female Seminary............................ 1839

SCHOOL COMPANIES AND ASSOCIATIONS

There were also incorporated during the same period twenty-three school or education societies whose purpose was to found academies or other schools, or in some way offer better educational facilities to the communities interested.

The denominational influence does not seem to have been great in founding these secondary schools. Some twenty-one of the schools and societies are more or less denominational in control or in sympathy, as indicated by the act of incorporation or the name. In six cases the Conference of the Methodist Episcopal Church either appointed the trustees or had some part in the appointment of them. The other schools and societies that show denominational influence are scattered among the Presbyterian, Baptist, Catholic, German Lutheran, and Quaker sects. It is true that prior to 1836 there were also eighty-four church incorporations in which the churches were given a right to maintain a school by the articles of incorporation. The usual form in which this was done was by limiting the use of funds to the support of a church "and to any institution of charity or education connected therewith." In 1836[1] a general law was passed which gave any religious society incorporating after that date the right to apply property not exceeding an annual value of one thousand dollars to the support of public worship and such institutions of learning and charity as might be connected with such society. How far the rights thus extended were used by the churches to found schools of secondary grade the laws themselves give no hint. Only a careful search of church records could do this. It is probable, however, that a secondary school of any importance would have followed the custom of the time and sought independent incorporation. The financial limitations both in special and in general acts would have prevented an extensive educational institution.

The comparatively small denominational influence exerted on secondary schools was not due to any lack of religious or sectarian interest. Numerous sects and varied religious beliefs[2] were common, but this very multiplicity was a source of religious toleration, and in the founding of schools for the children of the community a common interest was found, in support of which the adherents of creeds that were not too divergent often united.

There are frequent indications in the articles of incorporation of an effort to keep the schools free from any cause of religious

[1] O.L., XXXIV, 17.
[2] Chaddock. *Ohio Before 1850. A Study of the Early Influence of Pennsylvania and Southern Populations in Ohio*, p. 313.

controversy. Sections appear prohibiting the introduction or teaching of any religious tenets peculiar to any Christian sect.[1] Sometimes there is recognition of the fact that there are other possible causes of dissension, as when a clause appears providing that "no political, religious, moral or literary association shall have an ascendancy in the directory."[2]

The curriculum was not usually specified in the articles of incorporation, but was frequently hinted at in the right given to the trustees to determine what branches of the "arts and sciences" should be taught, or sometimes the phrase ran "learned languages, arts and sciences," or branches of a "polite and liberal education."

The manual labor influence first appeared in 1834 with the incorporation of Stephen Strong's Manual Labor Seminary.[3] The Ashtabula Institution of Science and Industry had been founded as early as 1831,[4] but in 1835[5] the name was changed to the Grand River Institute, and there is nothing but the earlier name to indicate anything other than the ordinary secondary institution. The name of Pestalozzi's one-time associate, Fellenberg, was doubtless in the minds of the incorporators of the Fellenburgh Institute in Medina County in 1835,[6] though no mention is made of manual labor in the articles of incorporation. There are only four other secondary institutions whose articles of incorporation make any mention of this phase of education.[7] One of these, Bishop's Fraternal Calvanistic [sic] Seminary, chartered in 1835, specifies that there shall be manual labor for both males and females.[8]

The only control the state exercised over these institutions was in limiting the amount of property they might hold, the amount of the annual income, or the amount of stock that might be issued. It was also common to find an express stipulation forbidding an incorporated company of this character to engage in the banking business or to issue any medium of exchange. The legislature, too, commonly reserved the right to alter the articles of incorpora-

[1] O.L., XIII, 132; O.L., XX, 11; O.L., XX, 27; O.L., XXII, 14.
[2] O.L., XIII, 132.
[3] O.L., XXXIII, local, 5.
[4] O.L., XXIX, local, 137.
[5] O.L., XXXIII, local, 79.
[6] O.L., XXXIII, local, 112.
[7] The Sheffield Manual Labor Institute, Bishop's Fraternal Calvanistic [sic] Seminary, the Huron Institute, and Berea Seminary.
[8] O.L., XXXIII, local, 328.

tion at any time, and in 1839[1] a general act was passed to regulate incorporated literary societies, which included all associations for literary purposes except common schools, colleges, and universities. The first general provision of this kind was enacted as early as 1817, in a rather cumbersome act "to provide for the incorporation of schools and library companies."[2]   By the terms of this law the association that wished to incorporate submitted the articles they had prepared to the "President of the court of common pleas," in the circuit in which the association was to be established.   If the "president" approved, he indorsed the same and submitted them to the inspection of two judges of the supreme court.   They were then examined by these judges and, if found comfortable to the provisions of the law, were approved and indorsed, and deposited with the recorder of the county in which the association was located.

This procedure established the association as a body politic and corporate under the laws of the state.   It seems to have been from the first a dead letter, although not formally repealed.   It was the first general law of the Ohio legislature that had primary reference to education, or educational institutions, and is of interest for this reason.

By the provisions of the act of 1839 the capital stock and property of academies could not exceed forty thousand dollars, unless increased in the act of incorporation.   The act also stated that no part of the funds of such an institution should ever be used for banking, nor should certificates of deposit or drafts which in any manner could be used as a circulating medium be issued.   From this time on, too, the directors or trustees were held individually liable for all debts of the association.   There was no thought of state supervision or control of these institutions until 1838,[3] and then only to see that funds given were being used for the purpose for which they were donated.   The law at that time directed the state superintendent to collect information concerning all funds and property given in any way for education, except in the case of chartered colleges, and allowed him to direct procedure against the corporation by the local prosecuting attorney in case any misapplication of funds appeared.

[1] O.L., XXXVII, 49.
[2] O.L., XV, 107.
[3] O.L., XXXVI, 21.

HIGHER EDUCATION
UNIVERSITIES, COLLEGES, AND THEOLOGICAL INSTITUTIONS

A large number of institutions of higher learning were incorporated during this period of Ohio's history, the total number of such incorporations before 1850 being forty-four. Among these are a number which are still in existence, including some of the best known institutions in the state. In the period from 1803 to 1810 the Ohio University, 1804, originally chartered in 1802; Cincinnati University, 1807, and Miami University, 1809, were founded. Between 1821 and 1830 Kenyon College, 1824; Western Reserve University, 1826; Lane Seminary, 1829, were incorporated; followed in the period from 1831 to 1840 by Denison University, 1832; Marietta College, 1832; Oberlin College, 1834, and Muskingum College, 1837; while in the last ten years from 1841 to 1850 Wesleyan University, 1842; Wittenberg College, 1845; Otterbein University, 1849; Capital University, 1850; Urbana University, 1850, and Hiram College, 1850, appeared.

A number of these institutions were not incorporated under the names which they now bear. Ohio University was originally incorporated during the territorial period as the American Western University.[1] Kenyon College first appeared as the Theological Seminary of the Protestant Episcopal Church,[2] Western Reserve University as Western Reserve College,[3] Denison University as the Granville Literary and Theological Institution,[4] Marietta College as the Marietta Collegiate Institute and Western Teachers' Seminary,[5] Oberlin College as the Oberlin Collegiate Institute,[6] and Hiram College as the Western Reserve Eclectic Institute.[7] In a few cases academies or other secondary schools were later given the right to confer collegiate degrees,[8] while in some instances institutions incorporated as colleges or universities were doubtless, in fact, secondary in character, and in other cases were never actually founded, the act of incorporation representing only the purpose and ideals of the incorporators.

[1] Nashee, *A Compilation of Laws, Treaties and Ordinances Which Relate to Lands in the State of Ohio*, p. 220.
[2] O.L., XXIII, local, 12.
[3] O.L., XXIV, local, 93.
[4] O.L., XXX, local, 88.
[5] O.L., XXXI, local, 18.
[6] O.L., XXXII, local, 226.
[7] O.L., XLVIII, local, 627.
[8] O.L., XLVI, local, 7; O.L., XXXVII, local, 308; O.L., XLIV, local, 65.

State influence on higher education.—The attitude of the state toward higher education as toward secondary education was marked by a willingness to legalize by incorporation the educational aspirations of any group of people, while taking on itself a minimum amount of responsibility for the resulting institution either through support or control.

Three townships had been set aside for the support of higher institutions of learning, two in the Ohio Company's Purchase[1] and one in the John Cleve Symmes Purchase.[2]   The Ohio University at Athens and the Miami University at Oxford grew out of these two grants.   These two institutions were under limited state control.   The General Assembly appointed their trustees, determined by legal enactment the manner in which their lands were to be disposed of, and in the acts of incorporation laid down certain regulations, but in no real sense did the state in this period assume any responsibility for them.

Ohio University.—On December 18, 1799,[3] the territorial legislature, by resolution, requested Rufus Putnam, with two associates, to lay off in the college townships (Townships 8 and 9 in Washington County) a town plat with a square for the colleges and lots for the president and professors, "bordering on or encircled by spacious commons."   The following year the report of "said Putnam" was accepted, and the town of Athens established,[4] and on January 9, 1802,[5] the university was incorporated under the name of the American Western University, with Rufus Putnam and Return Jonathan Meigs, afterward governor of Ohio and Postmaster-General of the United States, as members of the first Board of Trustees.

In 1803 Ohio was admitted as a state, and at the second session of the legislature, February 18, 1804,[6] a second act of incorporation was passed, in which the name was changed to "Ohio University." A board of twelve trustees, exclusive of the governor of the state and the president of the university, *ex-officio* members, was appointed, and power was given to them to appoint teachers and

---

[1] Nashee, *A Compilation of Laws, Treaties and Ordinances Which Relate to Lands in the State of Ohio*, p. 154.

[2] O.L., III, Enabling Act, 69.

[3] Nashee, *A Compilation of Laws, Treaties and Ordinances Which Relate to Lands in the State of Ohio*, p. 219.

[4] *Ibid.*, p. 220.

[5] *Idem.*

[6] O.L., II, 193.

officers.   Vacancies in the board could be filled temporarily by the board itself until appointments by the legislature at its next session.

The faculty was directed to report to the corporation "from time to time" and to hold public examinations of the students of each class quarterly.   Two townships were set aside "for the sole use, benefit and support of the state university forever," and directions were given for laying off, appraising, and leasing the lands. This latter provision directed that the land should be leased on ninety-year liens, renewable forever with an annual rental of 6 per cent, revaluation at thirty-five and sixty years, and another revaluation at the end of the ninety-year period.   All the land in the two townships, together with the buildings, was exempted from all state taxes.

The statement given above includes all the points in which the state exercised any control.   It appointed the trustees, it directed the faculty to report "from time to time" to the trustees, it directed that quarterly examinations of the students should be held, and it specified how the land granted for the use of the university was to be leased.

The next year[1] the legislature changed the form of the lease to ninety-nine-year leases, renewable forever, omitting the clause calling for a revaluation, and forbade the leasing of any land at less than one dollar and seventy-five cents per acre, but in 1807[2] the trustees were authorized to lease the land that had been appraised at less than one dollar and seventy-five cents at its appraised value.

The legislation of the next ten years is concerned only with different phases of leasing of the land and the appointment of trustees, but in 1817,[3] an act was passed authorizing a lottery to raise the sum of twenty thousand dollars "to defray the expense of completing the college edifice lately erected at Athens, and to purchase a library and suitable mathematical and philosophical apparatus for the use of Ohio University."   On February 1, 1825,[4] an appropriation of one thousand dollars was made for the purpose of paying debts and purchasing philosophical apparatus.   In 1826,[5] during the same period in which the sale of school lands was begun,

[1] O.L., III, 79.
[2] O.L., V, 85.
[3] O.L., XVI, 37.
[4] O.L., XXIII, 19.
[5] O.L., XXIV, 52.

the trustees were authorized to sell the remaining lands in the college townships which were not encumbered by leases, and to convey title in fee simple to lessees who paid a sum which would yield at 6 per cent a revenue equal to the yearly rental.   The money received from such sales was to be deposited with the state treasurer, and the state pledged itself to pay 6 per cent on the sums so deposited and reserved the right to repay the money at any time.[1]

In 1836[2] and again in 1837[3] the legislature passed resolutions demanding reports from the university, particularly as to the expenditures and receipts, and in the second resolution asking for the number of professors engaged, the branches of literature and science taught by each, and a list of the number of students of each year from 1826 to 1837.   In 1838[4] the commissioners of the Canal Fund were authorized to loan five thousand dollars to the university to be paid back in annual instalments of one thousand dollars each, with interest at 6 per cent, and in 1847[5] the president and trustees were authorized to fund the debts of the university in an amount not to exceed ten thousand dollars, and the debt so funded was exempt from taxation.

In 1843[6] the legislature passed an act declaring that it was the true intent of the law passed in 1805, authorizing ninety-nine-year leases, that the land should never be revalued.   This meant a great annual loss to the university, as the lands were originally appraised and leased at a low valuation and rental, and by this act the rental could never be increased.   The Supreme Court of the state had already passed on this question and had decided that the lands were legally subject to reappraisal.   The act of 1843 was passed to nullify that decision.[7]

These chief points in the legislation concerning Ohio University in the period from 1803 to 1850 show how little there was of either state aid or state direction.   One appropriation of one thousand dollars, authority to raise twenty thousand dollars by means of a lottery, a loan of five thousand dollars, and the privilege of funding a debt of ten thousand dollars without taxation, and the exemption

---

[1] The amount received from these sales was comparatively small.   The state auditor's report from 1838 to 1848 shows a credit of $1,897.39 to Ohio University from this source.

[2] O.L., XXXIV, local, 643.

[3] O.L., XXXV, local, 543.

[4] O.L., XXXVI, local, 204.

[5] O.L., XLV, local, 176.

[6] O.L., XLI, local, 144.

[7] F. W. Blackmar, *The History of Federal and State Aid to Higher Education in the United States*, p. 217.

of the lands in the college townships from state taxation comprise all the assistance of a financial nature given by the state.

The appointment of trustees, the requirement of a report asked for twice, and certain general requirements specified in the charter include all of the control or guidance on the educational side. It is evident that the institution was not regarded in any true sense as a state university, if by that term is meant an institution supported by the state and governed by policies of state initiation. If further evidence were needed, it is found in a memorial addressed to Congress by the legislature in 1829,[1] asking Congress to grant two townships of land for the support of colleges and universities. The memorial states that Ohio "has no adequate means of creating and fostering scientific institutions without resorting to the odious measure of direct taxation." "Possessing no national domains and having amongst its citizens few or none whose love of literature would prompt at the same time their wealth would make them able, to endow public seminaries of learning. . . . the interests of science must be neglected and languish, unless aid can be obtained in the mode now proposed."

"Ohio has received no grant of this character, unless the land included in the Ohio Company's Purchase and Symmes' Purchase should be so considered, but neither the state nor the inhabitants of those districts have ever thus regarded them." They were intended to be for the special benefit of the inhabitants of those districts, and the location of the seminaries was confined to them.

Miami University.—The legislation concerning Miami University is of the same general type. The college township was located in 1803[2] and the university incorporated in 1809.[3] By the act of incorporation all benefits and advantages were to be open to all citizens of the state. A board of twelve trustees was appointed, and the faculty was directed to hold at least once in every year a public examination of the students in each class. Succeeding legislation was concerned only with the appointment of trustees, the leasing of college lands, and the collecting of rents, with the exception of an act in 1814[4] which required the trustees to make an accurate statement of all proceedings "both as respects the

[1] O.L., XXVII, local, 174.
[2] O.L., I, 66.
[3] O.L., VII, 184.
[4] O.L., XII, 83.

disposal of land, as well as the state of the funds arising from the proceeds," to the legislature. There seems to have been no financial aid of any kind extended to Miami University prior to 1850, and, as in the case of Ohio University, no control or initiation of educational policies. The state for the first time shows an awakening responsibility in 1849[1] by the appointment of a committee of three "to examine into and report to the next General Assembly the condition of the Miami University and the cause of its decline, with such recommendations as they may deem proper to make."

Other institutions.—A grant of five hundred dollars each was made to two other institutions by the legislature by an act passed in 1836.[2] The two institutions receiving this aid were the College of Ripley in Brown County and Franklin College in Harrison County. The act of incorporation for the College of Ripley[3] specified that vacancies in the Board of Trustees were to be filled by the General Assembly. Aside from this, these two institutions seem in no way to differ from others founded during the same period. The appropriation made was evidently incidental and due to local influence, and did not indicate any general policy of state aid. It is also an indication that the state regarded other institutions in about the same way that it regarded Ohio and Miami universities.

In 1828[4] the legislature warmly seconded the efforts of Philander Chase, the president of Kenyon College, in his attempt to obtain a grant of lands from Congress for the support of that institution, and requested its senators and representatives to use their efforts in Congress to support such legislation. These instances include all of the state's activities in the interests of higher education.

In the case of other institutions chartered, the state exercised no control, except that it became customary after 1830 to specify in the incorporating act that the right to amend or alter the charter was reserved by the legislature. There also appeared frequent limitations as to the amount of real property that might be held, or the annual income that might be derived from it.

Denominational influences.—It is impossible to say from a study of the acts of incorporation how far denominational influence was instrumental in the founding of the large number of colleges and

[1] O.L., XLVII, local, 398.
[2] O.L., XXXIV, local, 610.
[3] O.L., XXVIII, local, 88.
[4] O.L., XXVI, local, 176.

universities that appeared during this period. It was certainly much more influential than in the case of secondary institutions. Twenty-one of the forty-four schools show evidence of denominational influence either in the act itself or in the name given, while a few of them had from the first the preparation of ministers for a particular sect in mind. It is quite probable that others were under denominational influence where nothing in the charter or name indicates it.

Agricultural schools.—It is interesting to note that as early as 1846[1] a Farmers' College was incorporated in Hamilton County, whose purpose was declared to be "to direct and cultivate the minds of the students in a thorough and scientific course of studies particularly adapted to agricultural pursuits." This institution was the result of private initiative and was founded by a stock company.

Summary.—The period was one of activity and interest in higher education with a determined effort to afford the advantages of college and university training to the young people of the state without the necessity of going beyond the state border for it. The state's attitude was shown in its willingness to assist through legalizing such efforts by acts of incorporation, but with no conception of any adequate responsibility in the matter, even for those institutions which might naturally have been considered state foundations.

MEDICAL EDUCATION

During the first eight years of the state's history there was no legislation that bore in any way upon medical practice or indicated any state requirements for entering the profession. In 1811[2] an act was passed to regulate the practice of physic and surgery. The state was divided into five medical districts each having three medical censors or examiners, and it was made obligatory upon anyone who wished to practice medicine as a means of livelihood to obtain a license from one of these boards of examiners. The qualifications for a license included satisfactory evidence that the candidate was of good moral character, and that he had attended three full years to the theory and practice of medicine under the guidance of some able physician or surgeon, or that he had a license from some medical society showing that he had been admitted as

[1] O.L., XLIV, local, 165.
[2] O.L., IX, 19.

a practitioner.   He was also required to give satisfactory answers
to such questions as might be put to him by the examiners in
"Anatomy, Materia Medica, Chymistry, and the Theory and Practice of Physic."

In 1812[1] a medical society was incorporated, the state divided
into seven medical districts, and the society given power to appoint
examining committees to examine and license candidates and also
to grant honorary degrees to such of the faculty as they might find
of distinguished merit.   Practicing without a license from some
medical society or college of physicians was forbidden, and a penalty
from five to one hundred dollars was imposed for each offense.

In 1817[2] the candidate was required, in addition to the examination, to deliver a thesis upon some medical subject, and in 1818[3]
those who had received the degree of Doctor of Medicine in any
university or other medical institution within the United States
were exempted from the necessity of being examined for a license.

In 1819 [4] the first medical school in the state was incorporated in
Cincinnati under the name of the Medical College of Ohio.   The
preamble recites that the students of medicine in Ohio are so distant
from any well-regulated college as to labor under serious disadvan-
tages in the prosecution of their studies.   The purpose of the college
was to give instruction in physic and surgery and the auxiliary
sciences.   There were four incorporators, and the act of incorporation
evidently followed the desires of those responsible for the institution.
Six professorships were created, and the subjects of instruction of
each were indicated.   The state very early assumed a certain
amount of control of this institution, at first indirectly, through
authorizing[5] the State Medical Convention to appoint two delegates
annually to attend the commencement of the medical college, take
part in the examination, vote on the candidates, and sign diplomas
on behalf of the convention.   This Medical Convention consisted
of delegates from the various medical districts in the state, and was
given at the same time (1821)[6] the exclusive right to grant licenses
for practice.   It was allowed to select each year two indigent

[1] O.L., X, 58.
[2] O.L., XV, 195.
[3] O.L., XVI, 105.
[4] O.L., XVII, 37.
[5] O.L., XIX, 28.
[6] *Idem.*

medical students and recommend them to the Medical College, whose duty it was to give them instruction gratuitously.

In 1822[1] on recommendation of the Medical Convention, a board of thirteen trustees of the college was appointed by the General Assembly, and they were given general control of the institution, and it was provided that from this time the trustees were to be so appointed.

In 1825[2] the legislature directed that the moneys raised by auction fees in Hamilton County should be appropriated for four years to the use of the Medical College, unless otherwise directed by the General Assembly.[3] This was extended to five years at the next meeting of the legislature, and in 1831[4] one-fourth of the money from the same source was appropriated for five years, not, however, to exceed twenty thousand dollars for the period. In 1838[5] there were fifteen hundred dollars appropriated outright from the state treasury to be applied to liquidate any unsatisfied claims against the school.

There were no other provisions for financial aid, but in 1833[6] the medical examiners were allowed to appoint one indigent student from each medical district for free instruction, and on the same date the governor was requested to appoint a committee of five to investigate the organization, government, and condition of the Medical College, and to report to the General Assembly, suggesting "the proper means of advancing the prosperity and utility of the state medical college as an institution of the state, and of medical science therein."

For the first thirty-five years there was no medical institution incorporated in any of the other cities of the state. Two other institutions were chartered in Cincinnati in 1828,[7] the Western Eye and Ear Infirmary, whose trustees had power to appoint "surgeons, advising physicians, lecturers, and teachers," and the Cincinnati Medical Academy,[8] designed to give a systematic course preparatory to admission to a medical college.

[1] O.L., XXI, 4.
[2] O.L., XXIII, 19.
[3] O.L., XXIV, 4.
[4] O.L., XXIX, local, 66.
[5] O.L., XXXVI, 37.
[6] O.L., XXXI, local, 269.
[7] O.L., XXVI, local, 28.
[8] O.L., XXVI, local, 54.

From 1839 to 1850 eight other institutions were chartered in the state for various types of medical instruction. There were also incorporated nine local and county medical societies, evidently associations of physicians organized for the advancement of medical science. The State Medical Society was incorporated in 1848[1] with power to organize auxiliary societies. The state took no part in the control or support of the later institutions incorporated.

LEGAL EDUCATION

There is almost no legislation bearing on legal education prior to 1850. In 1819[2] a law was passed that no person should be licensed to practice as an attorney unless he had studied law attentively for the period of two years previous to his application for a license. In 1846[3] appeared the first indication of any definite legal instruction in an act authorizing any male citizen of the state of good moral character to take the oath of office and receive a license to practice on producing to two judges of the Supreme Court a certificate from the law department of the Cincinnati College.

COLLEGES, UNIVERSITIES, AND THEOLOGICAL SEMINARIES CHARTERED IN OHIO:
1803–50

1.	Ohio University	1802
2.	Miami University (locating college townships)	1803
	Miami University (charter)	1809
3.	Cincinnati University	1807
4.	Worthington College	1819
5.	Kenyon College	1824
6.	{ College of Alma	1825
	{ Franklin College (name changed)	1826
7.	Western Reserve College	1826
8.	Lane Seminary	1829
9.	College of Ripley	1830
10.	The Trustees of the Granville Literary and Theological Institution	1832
11.	Marietta Collegiate Institute and Western Teacher's Seminary	1832
12.	Oberlin Collegiate Institute	1834
13.	Willoughby University of Lake Erie	1834
14.	German Reform Synod of Ohio	1836
15.	St. Clairsville Collegiate Seminary	1837
16.	Muskingum College	1837
17.	Baptist Literary and Collegiate Institute of Huron County	1837
18.	Wesleyan Collegiate Institute	1837
19.	Logan College	1838

[1] O.L., XLVI, local, 231.
[2] O.L., XVII, 92.
[3] O.L., XLIV, local, 157.

20. Theological Seminary of the Associated Reform Synod of the West. 1838
21. Central College of Ohio.. 1842
22. St. Xavier College.. 1842
23. Ohio Wesleyan University..................................... 1842
24. Lafayette University.. 1842
25. Germania College.. 1843
26. Providence College... 1843
27. Beverly College.. 1843
28. { Methodist Female Collegiate Institute........................ 1843
     Wesleyan Female College (name changed)...................... 1846
29. Bellefontaine College... 1843
30. English Lutheran Theological and Collegiate Institute of Wooster.. 1844
31. Ft. Meigs University.. 1845
32. Protestant University of the United States..................... 1845
33. Wittenberg College... 1845
34. Farmers' College 1846
35. Marietta Female College...................................... 1847
36. { Muhlenberg College.. 1848
     Judson College (name changed).............................. 1849
38. Newton College.. 1848
39. Edinburgh College.. 1848
40. Mt. Washington College....................................... 1849
41. Otterbein University.. 1849
42. Capital University.. 1850
43. Cambridge College.. 1850
44. Geneva Hall... 1850
45. Urbana University.. 1850

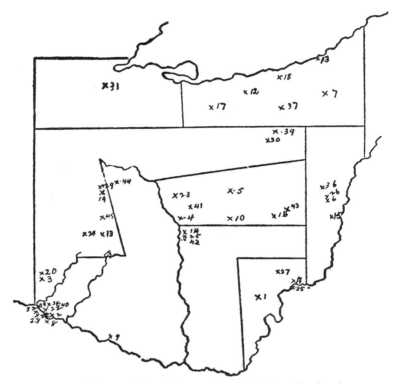

Fig. 4.—Colleges, universities, and theological seminaries chartered in Ohio from 1803 to 1850

NOTE: 37 shown on map is Medina Academy

CHAPTER V

THE EDUCATION OF DEFECTIVES, DEPENDENTS, AND DELINQUENTS

The institutions for the education of the deaf and dumb and the blind were definitely recognized as a state responsibility, and ample and intelligent provision was made by the state for children of this class. This conception of the state's responsibility was not recognized at once, however, but was a matter of gradual growth. The deaf and dumb school preceded the school for the blind by ten years, and in the legislation that centers about it the gradual development of the idea of state responsibility for financial support can be seen.

THE EDUCATION OF DEFECTIVES

Education of the deaf and dumb.—In an act passed in 1822[1] the Court of Common Pleas was authorized to appoint guardians for deaf and dumb persons, and the power of the guardians was expressly extended to the protection, education, and maintenance of their wards. In case the guardian or parent was unable to teach such children to read and write, the law permitted the county commissioners, on application, to appropriate money from the county treasury for such instruction. The law was wholly permissive in character and simply legalized appropriations for the instruction of deaf and dumb children in cases in which the county commissioners saw fit to grant aid. By the same law the township officers were required to report to the county auditors the number of deaf and dumb persons in the township, and the auditors were directed to report the results to the state auditor.

This was followed at the next session in 1822[2] by an act the sole purpose of which was to ascertain the number of deaf and dumb persons in the state. Five years later, in 1827,[3] an act was passed to incorporate the "Trustees of the Ohio Asylum for Educating the Deaf and Dumb." Eight trustees were named in the act of incorpora-

[1] O.L., XX, 49.
[2] O.L., XXI, 5.
[3] O.L., XXV, 87.

tion, and they were authorized to receive gifts and bequests for the purpose of educating the deaf and dumb, and were directed to report to the next General Assembly as to the location of the schools, the kind of buildings needed, with an estimate of expense for buildings and instruction, and a plan for its organization and government. The funds of the institution were to be under the management of the trustees subject to the regulation of the General Assembly, and reports were required annually as to the expenses, number of students, number taught at state expense, and the number who paid tuition, together with general information as to the status of the school.

The trustees were allowed to draw on the treasury of the state for the support of one indigent student from each judicial circuit an amount not to exceed one hundred dollars for any student, and no student was to receive such aid longer than three years. The governor was *ex-officio* president of the Board of Trustees, and it was specifically stated that the incorporated body was under the control and direction of the General Assembly.

The idea of the legislature seems to have been to organize an institution under state management and control, but financed by private donations, with the state giving a minimum amount to the support of indigent students. The following year, 1828, the first appropriation of state money was made, amounting to $376.76.[1] In 1829[2] the trustees were authorized to open the asylum in rented houses until suitable buildings were erected, and an additional appropriation of one thousand dollars was made. The same year it was decided to locate the institution permanently in Columbus,[3] and the trustees were authorized to receive any donations of land or to purchase a site. In the meanwhile Congress had been urged[4] to appropriate a township of land, or an amount equivalent to that, located in smaller tracts, to aid in the education of the deaf and dumb. The grant was not made, and in 1830[5] another appropriation of one thousand dollars was made, and the trustees were again authorized to receive one indigent student from each judicial circuit at state expense, but the amount to be expended was reduced from

[1] O.L., XXVI, 4.
[2] O.L., XXVII, 63.
[3] O.L., XXVII, local, 171.
[4] O.L., XXV, local, 113; O.L., XXVI, local, 178.
[5] O.L., XXVIII 30.

one hundred dollars to seventy-five dollars for each student.[1]   The next year the number of students receiving state aid was increased to two from each circuit,[2] a total of eighteen, and an appropriation of sixteen hundred dollars[3] was made for expenses.   This was followed in 1832 by an act appropriating one-fourth of the money arising from sales at auction in Hamilton County[4] and by another fifteen-hundred-dollar appropriation from the treasury.[5]

The state had not reached a point where it was ready to assume the burden of the school, and it again applied to Congress in the same year[6] for assistance through a land grant.   In this memorial it was estimated that a proper housing and equipment would cost from fifteen thousand to twenty thousand dollars, with a total annual expenditure of nearly ten thousand dollars.   It was pointed out that Ohio, in common with many other states, did not possess land of her own which might be appropriated, and that the only resource, unless Congress came to the state's aid, was by drawing from revenue derived by direct taxation for other purposes.   The memorial declares that everyone will admit that this measure is impolitic and ought to be avoided, and that it may be deemed quite sufficient to provide in this way for indigent students.[7]

From this time on appropriations of fifteen hundred to three thousand dollars were common until 1846,[8] when a systematic budget was evidently adopted and regular appropriations made to meet it.   The appropriation for expenses in this year amounted to nine thousand dollars, with an added four thousand dollars for building needs.   Provision was made in 1838[9] by a two-thousand-dollar appropriation for the erection of workshops and the introduction of mechanical employment as a part of the work of the institution.[10]

[1] There were nine judicial circuits.   The expense involved amounted to $675.

[2] O.L., XXIX, 427.

[3] O.L., XXIX, local, 246.

[4] O.L., XXX, 20.

[5] O.L., XXX, local, 318.

[6] O.L., XXX, local, 336.

[7] This memorial states that Ohio had established such a school, that it had been in operation two years, and that it had three teachers and nearly thirty pupils, with a prospect that the number of pupils would be doubled as soon as accommodations were furnished.

[8] O.L., XLIV, 130.

[9] O.L., XXXVI, 92.

[10] The legislature voted a grant of one hundred dollars annually in 1828 for two years to the trustees of a private school for educating deaf and dumb persons, located in Tallmadge Township, and bearing the name of the Tallmadge School for the Education of the Deaf and Dumb.   This is the only hint that appears in the legislation of a private institution of this kind (O.L., XXVI, local, 169).

Education of the blind.—With the exception of two special acts to assist individuals, one afterward repealed, the state took no steps looking toward the education of the blind until 1835.[1]   In this year the governor was requested to direct the county auditors to make a complete report on the number of blind persons in the state,[2] and in the following year[3] a committee was appointed to study the question of the education of the blind in letters and mechanical arts and to report to the General Assembly the results of their findings with an estimate of the probable expense of establishing a public school for that purpose.

This committee made a careful study of the subject.   They quote largely in their report[4] from the address of Dr. S. G. Howe, director of the New England Institution for the Blind, which he had made to the trustees of that institution.   In this address of Dr. Howe's there is given a synopsis of the development of the education of the blind in the different European nations and some description of the beginnings of such work in the New York and New England institutions.

In addition to the information so gained the committee addressed a list of specific questions to the directors of the New York, New England, and Pennsylvania institutions for the blind asking for definite information about expense, number of teachers needed, textbooks available, types of industry suitable to be taught in a school of this kind, and other questions of a similar nature.   Provision was also made for Dr. Howe to visit Columbus during the session of the legislature to "deliver lectures and exhibit one or two of the pupils in such a manner as to prove their attainments."

The committee estimated the number of blind in the state as 500, basing the estimate on the United States census and the reports made by the county auditors.   Of this number there were 60 under sixteen years of age whose names and residences were known.

The report closes with the following recommendation:

In order to commence a school it will be necessary to rent a suitable house, and furnish the books and apparatus for a class, and procure one teacher who is qualified to give instruction, and provide for the support of those children who

[1] O.L., IX, 68; O.L., X, 68; O.L., XVII, 7.
[2] O.L., XXXIII, local, 453.
[3] O.L., XXXIV, local, 648.
[4] Ohio Documents, 35th G.A., Doc. No. 10, pp. 1-24.

are indigent.   For this purpose it is supposed that, if the Legislature shall determine in favor of the measure, an appropriation of $1,500 will be necessary.—
And if it shall be deemed expedient to purchase a site on which permanent buildings may hereafter be erected, a further sum of $1,000 may be needed.   It is
desirable also, that as early as practicable, musical instruments may be procured,
and the necessary arrangements may be made, for teaching music, not only as
a solace and a pleasure to the blind in their disconsolate condition as strangers
to sight; but as a means of contributing to their own support in the school, and
afterward also.   And it is especially desirable, and indeed highly important, that
a superintendent of work, together with implements and materials for some prof-
itable manufactures, should be furnished; and thus every pupil, when discharged,
may be able to make his own living.

In conclusion the Trustees . . . . beg leave, most respectfully and most
earnestly, to recommend to the General Assembly the immediate establishment
of an Institution for the instruction of the Blind.[1]

On the Fourth of July, in 1837, the first "school was opened
with prayer, in the Presbyterian Church in the presence of the
Teachers and scholars of the Sunday Schools connected with the
different denominations in Columbus, who, to the number of 900,
had assembled to celebrate the sixty-first anniversary of Indepen-
dence.   On this day the Teacher and five pupils were present.   This
number was increased to nine, at the middle of September, and
still further to eleven in the month of November."[2]

The experience of the legislature with the deaf and dumb school
had prepared it to accept the responsibility for the school for the
blind in a larger way, and in 1837[3] trustees were appointed, and a
sum of fifteen thousand dollars was authorized for buildings and
ten thousand dollars appropriated for the purpose of building
materials and to pay the expense of beginning the school at once.
In 1838[4] fifteen thousand dollars was appropriated to complete
the building, and the trustees were authorized to receive twelve
students at state expense.   A tuition and maintenance fee not to
exceed one hundred and twenty dollars annually was fixed for other
students.   The trustees were authorized to procure all necessary
material and implements for the purpose of instruction in useful
arts and trades.

In 1843[5] the limitation as to the number of students received at
state expense was removed, and it was left to the discretion of the

[1] Ohio Documents, 35th G.A., Doc. No. 10, p. 23.
[2] Ohio Documents, 36th G.A., Doc. No. 10, p. 4.
[3] O.L., XXXV, 116.
[4] O.L., XXXVI, 49.
[5] O.L., XLI, 57.

trustees. The regulations on this subject appear to have been administered leniently, both in the case of the school for the blind and in that for the deaf and dumb, as frequent resolutions appear allowing exceptions in special cases.

In 1845[1] the legislature made another appeal to Congress for a land grant to assist in the education of the blind and the deaf and dumb, asking that such a grant be made in all the states where it had not been done; but the grant was not made, and the state was forced to assume full responsibility for both institutions.

THE EDUCATION OF DEPENDENTS

The first appropriation authorized from the state treasury of Ohio for educational purposes of any kind is found in the case of an Indian orphan girl whose mother had been shot by a citizen without provocation. In 1820[2] three hundred and fifty dollars was voted to pay for her support and education for seven years. This was repealed the following year,[3] but in 1823[4] twenty-five dollars annually was definitely appropriated for that purpose until she should reach the age of twelve years. This is the only time the state made any financial provision for the education of dependent children prior to 1850. In 1806[5] in an act concerning apprentices and servants it was directed that in all indentures for binding or putting out a child as servant or apprentice there should be a clause that every master or mistress should at least cause such child "to be taught and instructed to read and write." In 1824[6] this was extended to embrace as much arithmetic as would include the single rule of three, and the further provision that at the expiration of the term of service each minor child was to receive a new Bible and two suits of wearing apparel.

This embraces all the state provisions on the subject from 1803 to 1850, and it is interesting to note that the two laws last cited are the only laws passed during the period that in any way touch upon compulsory education, and these carry no penalties for failure to obey.

[1] O.L., XLIII, local, 434.
[2] O.L., XVIII, 66.
[3] O.L., XIX, 144.
[4] O.L., XXI, 39.
[5] O.L., IV, 72.
[6] O.L., XXII, 381.

Orphan asylums and schools for poor children.—Orphan asylums were incorporated in Cincinnati in 1833,[1] in Cleveland in 1837,[2] in Columbus in 1838,[3] and in Dayton in 1844.[4] These four institutions were all incorporated by women, and were to be under the management of women, as indicated in the acts of incorporation. A second asylum was incorporated by a Catholic society in Cincinnati in 1843,[5] and in 1845[6] an asylum for colored children was incorporated in the same city. The Stark County Orphans' Institute appeared in 1837,[7] but its charter was revoked three years later because it had embarked in the banking business.[8] There were also three endowed schools incorporated for the benefit of poor children, one in Cincinnati in 1827,[9] one in Zanesville in 1834,[10] and one in Kendal in 1826.[11] Their purpose, however, was to afford instruction free to children whose parents were unable to pay for it, not primarily to care for the wholly dependent. These three schools were the Woodward Free Grammar School, the M'Intire Poor School, and the Charity School of Kendal.

THE EDUCATION OF DELINQUENTS

Education of delinquents.—No state provision was made for the education of delinquents prior to 1850, and but little was done through private or municipal effort. In 1843[12] an act was passed for the regulation of county jails, which directed that each prisoner should be supplied with a Bible, and that the sheriff should keep a record of the means furnished for literary, moral, and religious instruction. In 1845[13] the directors of the penitentiary were authorized to employ some suitable person as a religious and moral instructor, and in the same year the city of Cincinnati was authorized to erect a house of correction.[14]

These three laws, one of them local in application, comprise the entire activity of the state for the moral and intellectual advance of delinquents prior to 1850.

---

[1] O.L., XXXI, local, 52.
[2] O.L., XXXV, local, 513.
[3] O.L., XXXVI, local, 185.
[4] O.L., XLII, local, 172.
[5] O.L., XLI, local, 112.
[6] O.L., XLIII, local, 101.
[7] O.L., XXXV, local, 201.
[8] O.L., XXXVIII, local, 87.
[9] O.L., XXV, local, 62.
[10] O.L., XXXIV, local, 514.
[11] O.L., XXIV, local, 36.
[12] O.L., XLI, 74.
[13] O.L., XLIII, local, 446.
[14] O.L., XLIII, local, 393; O.L., XLV, local, 112.

CHAPTER VI

THE TRAINING OF TEACHERS

In the preparation of teachers, as in other phases of educational activity, Ohio depended upon the sentiment and effort of individuals and communities, and did nothing through state aid or direction other than to legalize through incorporation the concerted efforts of groups of teachers or charter institutions established by private initiative. As a result of the educational awakening that accompanied the passage of the general school law of 1838, and the appointment of a state superintendent, some attention was given by the legislature to the state's responsibility, and the state superintendent was asked in the same year[1] to report to the next General Assembly "first, upon the expediency of establishing a state university or universities for the education of teachers and other students; second, if he shall deem it expedient to establish such university or universities then upon the subject of the proper system therefor, and the proper location thereof; third, also upon the proper mode of supporting same, the probable expense thereof to the state, and such other views and information in relation to the subject generally as he may deem it proper to communicate."

Mr. Lewis in his report strongly urged the necessity for the need of schools to train those expecting to teach,[2] but no action was taken by the General Assembly to found such an institution.

It was through the activity of voluntary associations of teachers and friends of education that the first efforts were made to raise the standard of the teaching profession. As early as 1829[3] such an association had been meeting regularly in Cincinnati for the discussion of educational problems, and at a general convention to which friends of education throughout the Mississippi Valley were invited an association was formed called the Western College of Teachers. As one result of this association the first educational

[1] O.L., XXXVI, local, 418.
[2] Ohio Documents, 37th G.A., Part 2, Doc. 72.
[3] Taylor, *A Manual of the Ohio School System*, p. 333.

journal in the Northwest, *The Academic Pioneer*, was established and continued for some ten years.

The original association was incorporated by legislative action February 13, 1832,[1] under the name of the Western Academic Institute and Board of Education, and its purpose was declared to be the promotion of "harmony, co-operation and efficiency in the diffusion of elementary knowledge, and discussing such subjects as may be considered conducive to the advantage of education generally." This association was intended to exercise an influence through the Mississippi Valley, and of its four vice-presidents one was from Harrodsburg, Kentucky, and another from Rising Sun, Iowa.

Two years later, through the leadership of many of the same men, an act was passed to incorporate[2] "The Teachers' Institute." The preamble and first section are of interest and show an advanced educational sentiment on the part of the incorporators and a definite attempt to meet the needs for better trained teachers, and illustrate the general legislative willingness to legalize educational effort through incorporation.

Whereas it has been reported to the General Assembly that a literary institution devoted to the instruction of professional teachers is much wanted within this state, and would be of much public utility. Therefore, be it enacted, etc., that there shall be established and instituted in the name hereinafter directed, a college for the instruction of candidates for professional school teachers, and for the purpose of qualifying such teachers in the best manner to instruct and govern schools, and other seminaries of learning, and to advance the intellectual and moral cultivation of youth.

Among the incorporators were many warm friends of the public schools. The names of Lyman Beecher, John P. Foote, Nathan. Guilford—through whose efforts the school law of 1825 took final form—Robert Picket, David L. Talbott, and others appear. The school for teachers that these men had in mind did not materialize, but there were continued until 1845 regular conventions of teachers and friends of education, and their discussions and influence were instrumental in awakening educational sentiment throughout the state.[3]

[1] O.L., XXX, local, 232.
[2] O.L., XXXII, local, 217.
[3] Taylor, *A Manual of the Ohio School System*, p. 334.

In 1832[1] the Marietta Collegiate Institute and Western Teachers' Seminary, which three years later became Marietta College, was incorporated. The original purpose was declared to be "the instruction of youth in the various branches of useful knowledge, and especially the education of teachers for common schools."

Other incorporations were the Wayne County Ohio Teachers' Association in 1833,[2] the Teachers' Institute at Fairmound,[3] the Meigs County High School and Teachers' Institute,[4] and the American Lyceum of Education in Cincinnati.[5]

This last institution planned to establish a common school "for the purpose of furnishing a model school, and one in which experiments might be made as to the best modes and means of instruction, with a view to advancing the interests of common school education throughout the state."

In 1847[6] the state passed a permissive act allowing teachers in eleven counties of the state to incorporate teachers' institutes. Ten of these counties were located in the Western Reserve. This act allowed the county commissioners in the counties named to use a portion of the money derived from the surplus revenue fund for the support of the institutes so organized. The counties had been held responsible by the act distributing the surplus revenue[7] for the payment of 5 per cent annually for the use of common schools. Any amount derived over this the counties had been allowed to devote to the support of common schools, the promotion of internal improvements, or the building of academies. They were now allowed in the eleven counties named to include teachers' institutes among the objects to which aid from this extra fund might be extended. The money was to be used under the direction of the school examiners of the county in the employment of instructors and lecturers, and in the purchase of a common school library for the use of the association.

This act was made general for the state in 1848[8] by the same act that permitted counties to provide for county superintendents

[1] O.L., XXXI, local, 18.
[2] O.L., XXXI, local, 193.
[3] O.L., XXXV, local, 417.
[4] O.L., XXXVII, local, 257.
[5] O.L., XXXVIII, local, 192.
[6] O.L., XLV, 67.
[7] O.L., XXXVI, 79.
[8] O.L., XLVI, 86.

if they wished to do so. The following year, 1849,[1] the county commissioners were allowed to appropriate from other sources whatever sum was needed to bring the total annual amount for this purpose up to one hundred dollars, but before doing so the teachers petitioning for such an institute were required to present evidence to the commissioners that they had already raised one-half of the total amount needed for the support of the institute, and the petition had to have the signature of forty regular teachers within the county, and also of the county board of examiners.

The Farmington Normal School in Trumbull County on the Western Reserve was incorporated in 1849[2] through the efforts of the citizens of Farmington, who gave a site and raised by voluntary subscription $2,575.00 for its support. A stock company was formed with shares selling at twenty-five dollars each. "One great object" of the school was declared to be "a thorough education of common or elementary school teachers, of both sexes, and to secure a course of intellectual and moral discipline for the youth of the country."

Nothing else appears in the legislation of the state prior to 1850 that has any reference to the training of teachers. Many of the academies assisted in supplying the deficiency and special courses were often organized in them for training teachers. The state, however, had no direct contact with this work. Governor Bartley voiced a feeling that was held by many friends of education that the state ought to take an active part in training teachers when he said in his message of December 3, 1844 :[3]

The subject of normal schools or seminaries for the education of teachers is attracting much attention in several of the states of the Union, and in other countries, and by the pre-eminent advantages afforded by this means for advancing the cause of education, it commends itself to your favorable consideration. Departments for the education of professional teachers in Ohio and Miami Universities could be established under the authority of the state, and by a part of the means derived from the large endowments which these institutions have received from the government.[4]

[1] O.L., XLVII, 19.
[2] O.L., XLVII, local, 261.
[3] Taylor, *A Manual of the Ohio School System*, p. 180.
[4] The plan proposed by Governor Bartley was the one finally followed by the state fifty-seven years later in establishing normal departments in these two schools.

CHAPTER VII

SUPPLEMENTARY EDUCATIONAL AGENCIES

LIBRARIES

The first recognition of libraries in the laws of the state is found in the charter of the Dayton Library Society, February 21, 1805.[1] There is plenty of evidence, however, that the early settlers established libraries before this, but had not sought the legal sanction of a state charter. Venable[2] says that the first library in the territory northwest of the Ohio was at Belpre, near Marietta. This was organized in 1796, and was first known as the Putnam Family Library, later as the Belpre, or Belpre Farmers' Library. This library was owned by a joint stock company, the common method of procedure in the formation of later libraries and library companies.

Another of these early ventures, much better known than the preceding, was the so-called 'Coon-skin Library. This was located at Ames, Washington County, also near Marietta. The reason for the name popularly given to it and the circumstances of its beginning are thus told by one of the founders:

At a public meeting of the inhabitants of Ames, called to devise means to improve our roads, and to consult about making one to connect the settlement at Sunday creek with that on Federal creek, held in the autumn of 1802, the intellectual wants of the neighborhood became the subject of the conversation. It was suggested that a library would supply what was needed, but the settlers had no money, and with few exceptions were in debt for their lands. Mr. Josiah True, of Sunday creek settlement, proposed to obtain the means by catching 'coons, and sending their skins to Boston by Samuel Brown, Esq., who expected to go east in a wagon the next summer. Esquire Brown was present and assented to this proposition. Our young men were active hunters; the 'coon skins and other furs were furnished and sent to market, and the books were bought. The Rev. Thaddeus Harris and the Rev. Dr. Manasseh Cutler selected for us about fifty volumes of choice books, and to these additions were made from time to time. As the settlement increased and children grew up, readers were multiplied, and all could have access to the library.[3]

[1] O.L., III, 288.
[2] Venable, *Beginnings of Literary Culture in the Ohio Valley, Historical and Biographical Sketches*, p. 135.
[3] Cutler, *Life and Times of Ephraim Cutler*, p. 50.

These early attempts to furnish opportunity for community study and improvement were followed by an increasing number of similar organizations during the first four decades of the nineteenth century.

Atwater, writing in 1838,[1] said that most of the towns in Ohio had reading-rooms where a traveler could read all the principal newspapers and periodicals, and that libraries were increasing in number as well as size. The record of incorporations in the session laws bears witness to the probable truth of his statement. One hundred and ninety-two library societies had been incorporated by 1850. The record of incorporation in the preceding decades is as follows:

1805–10	6
1811–20	15
1821–30	45
1831–40	95
1841–50	31
	192

The State Library at Columbus received regular appropriations from 1824[2] on. In 1846[3] district school libraries were authorized, but their support was left wholly to the initiative of the district. The law authorized the district to raise by taxes a sum not to exceed thirty dollars for the first year, and not more than ten dollars for each succeeding year. The decision was left to a meeting of the taxpayers of the district, called for the purpose of voting on the question.

LYCEUMS, INSTITUTES, ATHENAEUMS, AND LITERARY SOCIETIES

In addition to the library societies, there were frequent incorporations of lyceums, athenaeums, institutes, and literary societies, the total number of such incorporations being 64. These developed rapidly after 1830, prior to that time only three institutions of this type being incorporated. The record of their incorporation is as follows:

[1] Atwater, *A History of the State of Ohio, Natural and Civil*, p. 348.
[2] O.L., XXII, local, 36.
[3] O.L., XLIV, 81.

These latter institutions seem designed to afford meeting-places for their members for discussion and opportunity for reading and study. The use of their funds is usually limited to the purchase of books, maps, charts, pamphlets, and newspapers. Among them were eight mechanics' institutes, seven of these incorporated after 1831. The first one of the latter was the Ohio Mechanics' Institute of Cincinnati in 1829,[1] and its purpose was declared to be for "advancing the best interests of the Mechanics, Manufacturers and Artizans by the more general diffusion of useful knowledge in these important classes in the community."

COLLEGE SOCIETIES

The first college literary society incorporated was the Erodelphian Society of Miami University in 1831,[2] followed in the same year by the Philomathesian Society of Kenyon College.[3]

By 1850 twenty-three college and university societies were thus given sanction. Four of the number were incorporated under Greek-letter names.

MISCELLANEOUS

In addition to the various types of educational endeavor represented in the preceding paragraphs there were also incorporated the following institutions, whose names indicate a wide range of literary and artistic interest supplementary to the regular educational agencies: the Historical Society of Ohio, 1822;[4] the Cincinnati Academy of Fine Arts, 1828;[5] the Lancaster Harmonic Society, 1830;[6] the Historical and Philosophical Society of Ohio, 1831;[7] the Eclectic Academy of Music in Cincinnati, 1835;[8] the

[1] O.L., XXVII, local, 92.
[2] O.L., XXIX, local, 74.
[3] O.L., XXIX, local, 196.
[4] O.L., XX, local, 47.
[5] O.L., XXVI, local, 30.
[6] O.L., XXVIII, local, 179.
[7] O.L., XXIX, local, 122.
[8] O.L., XXXIII, local, 161.

New Paris Musical Institute, 1843;[1] the Western Academy of Natural Sciences, 1836;[2] the Cleveland Academy of Natural Sciences, 1840;[3] the Cincinnati Astronomical Society, 1844;[4] the Ohio Institute of Natural Sciences, 1849;[5] the Western Art Union, 1848;[6] the Columbus Art Union, 1849.[7]

[1] O.L., XLI, local, 174.
[2] O.L., XXXIV, local, 110.
[3] O.L., XXXVIII, local, 138.
[4] O.L., XLII, local, 122.
[5] O.L., XLVII, local, 256.
[6] O.L., XLVI, local, 228.
[7] O.L., XLVII, local, 267.

CHAPTER VIII

CONCLUSION

The two essential features of Ohio's educational policy as illustrated by the legislation passed from 1803 to 1850 are, first, the lack of any efficient central control of local educational activities, and, second, the permissive character of a large part of the legislation passed, and the lack of any compulsory features.

The large amount of educational legislation enacted shows that there was no lack of educational interest in the state, either in the public at large or in the people's representatives in the General Assembly. There was a widespread belief in universal education and a desire for it. While there was, as elsewhere, much opposition to taxation and to the idea of distributive responsibility for free schools, the general educational sentiment was good. The laws themselves show in many cases excellent educational possibilities. The weakness of the legislation was due to the fact that the theory followed seemed to be that the function of educational legislation was to establish general rules of organization and control in accord with which the communities might regulate their own educational activities and have legal sanction for them, but that it was not the function of the state to develop any legal machinery that would definitely bring about educational results.

The words of Samuel Lewis are so significant in this connection that they are quoted once more. Speaking of the law of 1838, far the best educational legislation of the entire period, he said:

> It gives to the people the power to do their own business whether in townships or districts as the majority may think best. The widest possible latitude is given for popular action: the most that the law does is to prescribe certain general rules within which the people can act under the sanction of the law, and it gives to such popular action the aid of law to effect its purpose.[1]

This expresses as well as it can be done the state theory that seems to underlie all the educational legislation prior to 1850.

---

[1] *Third Annual Report of the Superintendent of the Common Schools*, made to the Thirty-eighth General Assembly of the State of Ohio, p. 4.

One result of this type of legislation was great freedom in educational experimentation, with legislative sanction when that was asked for.   In communities where the general school sentiment was high, as in Cincinnati, Cleveland, Akron, and some other towns and cities, this resulted in an excellent type of school system, and through this experimentation a legalized model was given to other communities throughout the state.   The results were excellent for those communities which chose to follow the example set, and there were many that did so.   On the other hand, there were no penalties in any of the legislation prior to 1850 to compel even towns and cities to organize schools other than those of the district type, and the only compulsion to organize schools of any kind was the loss of the community's share of the school tax if it did not do so.

Ohio early took an advanced position on the right and desirability of taxing all property in the state for school purposes.   This principle appeared in 1825, when the commissioners of each county were directed to levy a half-mill for school support, and it remained in all subsequent laws in some form.   With this principle established, the state did not concern itself further to compel either the taxation or the establishment of schools.   These were matters to be decided by smaller local areas.   The general idea seemed to be that self-interest and a desire to use the share of money to which each district was entitled would be sufficient incentive for the establishment of public schools in the districts throughout the state.   The results of the next fifteen years show that this belief was in large part justified.   Mr. Lewis estimated the number of district schools taught in Ohio in the year 1839[1] at 13,049, and he based this estimate on actual reports from 5,442 districts in which 7,295 schools were taught.   The state, however, took no responsibility for seeing that the children of the district attended the school so established, and but a minor responsibility for the activities that were carried on in it.

This lack of compelling power and lack of efficient administrative officers made the system a loose and ineffective one, under which the various communities continued largely to do that which was right in their own eyes.

The great educational blunder of Ohio was in the abolition of the office of state superintendent in 1840.   Although the office as

---

[1] *Third Annual Report of the Superintendent of the Common Schools*, made to the Thirty-eighth General Assembly of the State of Ohio, p. 48.

created in 1837 did not carry with it the possibility of exercising any large legal powers, and was confined largely to the gathering of school statistics and the dissemination throughout the state of educational information concerning the laws in force and other matters of educational interest, it did centralize the educational interest of the state in one office, and had in it great possibilities of usefulness. The law of 1838, with the state superintendent at the head of the system, contained much of educational promise. It is not too much to say that if Mr. Lewis or a leader of equal ability could have continued the work begun so ably by him from 1837 to 1840, the educational development of Ohio might have paralleled that in Massachusetts under the guidance of Horace Mann. The explanation of its failure to do so must be found in the fact that, in spite of much educational interest, the people as a whole were not ready for such leadership. Whatever the causes may have been, the result was to leave Ohio educationally a generation behind the position she might have occupied had she lived up to the full promise of the law of 1838.

Nowhere is there a better illustration of the need of a centralized administrative office capable of giving to the legislature advice founded upon knowledge of the facts, and of administering the policies adopted uniformly throughout the state, than in the legislation concerning Ohio school lands. Educational interest, state economic interests—such as the question of internal improvements—local interests, and, too often, individual interests were all presented to the legislature, which acted in many cases upon a one-sided presentation of the facts. The result was a mass of confused facts and conflicting legislation that as it multiplied left the legislators themselves in ignorance as to the exact law that applied in particular cases. Opportunities for carelessness and downright dishonesty in the local handling of the funds and the selling and leasing of the lands were afforded, and, as the records show, not all local officials were either careful or honest. Aside from carelessness and occasional dishonesty, the conflict between the immediate interest of a neighbor and the more distant interest of the schools, that often confronted the local appraisers of lands, must have been frequently disastrous for the schools. John Brough, the auditor of state, said in 1840 that "anyone who would seek the records and gather the melancholy facts they contained would be convinced of the waste that had taken place."

The state had no clearly defined state-wide policy applicable in all instances and under all circumstances, and it lacked efficient machinery of government to administer carefully the policies that were initiated.

It is not probable that dishonesty or wilful carelessness was the cause of the legislation that made great loss possible, but rather ignorance of conditions and a hand-to-mouth expediency to meet present needs. This could have been largely avoided through the establishment of a central office, interested primarily in preserving for the educational interests of the state the first state-wide grant made by the general government for the use of schools.

There is little to be said in summarizing the state's attitude toward secondary and higher education. Ohio lacked in the beginning, and failed to develop during the period, any state educational policy that embraced elementary, secondary, and higher education. Her interest in public education was an interest in public elementary education only, not in secondary or higher institutions. One explanation for this is doubtless found in the abundance of local secondary and higher institutions established by private initiative, and a second in the fact that the three townships granted by the government for higher education were located in the Ohio Company's Purchase and in the Symmes Purchase, and that the resulting institutions were regarded as largely local and only quasi-state in nature. With a lack of clearly recognized state institutions of college or university rank, there was no pressure from above for a system of preparatory schools under state control.

Secondary education was still generally regarded as a privilege to be obtained by those who could afford to pay for it, not as a recognized part of a free state system. Private secondary schools had been established in abundance. It was not surprising that the development of a state system of secondary schools came as a part of the general high-school movement that began to take on vigorous growth about 1850.

The characteristic features of Ohio's educational legislation during her first half-century of statehood left a strong impression upon the state's educational policy for the next fifty years. The lack of any efficient centralized control, the absence of compulsory local supervision of any kind, an abundance of excellent permissive laws, which legalized advanced educational procedure without compelling it, the passing of laws general in form but local in application, lack of any state agency for training teachers for her schools—these continued throughout the next half-century, from 1850 to 1900, as marked traits of the state's educational procedure.

It is only in very recent years that Ohio has freed herself from some of the most undesirable features of her early legislative inheritance and has adopted a modern, progressive, centralized state system of education, with state-wide supervision, that places her on a parity with her most advanced sister-states.

APPENDIX A

A CLASSIFIED COLLECTION AND ABSTRACT OF THE EDUCATIONAL LEGISLATION OF THE PERIOD: 1803–50

GENERAL LEGISLATION

ACTS TO INCORPORATE THE ORIGINAL SURVEYED TOWNSHIPS, INCLUDING PROVISIONS FOR DISTRICTING, ESTABLISHING SCHOOLS, APPORTIONING MONEY, ETC.

O.L., IV, 66, January 2, 1806.
O.L., VIII, 100, February 6, 1810.
O.L., XIII, 295, December 5, 1814.
O.L., XXIX, 490, March 14, 1831.

GENERAL SCHOOL LAWS

O.L., XIX, 51, January 22, 1821. An act to provide for the regulation and support of common schools. (The first school law.)
O.L., XX, 86, January 31, 1822. Resolution. Seven commissioners to report a system of common schools.
O.L., XXIII, 36, February 5, 1825. An act to provide for the support, etc.
O.L., XXV, 65, January 30, 1827. An act supplementary to the above.
O.L., XXV, 78, January 30, 1827. An act to establish a fund for the support of common schools.
O.L., XXVII, 73, February 10, 1829. An act to provide for the support, etc.
O.L., XXVIII, 56, February 18, 1830. An act in addition to the act to establish a fund, etc.
O.L., XXVIII, 57, January 14, 1830. An act to amend the school law.
O.L., XXIX, 414, March 10, 1831. An act to provide for the support, etc.
O.L., XXIX, 423, March 2, 1831. An act to establish a fund for the support of common schools.
O.L., XXX, 4, December 23, 1831. An act to amend the school law.
O.L., XXXI, 18, December 3, 1832. An amendment regulating fees of county treasurers for handling school funds.
O.L., XXXI, 24, February 13, 1833. An act supplementary to the act concerning the school fund.
O.L., XXXI, 24, February 25, 1833. An act to amend the school law.
O.L., XXXII, 25, February 28, 1834. An act to provide for the support, etc.
O.L., XXXIV, 19, March 12, 1836. An act to provide for the support, etc.
O.L., XXXIV, 654, March 11, 1836. Resolution for a committee to prepare a school district manual.

O.L., XXXIV, 654, March 14, 1836.   Resolution requesting C. E. Stowe to study and report on European schools.

O.L., XXXV, 82, March 27, 1837.   An act creating the office of superintendent of common schools.

O.L., XXXV, 560, April 1, 1837.   Resolution appointing Samuel Lewis superintendent of common schools.

O.L., XXXV, 97, March 28, 1837.   An act for the distribution, etc., of United States surplus revenue.

O.L., XXXVI, 79, March 19, 1838.   An act amending the preceding act.

O.L., XXXIX, 41, March 27, 1841.   An act further to amend the preceding.

O.L., XXXVI, 21, March 7, 1838.   An act for the support, etc.

O.L., XXXVI, 399, December 16, 1837.   Resolution granting certain privileges to the superintendent of schools.

O.L., XXXVI, 411, March 9, 1838.   Resolution appointing Samuel Lewis superintendent for five years.

O.L., XXXVI, 73, March 17, 1838.   An act concerning the distribution of the school fund in certain districts.

O.L., XXXVI, 85, March 19, 1838.   An act levying a tax for school purposes.

O.L., XXXVI, 90, March 19, 1838.   An act regulating the fees of county auditors.

O.L., XXXVI, 402, January 4, 1838.   Resolution concerning Professor Stowe's report on European education.

O.L., XXXVI, 404, January 4, 1838.   Resolution thanking Professor Stowe for the report.

O.L., XXXVI, 404, January 16, 1838.   Resolution appropriating $500.00 for Professor C. E. Stowe for his labor.

O.L., XXXVI, 410, March 7, 1838.   Resolution providing for the distribution of the report of the superintendent of schools and C. E. Stowe's report.

O.L., XXXVI, 412, March 13, 1838.   Resolution asking for the amount of school tax levied on colored people.

O.L., XXXVI, 415, January 16, 1838.   Resolution that 8,500 copies of the report of the superintendent of schools be printed and distributed.

O.L., XXXVII, 394, January 16, 1839.   Resolution that 9,500 copies of the annual report of the superintendent be printed and distributed.

O.L., XXXVII, 61, March 16, 1839.   An act amending the school law and creating permanently the office of superintendent.

O.L., XXXVIII, 130, March 23, 1840.   An act to abolish the office of superintendent of schools.

O.L., XXXIX, 44, March 29, 1841.   An act to amend the school law and all acts amendatory thereto.

O.L., XL, 49, March 7, 1842.   An act to amend the school law.

O.L., XL, 59, March 7, 1842.   An act making appropriations.   Reduces the school appropriation to $150,000.00.

O.L., XLI, 59, March 11, 1843.   An act further to amend the school law.

O.L., XLII, 38, March 6, 1844.   An act to increase the school fund.

O.L., XLII, 48, March 12, 1844.   An act to amend the school law.

O.L., XLIV, 81, February 28, 1846.   An act authorizing districts to establish school libraries.

O.L., XLIV, 114, March 2, 1846.   An act to amend the preceding act of March 11, 1843.

O.L., XLV, 26, February 8, 1847.   An act to amend the school law.

O.L., XLV, 60, February 8, 1847.   An act to amend the act for levying taxes.

O.L., XLV, 67, February 8, 1847.   An act to incorporate teachers' institutes.

O.L., XLV, 32, February 8, 1847.   An act to provide for the appointment of county superintendents.

O.L., XLVI, 28, January 21, 1848.   An act to secure the returns of school statistics.

O.L., XLV, local, 187, February 8, 1847.   An act for the support of common schools in Akron.   (This act made general in 1848.)

O.L., XLVI, 40, January 28, 1848.   An act to amend the preceding act.

O.L., XLVI, 48, February 14, 1848.   An act making general the Akron Act.

O.L., XLVI, 69, February 22, 1848.   An act to amend the act for levying taxes.

O.L., XLVI, 81, February 24, 1848.   An act to provide a department of common schools for colored persons.

O.L., XLVI, 83, February 24, 1848.   An act amending the school law.

O.L., XLVI, 86, February 24, 1848.   An act amending the act to encourage teachers' institutes.

O.L., XLVII, 17, February 10, 1849.   An act authorizing separate schools for colored children.

O.L., XLVII, 19, February 16, 1849.   An act amending the act to incorporate teachers' institutes.

O.L., XLVII, 22, February 21, 1849.   An act for the regulation of public schools in cities and towns.

O.L., XLVII, 39, March 6, 1849.   An act amending the school law.

O.L., XLVII, 43, March 12, 1849.   An act to amend the school law.

O.L., XLVII, 45, March 15, 1849.   An act to amend the Akron Act.

O.L., XLVII, 52, March 24, 1849.   An act to amend the school law.

O.L., XLVIII, 40, March 13, 1850.   An act to amend the law concerning public schools in cities and towns.

O.L., XLVIII, 41, March 22, 1850.   An act concerning school district taxes, etc.

O.L., XLVIII, 44, March 22, 1850.   An act for the appointment of a state board of public instruction.

O.L., XLVIII, 47, March 23, 1850.   An act supplementary to the preceding.

O.L., XLVIII, 728, January 28, 1850.   Resolution for the appointment of a committee to report on the defects of the present school system.

SPECIAL ACTS CONCERNING PUBLIC SCHOOLS

Special acts for the following purposes were passed during the period from 1829 to 1850:

Creating district or changing boundaries of districts   29

Allowing districts to make appropriations, borrow money or tax themselves for school purposes   26

Authorizing the sale of school lots or other lots for school purposes   18

Authorizing the apportionment of school funds when the school census had not been made   13

Changing the form or powers of the district organization   4

Governing the distribution of school funds in special cases   6
Relief of individual school officers   2

FINES, FEES, ETC., APPLIED TO THE SUPPORT OF PUBLIC SCHOOLS

O.L., XXVII, 11, January 28, 1829.   An act to regulate grocers and retailers of spirituous liquors.
Licenses, $5.00 to $50.00.   Fines for operating without license, permitting rioting, drunkenness, gambling, etc., $10.00 to $50.00.   All moneys to go to the schools of the county.

O.L., XXIX, 161, February 17, 1831.   An act for the prevention of immoral practices.

Sabbath-breaking—Fine	$1.00 to	$5.00
Selling liquor on Sunday—Not to exceed		5.00
Disturbing religious meetings—Not to exceed		20.00
Using profanity	.25 to	1.00
Exciting disturbance in a tavern, etc	.50 to	5.00
Playing bullets, shooting, running horses in towns	.50 to	5.00
Liquor dealer keeping nine-pin alley	10.00 to	100.00
Exhibiting a puppet show, juggling, etc		10.00
Tearing down public notices		10.00
Selling liquor within one mile of religious gatherings except by licensed dealers at place of business, etc		20.00
Bull-baiting, bear-baiting, etc., not to exceed		100.00
Cock-fighting—not to exceed		100.00
Horse-racing on public road	1.00 to	5.00

All moneys to go to the schools of the township in which offenses occur.

O.L., XXIX, 304, March 14, 1831.   An act regulating sales at auctions.
Selling without license 500.00
Failure to render account, not to exceed 1,000.00
All moneys to go to State Literary Fund.

O.L., XXIX, 313, March 14, 1831.   An act for granting licenses.
Peddling without license . . . .   20.00 to 100.00
All moneys to go to schools of district in which the offense occurs.

O.L., XXIX, 446, February 28, 1831.   An act to regulate public shows.
Exhibiting circus without permit 100.00
Money to go to schools of the county.

O.L., XXIX, 469, January 18, 1830.   An act to protect the fur trade.
Killing muskrats out of season 1.00
Money to go to schools of township.

O.L., XXIX, 477, March 9, 1831.   An act concerning the inspection of certain articles.
Neglecting to have fish inspected and barrels branded . . .   5.00
Failure to bury offal when fish are packed . . . .   5.00 to 50.00
Inspector violating regulations 50.00
Money to go to schools of the county.

O.L., XXXII, 20, February 27, 1834. An act to provide for the punishment of certain crimes.

Medical malpractice of various kinds.................. 100.00 to 500.00
Money to go to schools of the county.

O.L., XXXII, 47, March 3, 1834. An act for the inspection of salt.
Selling or removing salt liable to inspection. Per barrel. 1.00
Money to go to schools of the county.

O.L., XLVI, 36, February 7, 1848. Amending the act granting licenses, etc.
Peddler's license fees to go to state school fund.
Fine for peddling without license...................... 50.00
Money to go to schools of the township.

O.L., XLIII, 17, February 10, 1845. An act to prevent firing
of cannon upon public streets, etc. Money to go to
schools of the township............................ 50.00

O.L., XLIV, 10, January 17, 1846. An act to prevent gambling.
Proprietor of gambling-house or common gambler....... 500.00
Money to go to schools of the county.

O.L., XLIV, 76, February 28, 1846. An act to protect enclosures.
Fine not to exceed................................. 100.00

O.L., XLII, 37, March 6, 1844. An act to prevent the introduction and spreading of Canada thistles.
Allowing to mature or selling seed containing Canada
thistle seed.................................... 10.00 to 20.00
Money to go to schools of the township.

O.L., XXXII, 38, March 1, 1834. Obstructing navigation in
the Muskingum River............................ 50.00

O.L., XXXVI, 68, March 17, 1838. Officer or corporation
disregarding court orders in quo warranto procedure... 10,000.00
Money to go to schools of the county.

O.L., XXXVIII, 4, January 17, 1840. Keeping breachy or
unruly animals................................. .25 to 1.00
Money to go to schools of the district.

O.L., XXXVIII, 57, January 17, 1840. Harboring intoxicated
Indians....................................... 5.00 to 25.00
Money to go to schools of the district.

O.L., XXXIX, 34, March 26, 1841. Selling liquor within two
miles of a religious society gathered in a field or wood-
land.. 10.00
Money to go to schools of the township.

CITY AND TOWN SCHOOL CHARTERS

LAWS CONCERNING COMMON SCHOOLS IN CITIES AND TOWNS

O.L., XXIII, 65, January 8, 1825. An act authorizing the township meeting at Marietta to vote a sum for schools.

O.L., XXVII, 33, February 12, 1829. An act creating a school system in the city of Cincinnati.

O.L., XXXVIII, 157, March 19, 1840. Amending the preceding act.

O.L., XLIII, 413, March 12, 1845. Supplementary. City of Cincinnati.

O.L., XLIV, 91, February 11, 1846.   An act for the better classification of the common schools of Cincinnati and Dayton.

O.L., XLV, 193, February 6, 1847.   An act authorizing the City Council of Cincinnati to levy taxes for school purposes.

O.L., XLVIII, 662, March 23, 1850.   An act authorizing the appointment of a superintendent of common schools in Cincinnati.

O.L., XXXIV, 226, March 3, 1836.   An act incorporating the city of Ohio.   Provides for school system.

O.L., XXXV, 32, January 7, 1837.   An act incorporating the city of Toledo. Provides for school system.

O.L., XXXIV, 271, March 5, 1836.   An act incorporating the city of Cleveland. Provides for school system.

O.L., XLVI, 150, February 18, 1848.   An act for the better regulation and support of the Cleveland schools.

O.L., XXXVI, 329, March 16, 1838.   Amending the act to incorporate the town of Portsmouth.   School system adapted from the Cincinnati charter.

O.L., XXXVII, 194, March 12, 1839.   An act for the support and better regulation of the schools in the town of Zanesville.

O.L., XXXIX, 22, February 20, 1841.   An act to regulate schools in the town of Marietta.

O.L., XXXIX, 135, March 27, 1841.   An act to incorporate the city of Dayton. Adapts provisions of the Cleveland and Cincinnati schools.

O.L., XLIII, 57, February 3, 1845.   An act for the support and better regulation of schools in the city of Columbus.

O.L., XLVII, 230, February 16, 1849.   Amending the preceding.

O.L., XLIII, 150, February 26, 1845.   An act incorporating the town of Mt. Vernon.   Provides for the control of schools.

O.L., XLVII, 205, March 9, 1849.   An act concerning taxes, schools, and sewers in the city of Toledo.

O.L., XLIV, 261, March 2, 1846.   An act to regulate common schools in Maumee City, Lucas County, and in Elyria.

O.L., XLV, 121, February 8, 1847.   An act for the support and better regulation of schools in District 1, in Ravenna.

O.L., XLVI, 185, February 18, 1848.   An act for the support and better regulation of schools in Lithopolis.

O.L., XLVI, 199, February 19, 1848.   An act for the support and better regulation of schools in Lancaster.

O.L., XLVIII, 647, February 13, 1850.   Amending the preceding.

O.L., XLVI, 237, February 24, 1848.   An act for the support and better regulation of schools in Lebanon District, Warren County.

O.L., XLVII, 253, March 21, 1849.   An act repealing the Akron Act in the town of New Lisbon.

O.L., XLVIII, 648, March 22, 1850.   An act to repeal the provisions of the act for the regulation of schools in cities and towns etc., so far as it is in force in the town of Hanover.

O.L., XLVIII, 662, March 21, 1850.   An act to exempt Mt. Vernon from the provisions of the Akron Act.

O.L., XLVIII, 373, March 21, 1850.   Amending the act to incorporate the town of Fulton.   (Providing for schools.)

O.L., XLVIII, 421, March 19, 1850.   An act incorporating the city of Piqua. (Providing for schools.)

O.L., XLVIII, 446, March 21, 1850.   An act to incorporate the city of Springfield.   (Providing for schools.)

O.L., XLVIII, 648, March 1, 1850.   An act extending the provisions of the act for regulation of schools in cities etc., to Union School District No. 7 in Springfield and Suffield Townships in Summit and Portage counties.

O.L., XLVIII, 651, March 19, 1850.   An act authorizing the citizens of Wooster to vote for or against the provisions of the Akron Act.

ACTS CONCERNING LOCAL SCHOOL FUNDS

O.L., XXVII, 22, January 5, 1829.   An act establishing a fund for common schools in Clermont County.

O.L., XXVII, 180, February 11, 1829. ⎫
O.L., XXVIII, 56, February 2, 1830. ⎬ Acts supplementary to the preced-
O.L., XXVIII, 57, January 14, 1830. ⎬   ing act.
O.L., XXIX, 210, March 11, 1831.   ⎭

O.L., XXXII, 100, February 20, 1834; O.L., XXXVIII, 149, March 17, 1840. Acts establishing a common school fund in that part of Warren County in the Virginia Military District.

O.L., XXVIII, 93, February 18, 1830.   An act incorporating the trustees of the Windham School Fund.

O.L., XXXVII, 50, February 16, 1839; O.L., XLI, 26, January 16, 1843.   Acts supplementary to the preceding.

ACTS CONCERNING SCHOOLS FOR POOR CHILDREN

O.L., XXIV, 36, January 24, 1826.   An act to incorporate the Charity School of Kendal, Stark County.

O.L., XXVII, 76, February 10, 1829; O.L., XLVIII, 625, March 7, 1850.   Acts supplementary to the preceding.

O.L., XXV, 62, January 24, 1827.   An act to incorporate the trustees of the Woodward Free Grammar School.

O.L., XXXIV, 514, March 14, 1836.   An act to incorporate the M'Intire Poor School, in Zanesville.

O.L., XXXVI, 208, March 7, 1838.   An act to incorporate the Emigrants Friends Society of Cincinnati.

LAWS CONCERNING SCHOOL LANDS

GENERAL LAWS CONCERNING SCHOOL LANDS

Journals of the American Congress.   1774–88.   Vol. IV, 520.   May 20, 1785. An ordinance for ascertaining the mode of disposing of lands in the Western territory.

United States Statutes at Large.   Vol. I, 51.   July 13, 1787.   An ordinance for the government of the territory of the United States northwest of the River Ohio.

Journals of the American Congress. 1774–88. Vol. IV, Appendix, 17. Powers to the Board of Treasury to contract for the sale of the Western territory.

United States Statutes at Large. Vol. II, 175. April 30, 1802. Enabling Act for Ohio.

Nashee's *Compilation*, page 161, Territorial Act. November 27, 1800. An act authorizing the leasing of school lands, etc., in Washington County.

O.L., I, 61, April 15, 1803. An act to provide for the leasing of school lands.

O.L., III, 230, February 20, 1805. An act directing the mode of leasing Section 16.

O.L., III, 321, April 15, 1805. An act to provide for leasing school lands.

O.L., IV, 66, January 2, 1806. An act to incorporate the original surveyed townships. (Leasing school lands.)

O.L., VI, 125, January 14, 1808. An act accepting certain lands offered by Congress for the use of schools in the Virginia Military Tract, in lieu of those heretofore appropriated.

O.L., VII, 109, February 17, 1809. An act directing the manner in which the school lands in the Virginia Military Tract shall be surveyed and disposed of.

O.L., VIII, 100, February 6, 1810. An act to incorporate the original surveyed townships. (Leasing school lands.)

O.L., VIII, 254, February 16, 1810. Amending the act concerning the disposition etc., of the school lands in the Virginia Military Tract.

O.L., XIII, 295, December 5, 1814. An act supplementing the act to incorporate townships. (Leasing school lands.)

O.L., XIV, 418, February 26, 1816. An act directing the manner of leasing the school lands in the Virginia Military Tract.

O.L., XV, 202, January 27, 1817. An act to provide for leasing the school lands. (99-year leases.)

O.L., XIX, 161, February 21, 1821. An act to provide for leasing school lands in the United States Military District.

O.L., XX, 34, January 31, 1822. An act regulating the school lands in the Connecticut Western Reserve.

O.L., XXI, 33, January 27, 1823. An act to authorize the surrender of certain leases, etc. (School lands.)

O.L., XXV, 56, January 29, 1827. An act to provide for the sale of Section 16.

O.L., XXV, 103, January 19, 1827. An act to provide for obtaining the consent of the inhabitants of the United States Military District to the sale of school lands, and to authorize the surrender of leases and the receiving of certificates of purchase.

O.L., XXV, 45, January 29, 1827. An act to enable the inhabitants of the Virginia Military District to vote on the sale of school lands.

O.L., XXVI, 23, January 28, 1828. An act to provide for the sale of the school lands in the Virginia Military District and to authorize the surrender of leases and the receiving of certificates of purchase.

O.L., XXVI, 135, February 11, 1828. An act to enable the inhabitants of the Connecticut Western Reserve to give their consent to the sale of their school lands.

O.L., XXVI, 80, February 11, 1828. An act to provide for granting temporary leases of certain school lands.

O.L., XXVIII, 16, February 9, 1830. An act to amend the act providing for the sale of Section 16.

O.L., XXVIII, 18, December 31, 1829. An act to enable the inhabitants of the Connecticut Western Reserve to give their consent to the sale of their school lands.

O.L., XXIX, 490, March 14, 1831. An act to incorporate the original surveyed townships. (Management of the school lands.)

O.L., XXIX, 187, March 3, 1831. An act making further provision for the sale of Section 16.

O.L., XXXIII, 128, February 25, 1835. An act authorizing the electors in the several counties of the Western Reserve to give their assent to the sale of additional school land.

O.L., XXXVI, 63, March 16, 1838. Amending the act to provide for the sale of Section 16.

O.L., XXXVII, 78, March 18, 1839. An act for the relief of holders of leases on Section 16.

O.L., XXXVIII, 62, March 21, 1840. Amending the act providing for the sale of school lands in the United States Military District.

O.L., XXXVIII, 164, March 20, 1840. An act providing for the sale of three tracts of Moravian school lands in Tuscarawas County.

O.L., XLI, 20, February 2, 1843. An act to regulate the sale of ministerial and school lands and the surrender of permanent leases.

O.L., XLIII, 58, March 4, 1845. An act to fix the minimum price of school lands.

O.L., XLVI, 38, February 8, 1848. An act to enable the inhabitants of the Western Reserve to give their consent to the sale of their school lands.

O.L., XLVII, 232, February 17, 1849. An act to provide for the sale of the Western Reserve school lands.

SPECIAL ACTS CONCERNING SCHOOL LANDS

1803–17

Granting permanent leases... 25
Concerning other features of leases.................................. 5

1817–23

Concerning leases.. 18
Extending time of payment of rent.................................... 3

1823–27

Calling for a revaluation of land..................................... 4
Granting one-year leases.. 2
For the relief of lessees... 4
Leasing less than legal amount....................................... 1

1827–31

Calling for a revaluation of land..................................... 15
For surrendering leases... 15
Authorizing sales of school lands.................................... 12
Making special provisions for leasing................................ 5

Distributing funds from leased lands................................. 4
Leasing less than legal amount...................................... 2
For the relief of lessees.. 1

1831–38

Providing for sales... 47
Changing provisions for surrendering leases......................... 17
Postponing payments due.. 17
Leasing less than legal amount...................................... 7
Distributing funds from leased lands................................. 6
Special provisions in lease.. 3
Concerning a revaluation of land..................................... 5

1838–45

Concerning the surrender of leases.................................. 21
Postponing payments.. 14
Acts legalizing sales... 13
Special provisions for leasing....................................... 11

Sixty-four of the acts of this period included a minimum price ranging from two to thirty dollars per acre. The minimum price that appears most frequently is five dollars per acre, this appearing in forty-six of the sixty-four cases. This fixing of a minimum price occurs in these cases before any general act has been passed placing a minimum price on school lands.

1845–50

Authorizing sales of land, approximately............................. 100
Surrendering leases.. 8
Extending time of payment.. 7
Leasing... 2

In addition to the special acts classified above, there are a comparatively small number of miscellaneous acts concerning school lands that do not lend themselves easily to classification, and which are of very minor importance. The total number of special acts passed concerning school lands during this period is approximately 500.

SECONDARY AND HIGHER EDUCATION

ACTS INCORPORATING SECONDARY INSTITUTIONS

Acts incorporating academies, seminaries, institutes, high schools, etc. The acts incorporating these institutions are not given in full. Only the date of incorporation and the main points are indicated. These facts will indicate the incorporators, the control of the institution, the body supporting it, the property limitations, the curriculum and purpose, and the limitations placed upon the body by the act of incorporation. These provisions are not all indicated in the case of each act, but the points that appear are shown.

O.L., I, 117, April 16, 1803. The Erie Literary Society; David Hudson and twelve others; board of trustees of ten to fifteen members; to support a seminary of learning, either a college or an academy.

O.L., VI, 17, February 15, 1808. The Dayton Academy; James Walsh and seven others; stock company, shares five dollars each; nine trustees; annual income not to exceed three thousand dollars.

O.L., VI, 51, February 20, 1808. The Worthington Academy; James Kilburne and six others; seven trustees; stock company, shares five dollars each; annual income not to exceed ten thousand dollars.

O.L., VI, 156, February 18, 1808. Chillicothe Academy; Robert Wilson and eight others; seven to eleven trustees; stock company, shares ten dollars; annual income not to exceed ten thousand dollars.

O.L., VIII, 26, January 2, 1810. The New Lisbon Academy; Clement Vallandigham and eleven others; twelve trustees; stock company, shares five dollars; annual income not to exceed three thousand dollars; to erect and keep in repair a house for an academy, and such other academical purposes as they shall deem most conducive to the interest of said corporation.

O.L., IX, 39, January 26, 1811. An academy at Steubenville; Lyman Potter and fifteen others, twelve trustees; stock company, shares five dollars; annual income not to exceed five thousand dollars.

O.L., IX, 57, January 29, 1811. Gallia Academy in Gallipolis; Claude R. Menager and fifty-nine others; seven trustees; stock company, shares ten dollars each; annual income not to exceed five thousand dollars; to use the funds in that way most beneficial for the encouragement of literature, and to set apart a fund for the education of orphans and poor children.

O.L., XIII, 132, February 4, 1815. The Cincinnati Lancaster Seminary; William Lytle and nineteen others; seven directors; annual income not to exceed ten thousand dollars; no part of said funds shall be applied for the purpose of banking; no political, religious, moral or literary association shall have ascendancy in the directory, and no religious tenets peculiar to any Christian sect shall ever be introduced into the seminary.

O.L., XIV, 217, February 13, 1816. Montgomery Academy, Hamilton County; Daniel Hayden and six others; seven trustees; stock company, shares five dollars each; annual income not to exceed one thousand dollars.

O.L., XIV, 440, February 27, 1816. Tallmadge Academy, Portage County; Elizur Wright and twenty-five others; seven to eleven trustees; stock company, shares ten dollars each; annual income not to exceed three thousand dollars; no funds shall be applied to banking.

O.L., XV, 107, January 24, 1817. An act to provide for the incorporation of schools and library companies. This act provides that any association of six or more persons may, for the purpose of establishing a school and building a schoolhouse, or for the purpose of establishing a library, submit their articles of association to the president of the Court of Common Pleas and if he approve and indorse same, submit it to two judges of the Supreme Court. If they in like manner approve and indorse the articles of association, they shall be recorded and deposited with the county recorder, and the incorporators shall have the usual corporate powers.

O.L., XVI, 109, January 29, 1818. The Florence Academy of Arts and Science, Huron County; Luther Havriss and nine others; annual income not to exceed two thousand dollars; no part of stock to be used for banking or other purposes.

O.L., XVII, 97, February 1, 1819. Cadiz Academy, Harrison County; John Rea and eleven others; twelve trustees; stock company, shares five dollars each; annual income not to exceed three thousand dollars; no part of funds to be used for banking.

O.L., XVII, 186, February 6, 1819. Union Academy, Muskingum County; Andrew Howell and ten others; nine trustees; stock company, shares five dollars each; annual income not to exceed five thousand dollars; no funds to be used in banking.

O.L., XVIII, local, 85, February 23, 1820. Lancaster Academy; P. Beecher and six others; seven trustees; stock company; annual income not to exceed two thousand dollars; trustees shall have power "of directing what branches of literature and the arts and sciences shall be taught."

O.L., XX, local, 11, January 1, 1822. The Academy of Alma, New Athens, Harrison County; Joseph Anderson and eleven others; said corporation shall not deal in exchange, discount notes or follow any commercial business or pursuit; no religious doctrines peculiar "to any one sect of Christians shall be inculcated by any professor of said academy."

O.L., XX, local, 27, January 30, 1822. The Urbana Academy; John Reynolds and six others; seven trustees; stock company; annual income not to exceed two thousand dollars; no religious tenets peculiar to any Christian sect to be taught.

O.L., XX, local, 30, January 31, 1822. Rutland Academy, Meigs County; Abel Larkin and four others; seven trustees; stock company, shares five dollars.

O.L., XXII, local, 14, January 22, 1824. Franklin Academy, Mansfield; Ebon P. Sturges and fourteen others; fifteen trustees; stock company, shares five dollars; no religious tenets peculiar to any one sect of Christians shall be taught or inculcated in said academy.

O.L., XXII, 72, February 21, 1824. Norwalk Academy, Huron County; Timothy Baker and four others; seven trustees; stock company; annual income not to exceed two thousand dollars; trustees shall direct "what branches of literature and of the arts and sciences shall be taught."

O.L., XXXII, local, 85, February 17, 1834. Norwalk Academy changed to Norwalk Seminary; trustees to be appointed by the Ohio Annual Conference of the Methodist Episcopal Church; no teacher shall be allowed to teach any student the peculiar tenets of any sect or religious denomination without the consent of the parents or guardian.

O.L., XXII, local, 104, February 24, 1824. Belmont Academy, St. Clairsville, Belmont County; James Caldwell and four others; five trustees; stock company, shares five dollars each.

O.L., XXIII, local, 18, December 22, 1824. Circleville Academy; Andrew Houston and six others; seven trustees; stock company, shares ten dollars each; trustees shall determine what branches of literature and the arts and sciences shall be taught.

O.L., XXV, local, 96, January 23, 1827. Academy of Perry County.

O.L., XXVI, local, 167, January 24, 1828. The Nelson Academy; Jeremiah H. Fuller and eight others; nine trustees; stock company, capital stock not to exceed twenty-five thousand dollars; board "to direct what branches of literature shall be taught."

O.L., XXVII, local, 152, February 9, 1829. Hillsborough Academy, Highland County; William Keys and six others; board of seven trustees; stock company, shares five dollars each.

O.L., XXVIII, local, 116, February 22, 1830. The High School of Elyria, Lorain County; Heman Ely and four others; no part of the funds shall be applied to any other object than the support of the high school.

O.L., XXIX, local, 43, January 15, 1831. The Woodward High School, Cincinnati; five trustees; endowment; to educate such children as have no parents living within the limits of said city; the benefits of this trust shall not be confined to any religious sect or sects, but shall be open to all children coming within the provisions of this act, whatever may be or whatever may have been the religious creed of their parents.

Amended, January 7, 1836, O.L., XXXIV, local, 27.

SEC. 1. Enabling the trustees to establish a college department to be called "The Woodward College of Cincinnati."

SEC. 2. Granting power to confer all such degrees as are usually conferred in colleges and universities, provided that they shall not establish a medical, law or theological department.

O.L., XXIX, local, 100, February 9, 1831. The Columbus Female Academy; James Hoge and four others; three to five trustees; stock company, shares of one hundred dollars each; annual income not to exceed three thousand dollars; to be employed only for literary purposes.

O.L., XXIX, local, 137, February 22, 1831. The Ashtabula Institution of Science and Industry; Giles Cowles and nine others.

O.L., XXXIII, local, 79, February 17, 1835. Amended.

Changing name to the "Grand River Institute."

O.L., XXIX, local, 139, February 22, 1831. Delaware Academy; Ezra Griswold and eight others; nine trustees; income not to exceed five thousand dollars; no part of such property to be applied to any banking or commercial purposes.

O.L., XXX, local, 30, January 19, 1832. Kinsman Academy, Trumbull County; Isaac McIlvaine and ten others; property not to exceed ten thousand dollars.

O.L., XXX, local, 47, January 25, 1832. Canton Academy; William Christmas and nine others; seven trustees; annual income not to exceed five thousand dollars; no part to be applied to banking, nor other than purposes that are purely literary; to manage the academy buildings hereafter erected on the public-school ground of said town of Canton for the purpose of this corporation, and the general interest of education.

O.L., XXXI, local, 133, February 19, 1833. Repealed.

O.L., XXX, local, 62, January 26, 1832. Farmington Academy, Trumbull County; Theodore Wolcott and four others; annual income not to exceed two thousand dollars; no part of property to be used for other than literary purposes.

O.L., XXX, local, 111, February 6, 1832. Ashtabula Academy, Ashtabula County; Mathew Hubbard and seven others; three to five trustees; stock company, shares twenty-five dollars each; income not to exceed three thousand dollars; property shall only be employed for literary purposes.

O.L., XXX, local, 141, February 7, 1832. Huron Institute; Ebenezer Andrews and nineteen others; twenty trustees; to afford instruction to the youth of both sexes in the higher branches of an English education the learned languages, and the liberal arts and sciences, and the trustees as their ability shall increase may erect a separate or additional departments for the pursuit of these and any other branches of a polite and liberal education, and may provide the requisite means for the employment of the students in manual labor such portion of their time as their health and other circumstances may require.

O.L., XXXI, 188, local, February 21, 1833.   The Chillicothe Female Seminary; John Woodbridge and five others of Ross County; five trustees; annual income not to exceed two thousand dollars; property and funds shall be converted to no other use than the promotion of female education.

O.L., XXXII, local, 177, February 25, 1834.   The Ravenna Academy; Darius Lemon and six others; property not to exceed ten thousand dollars.

O.L., XXXII, local, 223, February 7, 1834.   Union Academy, Wayne County; James Snodgrass and nine others.

O.L., XXXII, local, 234, February 28, 1834.   Vinton Academy, Gallia County; Samuel W. Holcomb and eight others; nine trustees; stock company, shares five dollars each.

O.L., XXXII, local, 270, March 1, 1834.   The Springfield High School, Clark County; nine trustees; stock company, shares ten dollars each; property not to exceed ten thousand dollars; "said high school shall afford instruction to the youths of both sexes in the higher branches of an English education, or learned languages, or liberal arts and sciences, and such other branches of a polite and liberal education as may be prescribed by the trustees"; funds shall never be appropriated for any other purpose than that for which they were given.

O.L., XL, local, 114, March 7, 1842.   Ohio Conference High School.   The Springfield High School passes to the control of the Ohio Annual Conference of the Methodist Episcopal Church; nineteen trustees, trustees to be appointed by the Ohio Annual Conference of the M. E. Church, property not to exceed five thousand dollars.

O.L., XXXII, local, 333, March 3, 1834.   The Female Academy of Mt. Vernon; Hosmer Curtis and nine others; annual income not to exceed five thousand dollars; funds to be used exclusively for the purposes of education in literature and the arts and sciences; no part of the funds to be employed for banking purposes in any way whatever.

O.L., XXXIII, local, 5, December 17, 1834.   Stephen Strong's Manual Labor Seminary, Meigs County; seven trustees; instruction of youth in the various branches of useful knowledge; the rules and regulations concerning the admission of scholars shall give no preference on account of religious tenets or any cause, except good moral character and promise of future usefulness; that no religious tenets peculiar to any sect of Christians shall ever be taught or inculcated in the seminary, provided that nothing in the foregoing shall be so construed as to prevent a course or moral and religious instruction such as is consistent with the Christian religion, except such as is calculated to support sectarianism.

O.L., XXXIII, local, 21, January 22, 1835.   The Richmond Classical Institute, Richmond, Jefferson County; Thomas George and twelve others; thirteen trustees; annual income not to exceed five thousand dollars; property and funds shall be used for no purpose other than that of education.

O.L., XLVI, local, 7, December 28, 1847. Changing the name of the Richmond Classical Institute to Richmond College.

O.L., XXXIII, local, 48, February 12, 1835. Kingsville High School, Ashtabula County; stock company, shares ten dollars each; said property shall be applied to no other use than the establishment and maintenance of said school and the promotion of literature and sciences.

O.L., XXXIII, local, 51, February 14, 1835. Conneaut Academy; Ashbel Dart and six others; property not to exceed ten thousand dollars.

O.L., XXXIII, local, 87, February 19, 1835. The Windham Academy; Hiram Messenger and six others; income not to exceed two thousand dollars annually.

O.L., XXXIII, local, 87, February 19, 1835. The Granville Female Seminary; Henry Carr and eleven others; annual income not to exceed two thousand dollars; for aiding and promoting literary and scientific purposes, and for the construction or purchase of buildings for said seminary.

O.L., XXXIII, local, 112, February 23, 1835. Fellenburgh Institute, Brunswick, Medina County; John Berdan and ten others; funds shall be applied to the endowment, support and maintenance of a seminary of learning.

O.L., XXXIII, local, 153, February 27, 1835. The Western Female Seminary, Mansfield; Elizur Hedges and eight others; property not to exceed five thousand dollars.

O.L., XXXIII, local, 190, March 5, 1835. The Wadsworth Academy; William Eyles and four others; property not to exceed ten thousand dollars.

O.L., XXXIII, local, 199, March 5, 1835. The Academic Institution of Richfield, Medina County; Secretary Rawson and four others; property not to exceed ten thousand dollars.

O.L., XXXIII, local, 305, March 7, 1835. The Hamilton and Rossville Female Academy; John Woods and eight others; five directors; stock company, shares ten dollars each; annual income not to exceed five thousand dollars; directors have power to "direct what branches of literature and of the arts and sciences shall be taught; no part of the funds shall be used for banking."

O.L., XXXIII, local, 321, March 7, 1835. The Circleville Female Seminary; Guy W. Doan and seven others.

O.L., XXXIII, local, 328, March 7, 1835. Bishop's Fraternal Calvanistic [sic] Baptist Seminary; Samuel G. Bishop and five others; property not to exceed twenty thousand dollars; that students may pay any part or all of their board and tuition in cultivating said land (one hundred acres) at a fair reward for their labor, as it is given for that expressed purpose and no other, and if circumstances shall require, may erect shops thereon and furnish materials for mechanics for the same purpose; also furnish places for female labor—sewing, braiding, and all such other kinds of labor as may be deemed expedient; no one shall be eligible for the office of trustee or president to superintend the instruction of said seminary unless he is a member of the Calvanistic or Regular Baptist Denomination, so called; nothing in this act shall be so construed to authorize the establishment of a school for the practice of medicine; "other teachers and students may be received without regard to their religious tenets provided they are of a moral character, and be treated according to their merit."

O.L., XXXIV, local, 6, December 30, 1835.   The Universal School of Massillon; Alexander McCully and four others; funds shall not be applied for any other than literary or scientific purposes.

O.L., XXXIV, local, 190, February 29, 1836.   The Putnam Classical Institute; William H. Beecher and five others.

O.L., XXXIV, local, 242, March 4, 1836.   The Seneca County Academy; Samuel Waggoner and six others; annual income not to exceed two thousand dollars.

O.L., XXXIV, local, 242, March 4, 1836.   The Madison Liberal Institute; Ebenezer Ward and four others; annual income not to exceed $2,000.00.

O.L., XXXIV, local, 386, March 11, 1836.   Wooster Academy; David Robinson and eight others; capital stock not to exceed twenty-five thousand dollars; stock company, shares five dollars; nine trustees; trustees have power "to direct what branches of literature and the arts and sciences shall be taught"; no part of funds shall ever be applied for banking purposes.

O.L., XXXIV, local, 408, March 12, 1836.   Shaw Academy, Cuyahoga County; Clifford Belden and sixty-nine others; nine trustees; endowment and stock company, shares ten dollars each; property not to exceed twenty thousand dollars, annual income not to exceed two thousand dollars; "to afford greater facilities for the instruction of youth in literature and sciences, and for the inculcating of good morals on Christian principles."

O.L., XXXIV, local, 458, March 14, 1836.   The Academy of Sylvania, Lucas County; William Wilson and eight others; nine trustees; stock company, shares five dollars each; stock not to exceed twenty-five thousand dollars; trustees may "direct what branches of literature and the arts and sciences shall be taught."

O.L., XXXIV, local, 460, March 14, 1836.   Granville Academy; Jacob Little and ten others; annual income not to exceed five thousand dollars; funds shall never be used for banking purposes.

O.L., XXXIV, local, 514, March 14, 1836.   Sharon Academy, Medina County; Thomas Briggs and five others; property not to exceed five thousand dollars; proceeds shall be applied to the support of a school and to no other purpose whatever.

O.L., XXXIV, local, 545, March 14, 1836.   Medina Academy; U. H. Peak and thirty-one others; stock company, annual income not to exceed two thousand dollars.

O.L., XXXIV, local, 547, March 14, 1836.   The Cleves Independent School, Hamilton County; "whereas the law regulating common schools does not sufficiently provide for schools such as would suit the wishes and circumstances of the people in every section of the state, and that the citizens of the village of Cleves and vicinity may have a school where the different branches of education may be taught such as has been contemplated by the provisions of the general school law"; Stephen Wood and four others; three trustees, a treasurer and secretary.

O.L., XXXV, local, 20, December 30, 1836.   Middleburg High School, Portage County; D. McNaughton and four others; five trustees; stock company, shares twenty-five dollars each; annual income not to exceed two thousand dollars; property not to exceed thirty thousand dollars.

O.L., XXXV, local, 133, March 3, 1837.   Warren Academy, Trumbull County; David Todd with eighteen others; nine trustees; stock company, shares fifty dollars each; annual income not to exceed five thousand dollars; funds to be used only for education; a seminary of learning for the instruction of young persons of either sex in science and literature.

O.L., XXXV, local, 139, March 7, 1837.   Sheffield Manual Labor Institute; Robbins Burrell with seven others of Lorain County; labor, arts and sciences; no part of funds shall be used for banking purposes.

O.L., XXXV, local, 185, March 10, 1837.   The Neville Institute, Columbiana County; Alexander Young and eight others; six trustees to be appointed by the legislature; endowment; annual income not to exceed two thousand dollars.

O.L., XXXV, local, 193, March 13, 1837.   New Hagerstown Academy, Carroll County; Richard Brown and thirteen others; annual income not to exceed two thousand dollars.

O.L., XXXV, local, 230, March 14, 1837.   Berea Seminary, Cuyahoga County; James Giltruth and eleven others; twelve trustees; stock company; "literary and manual labor departments."

O.L., XXXV, local, 262, March 16, 1837.   The Philomathean Literary Institute, Antrim, Guernsey County; annual income not to exceed ten thousand dollars.

O.L., XXXVII, local, 308, March 16, 1839.   Changing the name of The Philomathean Literary Institute to Madison College.

O.L., XXXV, local, 342, March 27, 1837.   Monroe Seminary, Monroe County; William Mason and eight others; nine trustees; stock company, shares ten dollars each; property not to exceed ten thousand dollars; "That it shall be the primary object of this institution to cultivate the intellectual and moral faculties of the youth who may resort to it for instruction, to teach them the art of self-government, and fit them by a judicious course of moral discipline for future usefulness and happiness; provided that no peculiar tenets of any religious sect shall ever be taught in such institution nor shall any denomination of Christians be excluded."

O.L., XXXV, 380, local, March 31, 1837.   Troy Academy, Miami County; nine trustees; stock company, shares twenty dollars; annual income not to exceed five thousand dollars; instruction of young persons of either sex in science and literature; funds to be used for no other purpose than education.

O.L., XXXV, local, 406, April 1, 1837.   New Philadelphia Academy, Tuscarawas County; Joshua Simons and ten others; three to five trustees; stock company, shares twenty dollars each; annual income not to exceed three thousand dollars; funds to be employed for literary purposes.

O.L., XXXV, local, 425, April 3, 1837.   Massillon Academy, Alexander McCulley and eight others.

O.L., XXXV, local, 511, April 3, 1837. The Cleveland Female Seminary; Henry Sexton and four others; annual income not to exceed five thousand dollars; trustees have power to assign professors and teachers "in the several departments of arts, science and literature."

O.L., XXXVI, local, 52, February 8, 1838. The Akron High School, Portage County; Simon Perkins and six others; seven trustees; stock company, shares twenty dollars each; property not to exceed twenty thousand dollars; "it shall be the primary object of this institution to cultivate and strengthen the intellectual and moral faculties of the youth who may resort to it for instruction"; no peculiar tenets of religion shall be taught nor any denomination of Christians be excluded.

O.L., XXXVI, local, 98, February 19, 1838. Cambridge Academy, Guernsey County; James Blackett and seven others; annual income not to exceed two thousand dollars.

O.L., XXXVI, local, 98, February 19, 1838. Massillon Female Seminary, Stark County; O. N. Sage and ten others; stock company, shares fifty dollars each; "moral, physical and intellectual improvement and education of young females."

O.L., XXXVI, local, 157, March 2, 1838. The Western Reserve Wesleyan Seminary; Isaac Winnans and twelve others; establishing and maintaining a seminary of learning in the town of Streetsborough.

O.L., XXXVI, local, 159, March 2, 1838. The Edinburgh Academy; Ira Eddy and ten others; establish an academy in the township of Edinburgh, Portage County.

O.L., XXXVI, local, 190, March 5, 1838. Wayne Academy; Ely B. Smith and eight others; nine directors; with power to increase to fifteen.

O.L., XXXVI, local, 210, March 9, 1838. Norwalk Female Seminary; Picket Latimer and nine others; nine trustees; stock company, capital stock twelve hundred dollars with privilege to increase to twenty thousand dollars, shares twenty dollars each; annual income not to exceed four thousand dollars; educating females only.

O.L., XXXVI, local, 223, March 10, 1838. Chester Academy, Geauga County; Austin Turner and four others.

O.L., XXXVI, local, 231, March 10, 1838. Eaton Academy, Preble County; five trustees; stock company, shares twenty dollars; annual income not to exceed five thousand dollars.

O.L., XXXVI, local, 235, March 10, 1838. Sandusky Academy, Huron County; Samuel B. Caldwell and twelve others; nine trustees, stock company, shares twenty dollars; capital stock not to exceed fifty thousand dollars; funds to be used only for education.

O.L., XXXVI, local, 287, March 14, 1838. Union Academy, Union County; Reuben P. Mann and ten others; eleven trustees; stock company, shares ten dollars; annual income not to exceed five thousand dollars; stock shall not be applied to banking purposes.

O.L., XXXVI, local, 317, March 15, 1838. Dover Academy, Tuscarawas County; Wright Warner and ten others; annual income not to exceed six thousand dollars; funds to be used only for purposes of education.

O.L., XXXVI, local, 362, March 16, 1838. Marion Academy, Marion County; Sanford F. Bennett and nine others; nine trustees; stock company, shares ten dollars; stock not to exceed fifty thousand dollars.

O.L., XXXVII, local, 49, March 7, 1839. "An act to regulate incorporated Literary Societies."

SEC. 1. "That all associations for literary purposes, except common schools, colleges and universities, which the General Assembly may hereafter incorporate, shall be regulated as follows." The persons named in the act of incorporation, their associates, etc., by their corporate names may have succession for thirty years. Usual corporate powers, etc.

SEC. 2. The capital stock and property of academies shall not exceed $40,000.00; that of libraries, lyceums and other literary associations, shall not exceed $5,000.00, unless extended in their respective acts of incorporation, and no part of funds shall ever be used for banking, nor shall such institutions issue certificates of deposit or drafts, which can in any manner be used as a circulating medium.

SEC. 3. Directors or trustees shall be held individually liable for all debts of their respective associations.

SEC. 4. Any future legislature may alter or amend any act of incorporation granted under this act when the public good requires such alteration.

O.L., XXXVII, local, 6, January 5, 1839. Bigelow High School, Xenia; William Ellsberry and seventeen others; board of directors of eighteen members and the Ohio Annual Conference of the M. E. Church may appoint a visiting committee of three, who shall for the time being be members of the board; property not to exceed fifty thousand dollars; to afford instruction in the common branches of a liberal education, and in the liberal arts and sciences; sectarian views of religion shall not be inculcated.

O.L., XXXVII, local, 30, February 1, 1839. The Martinsburg Academy, Knox County; William Mitchell and eight others.

O.L., XXXVII, local, 43, February 9, 1839. Blendon Young Men's Seminary; Mathew Westervelt and eleven others; vacancies in the board to be filled by the Methodist Annual Ohio Conference; partially by endowment; capital stock not to exceed fifty thousand dollars.

O.L., XXXVII, local, 44, February 13, 1839. Ashland Academy, Richland County; John P. Reznor and eight others; three trustees; stock company, shares ten dollars each; stock not to exceed thirty thousand dollars.

O.L., XXXVII, local, 79, February 26, 1839. Western Reserve Teachers' Seminary; Timothy Rockwell and ten others; twelve trustees; property not to exceed fifty thousand dollars; education of youth and preparation of teachers; trustees shall issue no circulating medium and shall be individually liable for debts.

O.L., XXXVII, local, 80, February 27, 1839. Oxford Female Academy; John W. Scott and six others; seven trustees; property not to exceed ten thousand dollars; education of females in the town of Oxford.

O.L., XXXVII, local, 109, March 5, 1839. Asbury Seminary, Chagrin Falls; John K. Halleck and twenty-nine others.

O.L., XXXVII, local, 141, March 9, 1839. Worthington Female Seminary; William Bishop and ten others; stock company, shares twenty-five dollars; controlled partially by the M. E. Church, and partially local.

O.L., XXXVII, local, 155, March 9, 1839. The Universalist Institute, Ohio City; Richard Lord and eight others; a board of trustees; stock company, shares five dollars; no rules of a sectarian character either in religion or politics shall be adopted.

O.L., XXXVII, local, 156, March 9, 1839. Parkman Academy, Geauga County; J. P. Converse and six others.

O.L., XXXVII, local, 172, March 12, 1839. The Barnesville Male Academy, Belmont County; Isaac Hoover and twelve others; thirteen trustees; stock company, shares ten dollars; capital stock not to exceed twenty thousand dollars; property to be used only for education; to cultivate and train the intellectual faculties of the youth who may resort to it for instruction, and rigorously to discountenance the inculcation of the peculiar tenets of any Christian sect or denomination.

O.L., XXXVII, local, 222, March 13, 1839. The Brooklyn Centre Academy; Joseph Weller and fifteen others; annual income not to exceed three thousand dollars.

O.L., XXXVII, local, 254, March 16, 1839. Auglaize Seminary, Wapakoneta; William Stockdale and twelve others; property not to exceed fifty thousand dollars; annual income not to exceed five thousand dollars.

O.L., XXXVII, local, 255, March 16, 1839. Lithopolis Academy; Samuel L. Wilson and twelve others; property not to exceed ten thousand dollars; no part to be used for banking.

O.L., XXXVII, local, 257, March 16, 1839. Meigs County High School and Teachers' Institute; Samuel Halliday and seventeen others; twenty trustees; stock company, shares ten dollars; annual income not to exceed five thousand dollars; "to afford great facilities for the instruction of youth in literature and science, and for the inculcating of good morals"; incorporation shall in no wise engage in the business of banking.

O.L., XXXVII, local, 262, March 16, 1839. Mount Pleasant Boarding School; John Benjamin Hoyle and three others; thirteen directors appointed by the Friends of Ohio; annual income not to exceed five thousand dollars.

O.L., XXXVII, local, 282, March 16, 1839. Cuyahoga Falls Institute; Boswell Brooks and four others; property shall be devoted to the purposes of education.

O.L., XXXVII, local, 291, March 16, 1839. Ravenna Female Seminary; board of twelve trustees; property not to exceed fifty thousand dollars; to afford instruction in the arts and sciences.

O.L., XXXVII, local, 344, March 16, 1839. New Hagerstown Female Seminary; Richard Brown and eight others; seven trustees; capital stock not to exceed ten thousand dollars.

O.L., XXXVIII, local, 29, January 29, 1840. Bascom Seminary of Waynesburgh; Daniel Schaeffer and seven others; stock company, shares twenty-five dollars each; capital stock ten thousand dollars.

O.L., XXXVIII, local, 127, March 12, 1840. Greenfield Institute, Huron

County; Jonas Childs and five others; promoting and encouraging education.

O.L., XXXVIII, local, 127, March 12, 1840. Streetsborough High School; John E. Jackson and ten others; stock company, shares five dollars each; promoting and encouraging education; capital stock not to exceed five thousand dollars.

O.L., XXXVIII, local, 155, March 17, 1840. Willoughby Female Academy; Jonathan Lapham and five others; annual income not to exceed five thousand dollars.

O.L., XXXVIII, local, 155, March 17, 1840. Protestant Methodist Academy of Brighton; Joseph Williams and five others; funds shall be exclusively applied to the education of literature and the arts and sciences.

O.L., XXXIX, local, 51, March 20, 1841; Edinburgh Academy, Wayne County; John Andrews and seven others.

O.L., XXXIX, local, 62, March 20, 1841. Burlington Academy, Lawrence County; Elijah Frampton and thirteen others.

O.L., XXXIX, local, 65, March 20, 1841. Athens Female Academy; E G. Carpenter and nine others; act to become null and void if the company do not organize within five years.

O.L., XXXIX, local, 125, March 27, 1841. Canton Male Seminary, Stark County; William Fogle and eight others; seven trustees, three to be elected by the Evangelical Congregation.

O.L., XXXIX, local, 134, March 27, 1841. Middletown Academy and Library Association, Butler County; Francis J. Titus and four others.

O.L., XXXIX, local, 134, March 27, 1841. Gustavus Academy, Trumbull County; Philo Gates and eight others; act shall be null and void if the academy fails to organize within five years.

O.L., XXXIX, local, 134, March 27, 1841. Kinsman Academy, Trumbull County; John Kinsman and eight others.

O.L., XL, local, 86, March 5, 1842. Pine Grove Academy in Porter; Stephan Sinon and four others.

O.L., XL, local, 116, March 7, 1842. Canaan Union Academy; Jonas Notestone and four others.

O.L., XL, local, 117, March 7, 1842. Tallmadge Academical Institute, Summit County; Asaph Whittlesey and seven others; president and six directors; stock company, shares five dollars each, property not to exceed ten thousand dollars; instruction in the higher branches of education of males or females or both.

O.L., XL, local, 119, March 7, 1842. Bath High School, Summit County.

O.L., XLI, local, 14, January 11, 1843. New Lisbon Academy, Columbiana County; Fisher A. Blocksom and fourteen others.

O.L., XLI, local, 46, January 25, 1843. St. Mary's Female Educational Institute of Cincinnati; Hortense Monseau and five other women.

O.L., XLI, local, 62, February 9, 1843. Maumee City Academy, Lucas County; John E. Hunt and nine others.

O.L., XLI, local, 127, March 7, 1843. Lebanon Academy, Warren County; Daniel Vorhees and four others; five trustees; stock company, shares ten dollars; property not to exceed ten thousand dollars; "maintenance of an academy for instruction in the various branches of education of males and females."

O.L., XLI, local, 148, March 10, 1843. Oakland Female Seminary of Hillsborough; Joseph J. Mathews and ten others; nine trustees; stock company, shares ten dollars; annual income not to exceed two thousand dollars; stock not to exceed six thousand dollars.

O.L., XLII, local, 80, February 9, 1844. Lebanon Academy; J. Martin Williams, Thomas Corwin and six others; twelve trustees; stock company, shares twenty dollars; property not to exceed twenty thousand dollars; no funds to be used in banking; "to educate males and females in the higher branches of learning than are usually taught in the common schools of the county, and to instruct them in the elements of morality and the great truths of the Christian religion"; the particular tenets or creed of any particular sect shall never be taught.

O.L., XLII, local, 107, February 26, 1844. West Lodi Academy, Seneca County; John Carey and nine others.

O.L., XLII, local, 115, March 4, 1844. Franklin Academy, Portage County; Thomas Earl and twelve others; buildings not to exceed ten thousand dollars; "to establish an academy and to promote and afford therein, both to males and females, instruction in the usual branches of a sound, practical and liberal education, and in the languages, arts and sciences."

O.L., XLII, local, 178, March 12, 1844. Salem Academy, Ross County; Hugh S. Fullerton and four others.

O.L., XLII, local, 184, March 12, 1844. Lorain Institute; Robert Cochran and six others; board of trustees; to afford instruction in literature, arts and sciences.

O.L., XLII, local, 191, March 12, 1844. Waynesville Academy, Warren County; Burrell Goode and eleven others; to establish an academy and promote and afford therein, both to males and females, instruction in the usual branches of a sound, practical and liberal education, and in the languages, arts and sciences.

O.L., XLII, local, 210, March 12, 1844. Keene Academy, Coshocton County; Robert Farewell and four others; to establish an academy and to promote and afford therein, both to male and females, instruction in the usual branches of a sound, practical and liberal education, and in the languages, arts and sciences; buildings not to exceed ten thousand dollars.

O.L., XLIII, local, 12, January 9, 1845. Tallmadge Academical Institute, Summit County; Samuel L. Bronson and four others; four directors; stock company, shares twenty-five dollars each; property not to exceed ten thousand dollars; the maintenance of an academy for instruction in the higher branches of education, both for males and females.

O.L., XLIII, local, 16, January 15, 1845. Bedford Seminary, Cuyahoga County; E. H. Holly and eleven others; twelve directors and a president; stock company, shares ten dollars; property not to exceed twenty-five thousand dollars; to maintain an institution for the instruction of youth in the various classes of education.

O.L., XLIII, local, 39, January 23, 1845. Cincinnati Classical Academy; Elbert T. Bledsoe and two others; a rector and five or more trustees; capital stock not to exceed fifty thousand dollars.

O.L., XLIII, local, 42, January 29, 1845. Name changed to St. John's College.

O.L., XLIII, local, 65, February 6, 1845. Columbus Academical and Collegiate Institute; H. M. Hubbell and nineteen others; twenty trustees; to afford instruction in literature and in the arts and sciences; not to confer collegiate honors or degrees until ten thousand dollars property shall be acquired.

O.L., XLIII, local, 75, February 10, 1845. Aurora Academical Institute, Portage County; John E. Jackson; nine trustees; stock company, shares ten dollars; stock not to exceed five thousand dollars.

O.L., XLIII, local, 87, February 10, 1845. Cooper Female Academy in Dayton; Samuel Forrer and five others including Robert W. Steele; annual income not to exceed five thousand dollars; trustees may direct what branches of literature and the arts and sciences shall be taught.

O.L., XLIII, local, 89, February 10, 1845. Akron Institute; Samuel Perkins and six others; seven trustees; stock company, shares twenty dollars.

O.L., XLIII, local, 121, February 26, 1845. Rocky River Seminary; Robert Cochran and ten others; literature, arts and sciences.

O.L., XLIII, local, 203, March 4, 1845. Findlay Academical Institute, Hancock County; J. Hughing and eight others; nine trustees; stock company, shares ten dollars; stock not to exceed fifty thousand dollars; shall not contract debts beyond the amount of the capital stock subscribed.

O.L., XLIII, local, 229, March 4, 1845. The Vermillion Institute; Harrison Armstrong and fifteen others; ten trustees; stock company, shares twenty dollars; property not to exceed fifty thousand dollars; to educate males and females in letters and the sciences, and to instruct them in the elements of morality and the great truths of the Christian religion; no part to be used in banking; the tenets or creed of any particular sect shall never be taught.

O.L., XLIII, local, 289, March 8, 1845. Cottage Hill Academy in Ellsworth; William Bottum and eight others; nine directors; stock company; annual income not to exceed ten thousand dollars.

O.L., XLIII, local, 292, March 8, 1845. The Normal High School, Carroll County; Joseph Cable and eight others; property not to exceed ten thousand dollars; "the promotion of a highly moral and intellectual education in languages, arts and sciences upon the normal plan"; a failure to organize said school within one year or to operate the school for the space of one year at one time shall act as a forfeiture.

O.L., XLIII, local, 384, March 12, 1845. The London Academy, Madison County; Patrick McLane and two others; three to seven trustees; stock company, shares ten dollars each; capital stock twenty thousand dollars.

O.L., XLIII, local, 409, March 12, 1845. West Jefferson Academical Institute, Madison County. James Burnham and eighteen others; nine trustees; stock company, shares five dollars each; capital stock not to exceed ten thousand dollars.

O.L., XLIV, local, 4, December 20, 1845. Baldwin Institute, Middleburg; Thomas Thompson and twelve others; trustees appointed by the North

Ohio Conference of the M. E. Church; annual income not to exceed three thousand dollars.

O.L., XLIV, local, 107, February 14, 1846.   Loudonville Academy, Richland County; C. N. Haskell and six others.

O.L., XLIV, local, 122, February 19, 1846.   Norwalk Institute; Joseph Lowry and four others; property shall not be devoted to any other purpose.

O.L., XLIV, local, 236, February 28, 1846.   Liverpool Seminary, Columbiana County; Alexander R. Young and twenty-five others; nine trustees; stock company, shares five dollars; stock not to exceed ten thousand dollars; instruction shall not be confined or restricted to pupils of any separate sect or denomination of religion.

O.L., XLV, local, 99, February 8, 1847.   Mansfield Academical Institute, Mordecai Bartley and nine others.

O.L., XLVI, local, 114, February 11, 1848.   The Xenia Academy; David Medsker and seven others; seven directors; stock company, shares twenty dollars each; stock not to exceed twenty-five thousand dollars.

O.L., XLVI. local, 126, February 14, 1848.   Richland Academic Institute; Logan County; Reverend G. G. Page and eight others.

O.L., XLVI, local, 135, February 14, 1848.   The Felicity Female Seminary, Clermont County; Robert Chalfert and fourteen others; three trustees; stock company, shares twenty-five dollars each; stock not to exceed ten thousand dollars; that instruction in said seminary shall not be confined or restricted to pupils of any separate sect or denomination of religion.

O.L., XLVI, local, 188, February 18, 1848.   Medina Academy; Stephen N. Sargeant and thirteen others; stock company, shares twenty dollars each.

O.L., XLVII, local, 238, February 23, 1849.   Oxford Female Institute, Butler County; Herman B. Mayo and eight others; nine trustees; stock company, shares twenty dollars each; real property not to exceed twenty thousand dollars; capital stock not to exceed twenty-five thousand dollars.

O.L., XLVII, local, 241, February 28, 1849.   Miller Academy in Washington; John E. Alexander and five others; the Presbytery of Zanesville in connection with the General Assembly of the Presbyterian Church and a board of five trustees; real property not to exceed twenty thousand dollars.

O.L., XLVIII, local, 618, March 23, 1850.   Under control of the Zanesville Presbytery in connection with the General Assembly of the Old School of the Presbyterian Church.

O.L., XLVII, local, 243, March 8, 1849.   Pomeroy Academy, Meigs County; Charles R. Pomeroy and six others.

O.L., XLVII, local, 263, February 17, 1849; Springfield Female Seminary, Clark County; J. S. Galloway and eight others; nine directors chosen by the Miami Presbytery; stock company, shares ten dollars each; stock not to exceed fifty thousand dollars; literature and the arts and sciences as directed by the board.

O.L., XLVII, local, 273, March 9, 1849.   Cadiz High School; Jonathan Dewey and six others; three trustees; stock company, shares fifty dollars each; property not to exceed ten thousand dollars; all the necessary and useful branches of a thorough and liberal education.

O.L., XLVII, local, 280, March 22, 1849.   Mansfield Female Seminary, Richland County; James Johnson and seven others; five directors; stock company, shares ten dollars; capital stock not to exceed twenty thousand dollars; literature and the arts and sciences as directed by the board.

O.L., XLVII, local, 284, March 28, 1849. Mount Pleasant Academy, Ross County; Timothy Stearns and four others; seven directors; stock company, shares ten dollars; capital stock not to exceed twenty thousand dollars.

O.L., XLVIII, local, 614, February 14, 1850. Elliott Female Seminary; Hugh Elliott and fourteen others; fifteen directors; capital stock not to exceed thirty thousand dollars; literature and the arts and sciences as directed by the board.

O.L., XLVIII, local, 617, March 21, 1850. Vinton High School, Gallia County; Herman Wilkins and four others; a board of three trustees; stock company, shares ten dollars; property not to exceed ten thousand dollars.

O.L., XLVIII, local, 625, March 23, 1850. Defiance Female Seminary, Defiance County; Sidney S. Sprague and five others; five trustees; stock company, shares twenty-five dollars each; stock not to exceed twenty thousand dollars; instruction shall never be confined or restricted to pupils of any separate sect or denomination.

O.L., XLVIII, local, 627, March 1, 1850. Western Reserve Eclectic Institute; George Paw and eleven others; stock company, shares twenty-five dollars each; stock not to exceed sixty thousand dollars; the instruction of youth of both sexes in the various branches of literature and sciences, especially the moral sciences based upon the facts and truths of the Holy Scriptures.

O.L., XLVIII, local, 630, March 21, 1850. Tiffin Academy, Seneca County; Henry Elbert and twenty-two others; seven trustees; stock company, shares twenty dollars each.

O.L., XLVIII, local, 637, March 22, 1850. Xenia Female Academy; Thomas C. Wright and eleven others; nine trustees; stock company, shares fifty dollars each; real property not to exceed twenty thousand dollars; capital stock twenty-five dollars each; the arts and sciences and all necessary and useful branches of a thorough and useful education such as may be taught in the best female colleges and academies.

O.L., XLVIII, local, 638, March 23, 1850. Hartford High School, Trumbull County; Seth Hayes and eight others; five trustees.

O.L., XLVIII, local, 639, March 22, 1850. Soeurs de Notre Dame Female Educational Institute, Chillicothe, Ross County; Julia Van Balton and four others (women).

ACTS INCORPORATING SCHOOL COMPANIES AND ASSOCIATIONS

O.L., XVI, 157, January 29, 1818. The Union School Association of the towns of Harpersfield and Madison; James A. Harper and twelve others; officers elected by the corporation; stock company, shares ten dollars, not to exceed seven hundred in number; property not to exceed ten thousand dollars; not to be used for banking.

O.L., XXII, local, 106, February 21, 1824. The Milford Union School Society, Milford, Clermont County; James MacDonald and twenty-five others; five trustees; stock company, shares twenty dollars each.

O.L., XXII, local, 109, February 10, 1824. The Jefferson School Association; Timothy Hawley and eleven others; four trustees and a president; stock company, shares ten dollars each; property shall not exceed twenty thousand dollars.

O.L., XXIII, local 44, January 28, 1825. The Literary Society of St. Joseph's; John A. Hill and three others; annual income not to exceed twelve thousand dollars; to erect and establish an academy at St. Joseph's in Perry County; an academy in Cincinnati, and an academy at Canton in Stark County; funds not to be used for any other than literary purposes.

O.L., XXIV, local, 92, February 7, 1826. Mesopotamia Central School Society; confirming incorporation under the general law because of doubts as to the constitutionality of said law.

O.L., XXVI, local, 67, January 29, 1828. The Goshen School Association, Logan County; Hardin Brown and four others.

O.L., XXVII, local, 131, February 12, 1829. The trustees of the Columbus Presbytery; twelve trustees; annual income not to exceed three thousand dollars; for the sole purpose of establishing and supporting an academy and of carrying into effect such benevolent, literary or religious plans as may be connected therewith.

O.L., XXVII, local, 147, February 11, 1829. The Education Society of Painesville, Geauga County; Isaac Gillett and eight others; stock company, shares ten dollars each (by an amendment of February 24, 1835); to establish an academy or other seminary of learning.

O.L., XXIX, local, 42, January 12, 1831. Bricksville Academical Association, Cuyahoga County; Isaac M. Gorman and four others.

O.L., XXXI, local, 4, December 17, 1832. The St. Mary's Female Literary Society, Elizabeth Sansberry and three others of Perry County; annual income not to exceed three thousand dollars; property of said society shall be converted to no other uses other than the promotion of female education.

O.L., XXXII, local, 46, January 30, 1834. The German Lutheran Seminary of the German Lutheran Synod of Ohio and adjacent states; annual income not to exceed ten thousand dollars; that the funds of the corporation shall never be used or employed for any other purpose than the promotion of religion, morality and learning.

O.L., XXXIV, local, 402, March 1, 1836. The North Union School Association of Carroll County; Jacob Everhart with seven others; money and funds of corporation shall be applied exclusively to the payment of a teacher and furnishing fuel for the school, and to no other purpose whatever except the purchase of a lot, the erection of a school building and dwelling house for a teacher. Amended March 12, 1844. O.L., XLII, local, 221. Authorizing said association to keep open four public schools and no more, and to own and equip four schoolhouses, and to draw a fair and equal proportion of the school funds of the county.

O.L., XXXIV, local, 411, March 12, 1836. Rome Academical Company; three trustees; property not to exceed ten thousand dollars.

O.L., XXXV, local, 3, December 17, 1836. The Springborough School Company, Warren County; Joseph Stanton and eight others; three trustees;

stock company, shares five dollars each; annual income not to exceed three thousand dollars; capital stock five hundred to five thousand dollars; to promote the organization of useful knowledge and a sound practical education.

O.L., XXXVI, local, 107, February 23, 1838. High Falls Primary Institute in Chagrin Falls, Cuyahoga and Geauga Counties; twelve trustees; property not to exceed fifteen thousand dollars; education of youth is the exclusive object of this corporation and its funds shall be exclusively devoted to the promotion of this object.

O.L., XXXVI, local, 371, March 17, 1838. Newark Association for the Promotion of Education; Asa Beckwith and twenty others; twenty-one directors; stock company, shares ten to fifty dollars; stock not to exceed twenty-five thousand dollars; "the object of this corporation is to establish a high school with suitable houses and means of instruction for the education of both males and females."

O.L., XXXVII, local, 166, March 12, 1839. Monroe Academical Association; David Kirkbridge and six others; three trustees and a president; stock company, shares fifty dollars; annual income not to exceed ten thousand dollars; "to cultivate and strengthen the intellectual and moral faculties of the youth who may resort to it for instruction, to teach them the art of self-government and to fit them by a judicious course of moral discipline for virtue, usefulness and happiness."

O.L., XXXVII, local, 169, March 12, 1839. The Harveysburg High School Company, Warren County; property not to exceed ten thousand dollars; to establish a high school and to promote and afford therein instruction in the usual branches of a sound, practical and liberal education, and in the languages, arts and sciences.

O.L., XXXIX, local, 11, January 29, 1841. The Cincinnati New Jerusalem Church School Association; Jacob L. Wayne and nine others; five trustees; annual income not to exceed five thousand dollars; not to issue any circulating medium or exercise any banking privilege; to establish and carry forward a school in the city of Cincinnati, wherein may be taught all branches of literature and science.

O.L., XXXIX, local, 103, March 27, 1841. Berkshire Education Society, Delaware County; David Prince and three others.

O.L., XLI, local, 85, February 17, 1843. Western Reserve Freewill Baptist Academical Society; S. B. Philbrick and nine others; promoting and encouraging education; if the managers shall receive blacks and mulattoes into the same upon equality with white persons it shall work a forfeiture of all the powers hereby granted.

O.L., XLII, local, 60, February 15, 1844. The Sylvania High School Company, Lucas County; John P. Pease and three others; property not to exceed ten thousand dollars; the establishment of a high school and to promote and afford therein instruction in the usual branches of a sound, practical and liberal education and in the languages, arts and sciences.

O.L., XLII, local, 163, March 12, 1844. The Western Reserve Freewill Baptist Educational Society; S. B. Philbrick and nine others; promoting and encouraging education and sustaining the Western Reserve Manual Labor Seminary in Chester.

O.L., XLIV, local, 161, February 23, 1846. Madison Education Society; Joshua Harkwell and eight others; nine trustees; stock company, shares twenty dollars.

ACTS CONCERNING HIGHER INSTITUTIONS

COLLEGES, UNIVERSITIES, AND THEOLOGICAL SEMINARIES

Ohio University:

Territorial Acts, Nashee's *Compilation*, p. 219, December 18, 1799. Resolution that Rufus Putnam, Ives Kleeman, Jonathan Stone, Esqs., be requested to lay off in Townships 8 and 9 in Washington County a town plat with a square for the colleges, lots for the president and professors, tutors, etc., bordering on or encircled by spacious commons.

Territorial Acts, Nashee's *Compilation*, p. 220, January 9, 1802. An act establishing a University in the town of Athens.

SEC. 1. That there shall be a university instituted and established in the town of Athens by the name and style of the American Western University, for the instruction of youth in all branches of the liberal arts and sciences, for the promotion of good education, virtue, religion and morality, and for conferring of the degrees and literary honors granted in similar institutions.

SEC. 2. Creating a body politic.

SEC. 3. Appointing the Honorable Rufus Putnam, Joseph Kleeman, Return Jonathan Meigs and seven others; created a body politic.

SEC. 11. Vesting Townships 8 and 9 granted by Congress in said corporation forever.

SEC. 18. The legislature may grant further powers or alter, limit or restrain any of the powers by this vested in this corporation.

O.L., I, 148, April 16, 1803. Resolution appointing three commissioners to appraise the college townships in Washington Township.

O.L., II, 193, February 18, 1804.

SEC. 2. Creating a body politic and corporate by the name and style of the President and Trustees of the Ohio University, to consist of the Governor of the state, the President, and not more than fifteen nor less than ten trustees.

SEC. 8. Vacancies caused by death shall be filled at the next meeting of the legislature.

SEC. 9. The faculty shall direct and cause to be holden quarterly in every year a public examination, at which time the faculty shall attend, when each class of the students shall be examined relative to the proficiency they shall have made in the particular arts and sciences or branches of education in which they shall have been instructed.

SEC. 13. Directing the trustees to lay off the town of Athens conformably to a plan made out by Rufus Putnam and others.

SEC. 14. Providing that the annual rents and profits shall be appropriated to the endowment of the University.

Sec. 17. Exempting the lands in the two townships appropriated, together with the buildings, from all state taxes.

O.L., III, 79, February 21, 1805. Amendatory, providing for appraising and leasing the land in the two college townships for ninety-nine years, renewable forever. No land to be valued for less than one dollar and seventy-five cents per acre.

O.L., V, 85, January 23, 1807. Amendatory, authorizing the trustees to lease the appraised lots that have been appraised at less than one dollar and seventy-five cents.

O.L., VII, 167, February 15, 1809. Sec. 2. Trustees shall have power until the the year 1811 to receive articles or produce from the lessees in payment of rent.

O.L., XVI, 37, December 29, 1817. An act to authorize the drawing of a lottery for the benefit of the Ohio University.

"WHEREAS the diffusion of science and literature has ever been found to be auspicious to the interests of liberty and the purity and permanence of republican institutions":

Sec. 1. Seven commissioners are authorized to raise by lottery a sum not to exceed twenty thousand dollars to defray the expenses of building a college edifice and to purchase a library and suitable mathematical and philosophical apparatus.

O.L., XXIII, 19, February 25, 1825. An act for the better regulation of the Medical College of Ohio and making certain appropriations therein named.

Sec. 7. That the sum of one thousand dollars be appropriated for the use of the Ohio University to be paid out of the lottery fund and to be applied by direction of the trustees for the purpose of paying any debts that may have been contracted for the purchase of philosophical apparatus or for any addition to the Library.

O.L., XXVII, 9, January 10, 1829. Amendatory, the Board of Trustees shall report annually to the Auditor of State the amount of money arising from the sale of lands situated in the college township; when the money is deposited with the Treasurer of State it shall be placed to the credit of the Ohio University.

O.L., XXXIV, 643, March 7, 1836. WHEREAS by a resolution of January 30, 1827, it is made the duty of the President and Trustees of the Ohio University annually to report the condition of said University:

Resolved, That the President and Trustees of the Ohio University be required to report to the legislature a statement of the condition of said University.

O.L., XXXV, 543, January 12, 1837. "WHEREAS the legislature of this state do possess a controlling power over the officers of the Ohio University, and whereas no report can be found on the files of this legislature made by the President and Trustees of said University":

Requiring a report on the total amount of revenue and its source, amount of disbursements and the purpose, state of buildings, amount of debts due, to whom and for what expended, the number of professors engaged, the branches of literature and science taught by each, and a list of the number of students in each year commencing with the first day of April, 1826 to the first day of January, 1837, inclusive.

O.L., XXXVI, 204, March 7, 1838.   An act providing for a loan to the Ohio University.

SEC. 1.   Authorizing the Commissioners of the Canal Fund to loan from the sinking fund five thousand dollars to the Ohio University to be paid back in annual instalments of one thousand dollars each, interest at six per cent.

O.L., XLI, 144, March 10, 1843.   An act to declare the true intent and meaning of the first section of the act entitled, "An act to amend an act entitled an act to establish a university in the town of Athens, passed February 21, 1805."

SEC. 1.   "That it is the true intent and meaning of said act that the leases granted under said act and the one to which that was an amendment should not be subject to a revaluation at any time thereafter."

O.L., XLV, 176, February 8, 1847.   An act to provide for the funding of debts for the Ohio University.

SEC. 1.   Authorizing the President and Trustees to fund any amount of the debts due from said University not exceeding ten thousand dollars in sums not less than one hundred dollars each, for such length of time and for such rates of interest not exceeding seven per cent per annum as may be agreed upon.

Miami University:

O.L., I, 66, April 15, 1803.   An act to provide for the locating of a college township in the District of Cincinnati.

SEC. 1.   That one township in the District of Cincinnati, or equivalent land equal to thirty-six sections, shall be located and entered for the use and support of an academy in lieu of the college township heretofore granted in trust to John C. Symmes and his associates.

SEC. 2.   Directing the Commissioners appointed to select such lands as are most valuable "having due regard to the quality of the land, the situation for health, the goodness of the water, and the advantage of inland navigation."

O.L., VII, 184, February 17, 1809.   An act to establish the Miami University.

SEC. 1.   For the instruction of youth in all the various branches of the liberal arts and sciences, for the promotion of good education, virtue, religion and morality, and for conferring all the literary honors granted in similar institutions; and benefits and advantages of the said University shall be open to all the citizens within this state.

SEC. 2.   Creating a body politic, a president and not more than fourteen or less than seven trustees.

SEC. 8.   The faculty shall cause to be holden in the said University at least once every year a public examination, at which time the faculty shall attend, etc.

SEC. 10.   Vesting the township granted by Congress in the Cincinnati District, in the said corporation for the sole use, benefit and support of the said University, with power to subdivide and sell the same for terms of ninety-nine years; renewable forever; subject to a revaluation every fifteen years; minimum price two dollars per acre.

SEC. 11. The clear annual rents and profits to be appropriated "in such manner as shall most effectually promote virtue, and morality" and knowledge of such languages, liberal arts and sciences as shall hereafter be directed from time to time by said corporation.

SEC. 15. Legislature shall have power to grant any further and greater powers or alter, limit or restrain any of the powers by this act vested.

SEC. 17. Alexander Campbell, the Reverend James Kilbourne and The Reverend Robert G. Wilson appointed to select a permanent seat for the University.

O.L., VIII, 94, February 6, 1810. Amendatory, That the trustees of the Miami University shall cause a town to be laid off on such part of land described in said act as they may think proper, to be known by the name of "Oxford."

SEC. 2. The said University is hereby established on said land and such place as the trustees may think proper, and they are authorized to direct such building and buildings to be erected as they deem necessary.

O.L., XII, 83, February 1, 1814. Amendatory.

SEC. 1. Trustees are required to make an accurate statement of all proceedings both as respects the disposal of land as well as the state of the funds arising from the proceeds to the legislature.

O.L., XVII, 131, February 5, 1819. Amendatory.

SEC. 1. Not more than four trustees shall reside out of the limits of the John Cleve Symmes Purchase; none of them shall reside within the college township.

O.L., XLVI, 291, February 7, 1848. Repealing so much of the act as provides that not more than four of the trustees shall reside out of the limits of the John Cleve Symmes Purchase.

O.L., XLVII, 398. (No date). Resolution appointing a committee of three to examine into and report to the next General Assembly the condition of the Miami University and the cause of its decline, with such recommendations as they may deem proper to make, and that said committee shall have power to send for reports and papers, and to administer all acts necessary to said investigation.

Cincinnati University:

O.L., V, 64, January 23, 1807. An act to incorporate the Cincinnati University. J. S. Gano and forty-eight others.

SEC. 3. "That all parcels of land, tenants, rents, annuities, profits on any goods, chattels, or any other effects . . . . and shall have power to appropriate any funds belonging to said corporation in improving the present university and making further improvements on the tract of land thereunto now belonging or for educating poor children"; stock company, shares ten dollars.

O.L., V, 120, February 3, 1807. An act authorizing the citizens of Cincinnati and its vicinity to raise six thousand dollars for certain purposes; authorizes the appointing of commissioners to raise by lottery a sum not to exceed six thousand dollars for Cincinnati University.

Cincinnati College:

O.L., XVII, 46, January 22, 1819. Jacob Burrett and nineteen others incorporated as trustees and faculty of the Cincinnati College; annual income not to exceed eleven thousand dollars; stock company, shares twenty-five dollars each; control thirteen trustees; the religious tenets that may be peculiar to any sect or denomination shall never be taught or enforced in the College; Board of Trustees may grant all or any of the degrees that are usually conferred in any college or university within the United States.

O.L., XLIII, 376, March 11, 1845. Authorizing the trustees to borrow not to exceed thirty-five thousand dollars.

O.L., XLIV, 157, February 21, 1846. Licensing law graduates.

Worthington College:

O.L., XVII, 155, February 8, 1819. An act to establish a college in the town of Worthington by the name and style of the "Worthington College" for the instruction of youth in all the liberal arts and sciences, in virtue, religion and literary honors granted in similar institutions. Philander Chase and eleven others created a body politic.

Kenyon College:

O.L., XXIII, 12, December 22, 1824. An act to incorporate the Theological Seminary of the Protestant Episcopal Church in the Diocese of Ohio.

Sec. 1. The Right Reverend Philander Chase, now Bishop of the Protestant Episcopal Church, and eight others, the present trustees, are created a body corporate; annual income exclusive of lands or tenants occupied by said seminary, not to exceed twenty thousand dollars.

The General Assembly may at any time hereafter modify or repeal this act, but no such modification shall divert the real and personal property of the seminary to any other purpose than the education of ministers of the gospel in the Protestant Episcopal Church in the United States of America.

O.L., XXIV, 39, January 24, 1826. Supplementary.

Sec. 1. The president and professors of said seminary shall be considered as the faculty of a college, and as such have the power of conferring degrees in the arts and sciences and of performing all such other acts as pertain to the faculties of colleges for the encouragement and reward of learning, and the name and style by which the said degrees shall be conferred and the certificate of learning given shall be that of the president and professors of Kenyon College in the State of Ohio.

O.L., XXVI, 176, January 11, 1828. *Resolved,* That this General Assembly approve of the object of the application of The Reverend Philander Chase to the Congress of the United States for a donation of a tract or tracts of public lands for the support of Kenyon College, and that the Senators and Representatives of this state in the Congress of the United States be requested to use their exertions in aid and support of the said application.

O.L., XXXVII, 353, March 6, 1839. Supplementary.

Sec. 1. Trustees shall have power in connection with said seminary to establish a college and halls for preparatory education.

Sec. 2. Power to confer degrees as president and professors of Kenyon College.

Sec. 3. The president and professors of said Theological Seminary shall have power to confer degrees in Theology by the name and style of the president and professors of the Theological Seminary of the Diocese of Ohio.

Franklin College:

O.L., XXIII, 22, January 22, 1825.   An act to incorporate the College of Alma in the town of Athens, Harrison County.   John Rhea and thirteen others are created a body corporate with full power to confer degrees.

O.L., XXIV, 49, January 31, 1826.   Amendatory.   Changing the name to Franklin College.

O.L., XXXIV, 610, March 14, 1836.   An act making an appropriation to Franklin College in the County of Harrison and Ripley College in the County of Brown.

Sec. 1.   Appropriating five hundred dollars to each college, to be applied in such manner as the Board of Trustees shall direct.

Western Reserve University:

O.L., XXIV, 93, February 7, 1826.   An act to incorporate the trustees of the Western Reserve College.

Sec. 1.   George Swift and eleven others are created a body politic to be styled the Board of Trustees of Western Reserve College with power to confer on those whom they may deem worthy all such honors and degrees as are usually conferred in similar institutions.

Sec. 2.   Said college shall be located in the Township of Hudson, Portage County, and erected in a plan sufficiently extensive to afford instruction in the liberal arts and sciences, and the trustees may erect additional departments for the study of any or all of the liberal professions.

O.L., XLII, 95, February 23, 1844.   Amendatory.

Sec. 1.   That the trustees of the Western Reserve College are authorized to establish a medical department in the City of Cleveland, and to confer degrees and other diplomas.

Lane Seminary:

O.L., XXVII, 118, February 11, 1829.   An act to incorporate the Lane Seminary in the County of Hamilton.

Sec. 1.   "That there shall be and hereby is established in the County of Hamilton a theological institution for the education of young men for the gospel ministry by the name of the Lane Seminary."

Sec. 3.   "That the officers and members of the Executive Committee shall reside in the City of Cincinnati or this vicinity, a majority of whom together with all the professors and instructors of said institution shall be members of the Presbyterian Church in good standing under the general care of the General Assembly of the Church in the United States." Board of Trustees shall have power to confer any of the degrees in divinity usually granted in the colleges and universities of the United States.

Sec. 5.   "That a fundamental rule or principle of said institution shall be that every student therein when in good health shall be required to spend not less than three nor more than four hours each day in agricultural or mechanical labor, the profits of which shall be applied to defray the expense of the institution and the board and tuition of the students."

O.L., XXXVI, 22, January 16, 1838. Amendatory. The Board of Trustees shall consist of not less than thirteen nor more than twenty-five.

College of Ripley:

O.L., XXVIII, 88, February 9, 1830. An act to incorporate the College of Ripley in the County of Brown. Allan Trimbell and twenty-one others are created a body politic with full power and authority to confer degrees; annual income not to exceed twenty thousand dollars; no religious doctrines peculiar to any sect of Christians shall ever be inculcated; vacancies in the trustees to be filled by the General Assembly.

Denison University:

O.L., XXX, 88, February 2, 1832. An act to incorporate the "Granville Literary and Theological Institution." Jonathan Atwood and six others; the present trustees of said institution are constituted a body politic; income from property not used by said institution or its officers or professors not to exceed five thousand dollars.

SEC. 2. Trustees have power to confer on those whom they may think worthy all such honors and degrees as are conferred by similar institutions.

SEC. 3. Trustees may increase their number, but not to exceed eighteen.

O.L., XXXII, 215, February 27, 1834. Amendatory. Trustees shall have power to increase the number of trustees not exceeding thirty-six nor less than twelve.

O.L., XLIII, 54, February 3, 1845. Amendatory. Changing the name to "The Granville College."

SEC. 2. The trustees may as their ability shall increase erect additional departments for the study of any or all of the liberal professions.

Marietta College:

O.L., XXXI, 18, December 17, 1832. An act to incorporate the Marietta Collegiate Institute and Western Teachers' Seminary. Luther G. Bingham and eight others are created a body politic; purpose, the instruction of youth in the various branches of useful knowledge and especially the education of teachers for common schools; annual income not to exceed five thousand dollars.

O.L., XXXIII, 53, February 14, 1835. An act to incorporate Marietta College.

SEC. 1. That there shall be and there is hereby established in the County of Washington an institution for the education of youth in the various branches of useful knowledge by the name of the Marietta College.

SEC. 4. Annual income not to exceed five thousand dollars; funds shall never be used for purposes of banking.

SEC. 6. Power to confer such honors and degrees as are usually conferred in similar institutions.

O.L., XLIII, 4, December 31, 1844. Amendatory. It shall be lawful for the board to increase the number of trustees not to exceed twenty-five.

Oberlin College:

O.L., XXXII, 226, February 2, 1834.   An act to incorporate the Oberlin College Institute.   Henry Brown and eight others are created a body politic to be styled the Board of Trustees of the Oberlin Collegiate Institute with power to confer on those whom they deem worthy such honors and degrees as are usually conferred in similar institutions.

SEC. 2.   That the said institution shall remain in Lorain County and shall afford instruction in the liberal arts and sciences and the trustees may erect additional departments for such other branches of education as they may think necessary or useful.

SEC. 3.   They may increase the number of trustees to twelve exclusive of the president.

SEC. 4.   The president shall be ex officio a member of the Board of Trustees and president of the same.

SEC. 6.   The funds to be applied in erecting suitable buildings and supporting officers and in securing books, maps, charts, and other apparatus necessary to the well-being of the institution.

O.L., XLVIII, 632, March 21, 1850.   Amendatory.   Changing the name of the Oberlin Collegiate Institute to Oberlin College.

Willoughby University of Lake Erie:

O.L., XXXII, 376, March 3, 1834.   An act to incorporate the Willoughby University of Lake Erie.   Nehemia Allan and two others are created a body politic.   Purpose—the instruction of young men and youth in the various branches of literature and sciences; annual income from real estate not to exceed five thousand dollars; power of conferring degrees in the arts, sciences, and professions.

O.L., XLV, 7, January 14, 1847.   Amendatory.

SEC. 1.   Trustees are authorized to transfer the medical department of said university from Willoughby and establish the same at the City of Columbus to be known as the Willoughby Medical College at Columbus.

German Reform Theological Seminary:

O.L., XXXV, 9, December 20, 1836.   An act to incorporate the German Reform Synod of Ohio.

SEC. 2.   For the purpose of furthering the interests of the German Reform Church in Ohio by erecting a house or houses for a theological seminary or for establishing all the necessary conveniences for an institution of learning wherein to prepare men for the gospel ministry.

St. Clairsville Collegiate Seminary:

O.L., XXXV, 55, January 30, 1837.   An act to incorporate the St. Clairsville Collegiate Seminary.   James Moore and thirty-eight others are created a body politic; "all property shall be for the purpose and no other of educating females"; annual income from funds not to exceed ten thousand dollars; instruction and the means of education in the said seminary whether in the primary or collegiate department shall never be confined or restricted to the tenets of any separate sect or denomination of religion.

Sec. 15. Corporation shall report annually to the General Assembly the number of scholars taught the preceding year and the condition of the corporation.

Muskingum College:

O.L., XXXV, 272, March 18, 1837. An act to incorporate the Muskingum College. Robert Wallace and eight others associated for the purpose of establishing a seminary of learning at or near the town of New Concord in Muskingum County are created a body politic; nine directors with power to increase same to fifteen.

Baptist Literary and Collegiate Institute:

O.L., XXXV, 347, March 29, 1837. An act to incorporate the Baptist Literary and Collegiate Institute of Huron County.

Sec. 1. For the education of young men.

Sec. 2. Board self-perpetuating, not less than twenty-one nor more than twenty-five.

Sec. 3. Officers and members of the Executive Committee shall reside in Huron County, a majority of whom, together with all the professors, tutors, teachers and instructors, shall be members of the regular Baptist Church in good standing.

Sec. 5. "The design of this institution shall be to give a thorough literary and collegiate education; the income and tuition of which shall be applied to defraying the expense of the institution and the board and tuition of the students."

Wesleyan Collegiate Institute:

O.L., XXXV, 378, March 31, 1837. An act to incorporate the trustees of the Wesleyan Collegiate Institute. Jacob Ward and nine others are created a body politic; to be located at Olmsted and erected on a plan sufficiently extensive to afford instruction in the liberal arts and sciences.

Logan College:

O.L., XXXVI, 203, March 7, 1838. An act to incorporate Logan College. James Wallace and twenty others are created a body corporate.

Theological Seminary, Reform Synod:

O.L., XXXVI, 34, January 22, 1838. An act to incorporate the Theological Seminary of the Associated Reform Synod of the West.

Sec. 1. That there shall be established at Oxford in Butler County a theological institution for the education of young men for the gospel ministry; annual income of property not to exceed two thousand dollars.

Central College:

O.L., XL, 77, March 2, 1842. An act to incorporate the trustees of the Central College of Ohio. H. L. Hitchcock and thirteen others are created a body politic with power to confer on those whom they may deem worthy all such honors and degrees as are usually conferred by colleges; said college shall afford instruction in the liberal arts and sciences usually taught in colleges; shall be allowed to have an academical department.

St. Xavier College:

O.L., XL, 84, March 5, 1842.   An act to incorporate the St. Xavier College.

"That there shall be and there is hereby established in the city of Cincinnati an institution, for the education of white youth in the various branches of useful knowledge, by the name of the Trustees of St. Xavier's College"; property not to exceed forty thousand dollars; no part of funds to be used in banking; trustees shall have power to confer honors and degrees.

Ohio Wesleyan University:

O.L., XL, 111, March 7, 1842.   An act to incorporate the trustees of the Ohio Wesleyan University.

WHEREAS, "The Ohio and North Ohio Annual Conference of the Methodist Episcopal Church have determined upon establishing an extensive university or college in this state to the support of which they are pledged to use their utmost efforts, and which university is ever to be conducted on the most liberal principles, accessible to all religious denominations, and designed for the benefit of our citizens in general," therefore:

SEC. 1.   William Neff and twenty others are created a body politic.

SEC. 3.   That the Ohio and North Ohio Conferences of the Methodist Episcopal Church, or such other conferences as may be formed out of these conferences, shall fill the vacancies occurring in the Board of Trustees, and shall annually appoint any number of visitors not exceeding three for each conference, who shall attend the meetings of the Board of Trustees and shall constitute a joint board in the appointment and removal of all officers of the said university.

SEC. 5.   The university shall be styled the Ohio Wesleyan University and shall be located in or near Delaware, Ohio.

O.L., XLI, 12, January 11, 1843.   An act to amend the charter of the Ohio Wesleyan University.   Trustees appointed by the Ohio and North Ohio Conferences of the M. E. Church.

Lafayette University:

O.L., XL, 119, March 7, 1842.   An act to incorporate Lafayette University at New Carlisle, Clark County.

SEC. 1.   There is hereby established "an institution for the education of youth in the various branches of useful knowledge''; William G. Serviss and twenty others are appointed trustees; annual income of real property not to exceed five thousand dollars; funds shall never be used for banking; the said corporation shall have power to confer honors and degrees.

Germania College:

O.L., XLI, 12, January 11, 1843.   An act to incorporate the trustees of the Germania College.   Jacob Leist and eight others are created a body politic for thirty years with power to confer honors and degrees; not less than eleven nor more than twenty-one trustees.

SEC. 5.   "The said college shall afford instruction in the liberal arts and sciences usually taught in colleges, and shall be allowed to establish an academical department for the instruction of students in the various branches of an academical education and general knowledge not included in the usual collegiate course, and for the instruction of those who design to be teachers of schools."

Providence College:

O.L., XLI, 63, February 9, 1843.   An act .to incorporate Providence College and that for the purpose of establishing a college for the education of youth in the various branches of useful knowledge. Wilson Shannon and twenty others are created a body politic with power to confer honors and degrees; trustees not less than eleven nor more than twenty-one.

SEC. 5.   "The said college shall afford instruction in the liberal arts and sciences usually taught in colleges and shall be allowed to have an academical department, etc."

SEC. 9.   The private and individual property of the incorporators shall be held responsible for the payment of debts of said college.

Beverly College:

O.L., XLI, 92, February 28, 1843.   An act to incorporate the Beverly College at Beverly for the purpose of educating youth in the learned and foreign languages, the liberal arts and sciences, and literature; Board of Trustees not to exceed twenty-one; A. M. Bryan and twenty others named as the first trustees incorporated a body politic; annual income not to exceed five thousand dollars; Board of Trustees to be elected by the Pennsylvania Synod of the Cumberland Presbyterian Church.

Methodist Female Collegiate Institute:

O.L., XLI, 146, March 10, 1843.   An act to incorporate the trustees of the Methodist Female Collegiate Institute of Cincinnati.   Thomas A. Morris and twelve others.

Wesleyan Female College:

O.L., XLIV, 171, February 24, 1846.   An act to incorporate the trustees of the Wesleyan Female College of Cincinnati.   Thomas A. Morris and twenty-one others; trustees to be chosen by the Board of Trustees of eight local Methodist Churches, and the ministers of the M. E. Church in Cincinnati, with the agents and editors of the Western Book Concern to be trustees ex officio; purpose—"the instruction of the pupils therein in the arts and sciences and in all necessary and useful and ornamental branches of an efficient and liberal education, such as is taught in the best female academies;" power to grant literary honors and degrees.

Bellefontaine College:

O.L., XLI, 220, March 13, 1843.   An act to incorporate the Bellefontaine, Ohio, College.   Joseph Stevenson and fourteen others; to afford instruction in the common branches of a liberal education and in the liberal arts and sciences; property not to exceed two hundred thousand dollars; a board of fifteen trustees.

SEC. 10.   If from any cause the corporation shall dissolve, the property of said institution, after its debts are paid, shall go to the Common School Fund of the State of Ohio.

English Lutheran Theological and Collegiate Institute:
O.L., XLII, 189, March 17, 1844.   An act to incorporate the Board of Directors of the English Lutheran Theological and Collegiate Institute of Wooster, Wayne County.   William Godfrey Keil and eleven others; property not to exceed ten thousand dollars; power to grant degrees in the liberal arts and sciences; trustees appointed by the English Evangelical Lutheran Synod.

Ft. Meigs University:
O.L., XLIII, 80, February 10, 1845.   An act to incorporate the trustees of Ft. Meigs University.   John C. Spink and eleven others, location— Perrysburg, Wood County; "to be erected on a plan sufficiently extensive to afford instruction in the liberal arts and sciences" and that trustees may erect additional departments for instruction in the languages, arts and sciences, and in all of the liberal professions; power to confer degrees; degrees shall not be conferred until the corporation shall have obtained property to the amount of ten thousand dollars; twelve trustees.

Protestant University of the United States:
O.L., XLIII, 338, March 10, 1845.   An act to incorporate the trustees of the Protestant University of the United States.   William Wilson and twenty-nine others; location—in or near Cincinnati; "the promotion and advancement of education, the cultivation and diffusion of literature, science, and the arts, in all their departments and formalities."
    SEC. 11.   The corporation shall have power to establish a sectarian religious test as a condition of enjoying the honors and privileges of the university, provided that it shall always be conducted in conformity to the Reformed Protestant religion as taught in the Holy Scriptures of the Old and New Testaments; degrees not to be conferred until the corporation shall have fifteen thousand dollars in property; annual income not to exceed twenty thousand dollars; said university shall report annually to the legislature.

Wittenberg College:
O.L., XLIII, 375, March 11, 1845.   An act to incorporate the Board of Directors of Wittenberg College; John Hamilton and fifteen others; degrees shall not be conferred until the corporation have acquired property to the value of ten thousand dollars; Board of Directors appointed by the English Evangelical Synod of Ohio and the Miami Synod.

Farmers' College:
O.L., XLIV, 163, February 23, 1846.   An act to incorporate the Farmers' College of Hamilton County.   Charles Cheney and fourteen others; stock company, shares thirty dollars.

SEC. 5. "The objects of this association shall be to direct and cultivate the minds of the students in a thorough and scientific course of studies, particularly adapted to agricultural pursuits"; real property not to exceed forty thousand dollars.

Marietta Female College:

O.L., XLV, 140, February 8, 1847.   An act to incorporate the Marietta Female College; David C. Skinner and four others; a board of three to fifteen trustees; stock company, shares twenty-five dollars each, capital stock not to exceed twenty thousand dollars; the instruction of females in all the necessary and useful and ornamental branches of a thorough and liberal education.

Muhlenberg College:

O.L., XLVI, 19, January 11, 1848.   An act to incorporate the Board of Directors of Muhlenberg College at the town of Jefferson, Harrison County.   Moses Bartholomew and fourteen others; directors appointed by the English branch of the Evangelical Lutheran Joint Synod of Ohio and adjacent states; degrees shall not be conferred until the corporation have property to the value of ten thousand dollars.

Judson College:

O.L., XLVII, local, 259, February 10, 1849.   An act to incorporate the Judson College at Jefferson, County of Harrison; transferring the rights, franchises, etc., of Muhlenberg College to the Board of Directors of Judson College.

Newton College:

O.L., XLVI, 211, February 19, 1848.   An act to incorporate Newton College, Hamilton County.   Joseph Jackson and eleven others; stock company, shares fifty dollars; twelve trustees; "to direct and cultivate the minds of the students thoroughly in literary, classical and scientific studies for a regular course, and studies for an irregular course as the trustees may deem proper;" degrees shall not be conferred until the corporation have property to the amount of ten thousand dollars; real property not to exceed two hundred thousand dollars.

Edinburgh College:

O.L., XLVI, 220, February 21, 1848.   An act to incorporate the Edinburgh College.   George Hackett and sixteen others.
SEC. 5.   The said college shall afford instruction in the liberal arts and sciences usually taught in colleges, and shall be allowed to have an academical department, etc.; the corporation shall not confer degrees until it have obtained property to the amount of ten thousand dollars.

Mt. Washington College:

O.L., XLVII, 236, February 21, 1849.   An act to incorporate the Mt. Washington College in Hamilton County; Thomas H. Whetstone and eight others;

stock company, shares fifty dollars each; eight trustees; property not to exceed two hundred thousand dollars; "to direct and cultivate the minds of the students thoroughly in literary, classical and scientific studies for a regular course" and also an irregular course as the trustees shall decide; corporation shall not grant degrees until the college shall have obtained property to the amount of ten thousand dollars.

Otterbein University:
O.L., XLVII, 257, February 13, 1849. An act to incorporate the Otterbein University of Ohio. Louis Davis and two others named of the Scioto Annual Conference of the Church of the United Brethren of Christ, and Jacob Barger and two others named of the Sandusky Annual Conference of the South Church; power to confer degrees; location—Westerville; the corporation shall afford instruction in the liberal arts and sciences usually taught in colleges, and be allowed to have an academical department; they may use funds in the erection of buildings, purchase of lots, mechanical implements wherewith to maintain the manual labor connected with said university; no part of the property to be used for banking; honors and degrees shall not be conferred until the corporation have property to the amount of ten thousand dollars.

Capital University:
O.L., XLVIII, 619, March 2, 1850. An act to incorporate the Capital University. James Manning and thirty others; purpose—the promotion of religion, morality and learning; trustees to be chosen by the Synod of the Evangelical Lutheran Church, and by the Board of Trustees created by the act of incorporation.

Cambridge College:
O.L., XLVIII, 621, March 22, 1850. An act to incorporate the Cambridge College. John Fordyce and eight others are created a body politic to be styled "the Trustees of the Cambridge College of the Methodist Protestant Church"; vacancies in the board to be filled by the Muskingum Annual Conference of the Methodist Protestant Church and one member of the Conference shall annually attend the meetings of the Board; purpose—the instruction of students in the arts and sciences, in the learned professions, and all branches of learning as are usually taught in the colleges of the country; "the college shall be conducted on the most liberal principles and open alike to all religious denominations and to the community in general."

Geneva Hall:
O.L., XLVIII, 622, March 7, 1850. An act to incorporate the Geneva Hall. J. B. Johnston and ten others; seven trustees; stock company, shares fifty dollars each; location—Northwood, Logan County; capital stock not to exceed fifty thousand dollars; the promotion of learning, morality and religion; power to establish a literary and theological department, the

theological department to be known by the name of "The Theological Seminary of the Reformed Presbyterian Church."

Urbana University:

O.L., XLVIII, 624, March 7, 1850.   An act to incorporate the Urbana University; a board of twelve trustees; Milo G. Williams and eleven others; purpose—to encourage and promote the diffusion of knowledge in all the branches of academic and scientific, and exegetic instruction, and to combine therewith instruction in the productive arts and practice of rural economy; power to confer degrees; to be under the management of persons recognized as belonging to the New Church.

ACTS CONCERNING PROFESSIONAL EDUCATION

MEDICAL EDUCATION

O.L., IX, 19, January 14, 1811.   An act regulating the practice of Physic and Surgery.   Five medical districts created, three medical examiners in each to license applicants.

O.L., X, 58, February 8, 1812.   An act to incorporate a Medical Society.   Seven medical districts.   Power to appoint examining committees.   Practicing without license $5.00 to $100.00 penalty for each offense.

O.L., XI, 28, January 18, 1813.   An act regulating the practice of physic and surgery.

O.L., XV, 195, January 28, 1817.   An act regulating the practice of physic and surgery.

O.L., XVI, 105, January 30, 1818.   Amendatory.   Allowing any person who has received the degree of Doctor of Medicine from any medical school in the U. S. to receive license without examination.

Medical College of Ohio:

O.L., XVII, 37, January 19, 1819.   An act to authorize the establishment of a medical college.   Name: Medical College of Ohio.   Location: Cincinnati. Professorships: Practice of Medicine, Anatomy, Surgery, Materia Medica, Obstetrics, etc., and Chemistry and Pharmacy.

O.L., XVIII, 43, December 30, 1819.   Amendatory.   Two-thirds of faculty necessary to create or abolish professorships.

O.L., XIX, 28, January 15, 1821.   An act regulating the practice of Physic and Surgery.   Creating the Medical Convention of Ohio, which may select annually two medical students destitute of means and recommend to the Medical College whose duty it shall be to extend to them gratuitously all its advantages.

O.L., XIX, 58, January 22, 1821.   An act establishing a Commercial Hospital and Lunatic Asylum for the State of Ohio.   Location: Cincinnati. Faculty of Medical College to give medical and surgical advice.   Students may witness treatment of patients.

O.L., XXI, 4, December 13, 1822. Amendatory. Medical College of Ohio. Corporate powers vested in a Board of Trustees instead of the faculty. Trustees appointed by the General Assembly.

O.L., XXII, 142, February 26, 1824. An act to incorporate Medical Societies, etc.

O.L., XXIII, 16, January 28, 1825. Amendatory to the preceding.

O.L., XXIII, 19, February 15, 1825. An act for the better regulation of the Medical College of Ohio. Making certain appropriations, etc.

O.L., XXIV, 4, December 31, 1825. An act to incorporate the Medical College of Ohio and to revise and repeal all existing laws concerning it.

O.L., XXXI, 269, February 25, 1833. Resolution. Free tuition in Medical College to one indigent student from each medical district in the state, on appointment of the censors.

O.L., XXXI, 272, February 25, 1833. Resolution. Governor to appoint a committee of five to inspect and report on the condition, etc., of the Medical College of Ohio.

O.L., XXXVI, 37, March 7, 1838. An act for the relief of the Medical College of Ohio. Appropriating $1,500.00.

Cincinnati Medical Academy:

O.L., XXVI, 54, January 18, 1828. An act to incorporate the Cincinnati Medical Academy. Benjamin Piatt and ten others.

O.L., XXIX, 66, January 31, 1831. Amendatory. The Medical College of Ohio. Appropriating one-fourth of the money arising from taxes on auction sales in Hamilton County for a five year period to the Medical College, not to exceed $30,000.00.

Ohio Medical Lyceum:

O.L., XXXI, 207, February 22, 1833. An act to incorporate the Ohio Medical Lyceum in the city of Cincinnati.

Medina Medical Lyceum:

O.L., XXXII, 9, December 24, 1833. An act to incorporate the Medina Medical Lyceum.

Lebanon Medical Society:

O.L., XXXVI, 347, March 16, 1838. An act to incorporate the Lebanon Medical Society.

Literary and Botanico Medical College of the State of Ohio:

O.L., XXXVII, 208, March 8, 1839. An act to incorporate the Directors of the Literary and Botanico Medical College of the State of Ohio.

O.L., XXXIX, 161, March 29, 1841. Amendatory. Locating the above corporation in Cincinnati during the continuation of the charter.

Eaton Medical Society:

O.L., XL, 83, March 3, 1842. An act to incorporate the Eaton Medical Society.

Morgan County Medical Society:
O.L., XLI, 145, March 10, 1843.   An act to incorporate the Morgan County Medical Society.

Dudley Medical University:
O.L., XLII, 179, March 12, 1844.   An act to incorporate the Dudley Medical University of Wadsworth.

Summit County Medical Society:
O.L., XLII, 183, March 12, 1844.   An act to incorporate the Summit County Medical Society.

College of Dental Surgery:
O.L., XLIII, 32, January 21, 1845.   An act to authorize the establishment of a College of Dental Surgery.   Location: Cincinnati.

Medical Institute of Cincinnati:
O.L., XLIII, 357, March 10, 1845.   An act to incorporate the Medical Institute of Cincinnati.   Name Eclectic Institute.   At least five professors.
O.L., XVII, 264, March 8, 1849.   Amendatory.   Increasing capital stock of preceding institution to $60,000.00.

Starling Medical College:
O.L., XLVI, 31, January 28, 1848.   An act to incorporate the Starling Medical College in the City of Columbus.   Lyne Starling gives $30,000.00 for support.

Medical and Surgical Society of the County of Ashland:
O.L., XLVI, 76, February 4, 1848.   An act to incorporate the Medical and Surgical Society of the County of Ashland.

State Medical Society of Ohio:
O.L., XLVI, 231, February 22, 1848.   An act to incorporate the State Medical Society of Ohio.

Cincinnati Medical Institute:
O.L., XLVII, 264, February 23, 1849.   An act to incorporate the Cincinnati Medical Institute.

Darke County Medical Society:
O.L., XLVII, 274, March 18, 1849.   An act to incorporate the Darke County Medical Society.

Western College of Homeopathic Medicine:
O.L., XLVIII, 629, March 1, 1850.   An act to incorporate the Western College of Homeopathic Medicine.

Cincinnati College of Pharmacy:
O.L., XLVIII, 634, March 23, 1850.   An act to incorporate the Cincinnati College of Pharmacy.

LEGAL EDUCATION

O.L., XVII, 92, January 28, 1819. Amendatory. An act to regulate the admission and practice of attorneys, etc. Candidates must have studied law attentively two years prior to application.

Cincinnati College:
O.L., XLIV, 157, February 21, 1846. Amendatory. Certificate from the law department of Cincinnati College shall entitle to admission to the bar.

ACTS CONCERNING THE EDUCATION OF DEFECTIVES, DEPENDENTS AND DELINQUENTS

EDUCATION OF DEFECTIVES

Education of the deaf and dumb:
O.L., XX, 49, February 2, 1822. An act to amend an act concerning the safekeeping of idiots, etc. Court of Common Pleas may appoint guardians of deaf and dumb persons. Guardians shall teach. If unable to do so County Commissioners may appropriate money for the purpose. All deaf and dumb persons to be listed in townships and be reported to the State Auditor.

O.L., XXI, 5, December 28, 1822. An act to ascertain the number of deaf and dumb persons in this state.

O.L., XXV, 87, January 30, 1827. An act to establish an asylum for the deaf and dumb persons. Eight trustees. Income not to exceed $30,000.00 Shall be forever under the control of the General Assembly.

O.L., XXVI, 4, January 16, 1828. Amendatory. Adds three trustees. Appropriation, $376.76.

O.L., XXVII, 63, January 28, 1829. An act to provide further for the establishment of the asylum. Authorizes opening in October 1829, at Columbus.

O.L., XXV, 113, January 9, 1827. Resolution. Instructing Senators and Representatives in Congress to try to obtain from Congress a grant equal to one township to aid in the education of the deaf and dumb in this state.

O.L., XXVI, 178, January 29, 1828. Resolution. Renewing preceding effort.

O.L., XXVII, 171, January 21, 1829. Resolution. Locating asylum at Columbus. Authorizing receiving donation of land or purchasing land for a site.   .

O.L., XXVIII, 30, February 18, 1830. Amendatory. Twelve trustees; $1,000.00 appropriation. Provisions for indigent students.

O.L., XXIX, 427, March 3, 1831. An act to establish an Asylum for the education of deaf and dumb persons and repealing all existing laws on that subject.

O.L., XXIX, 246, March 10, 1831. Resolution. Appropriating $1,600.00.

O.L., XXX, 20, February 13, 1832. Amendatory. One-fourth of all moneys arising from auction sales and licenses in Hamilton Co. appropriated to the use of the Deaf and Dumb Asylum.

O.L., XXX, 318, February 11, 1832. Resolution. Appropriating $1,500.00.

O.L., XXX, 336, January 5, 1832. Memorial. Asking Congress for a grant of a township of land for the use of the asylum.

O.L., XXXI, 24, February 25, 1833. Amendatory. Three indigent pupils to be admitted from each judicial circuit in the state.

O.L., XXXI, 237, February 25, 1833. Resolution. Appropriating $1,500.00.

O.L., XXXII, 39, March 3, 1834. Amendatory. Provision for educating all indigent deaf and dumb persons between ages of 12 and 20. Appropriation, $2,213.10.

O.L., XXXII, 427, March 3, 1834. Appropriation, $2,000.00.

O.L., XXXIII, 435, March 9, 1835. Appropriation, $3,000.00.

From this time on appropriations are usually made annually until 1846. From 1846 on regular budget appropriations are made.

O.L., XLIII, 434, January 11, 1845. Resolution. Urging Congress to grant a portion of the public domain for institutions for the education of the deaf and dumb or the blind, in states where such institutions may be established.

O.L., XLIV, 111, March 2, 1846. Amendatory. Salary of the Supt. to be $1,000.00. Six trustees to be appointed by the Gen. Assembly.

Education of the blind:

O.L., IX, 68, January 29, 1811. An act for the relief of David Phouts. Appropriating $150.00 annually for the relief of five children born blind.

O.L., X, 68, February 11, 1812. Repealing preceding act.

O.L., XVII, 7, December 23, 1818. An act for the relief of John Twaddle. County Commissioners of Jefferson County authorized to make an annual allowance. Nine children, six born blind.

O.L., XXXIII, 453, March 5, 1835. Resolution. Census of the blind

O.L., XXXIV, 648, March 11, 1836. Resolution. Three trustees appointed to gather information concerning the instruction of the blind and probable cost of commencing a school.

O.L., XXXV, 116, April 13, 1837. An act making provision for the instruction of the blind. Three trustees. Ohio Institution for the Instruction of the Blind. Provisions for site and buildings at or near Columbus. Authorizing $15,000.00 for building; provision for apparatus.

O.L., XXXV, 559, April 1, 1837. Resolution. Extending thanks to Dr. Howe for his work in behalf of the blind.

O.L., XXXVI, 49, March 10, 1838. An act making further provisions for the instruction of the blind. Authorizing completion of the building, receiving students from other states, giving free instruction to 12 indigent students, etc.

O.L., XLI, 57, March 11, 1843. Amendatory. Extending privileges to indigent students.

O.L., XLII, 21, January 27, 1844. An act reducing salaries. Superintendents of Blind Asylum not to exceed $700.00. Superintendent of Deaf and Dumb Asylum not to exceed $600.00.

O.L., XLII, 253, February 3, 1844. Resolution. Authorizing employment of oculist by the asylum.

O.L., XLII, 270, March 12, 1844. Resolution. Authorizing $150.00 for philosophical apparatus for the pupils.

O.L., XLIV, 111, March 2, 1846. Amendatory. Salaries of Superintendents of Asylums for the Blind and Deaf and Dumb to be $1,000.00 each. Repealing acts for support of pupils in these institutions.

EDUCATION OF DEPENDENTS

Individuals:

O.L., XVIII, 66, February 26, 1820. An act for the relief of an orphan Indian child.

O.L., XIX, 144, February 2, 1821. Repealing the preceding act.

O.L., XXI, 39, January 25, 1823. An act for the relief and benefit of an Indian orphan child. Mother killed by a citizen of the state; $25.00 annually appropriated for education and maintenance until age of 12 years.

Apprentices and servants:

O.L., IV, 72, January 27, 1806. An act concerning apprentices and servants. Children bound out must be taught to read and write.

O.L., XXII, 381, February 23, 1824. An act concerning apprentices and servants. Arithmetic to the rule of three added to the preceding requirements. A new Bible and two suits of clothes to be furnished at the end of the period of service.

Orphan asylums, etc.:

O.L., XXXI, 52, January 25, 1833. An act to incorporate the Cincinnati Orphan Asylum.

O.L., XXXII, 216, February 27, 1834. An act to provide a fund for the relief of the widows and children of the clergy of the Protestant Episcopal Church in Ohio.

O.L., XXXV, 201, March 13, 1837. An act to incorporate the Stark County Orphans' Institute.

O.L., XXXVIII, 87, March 3, 1840. Repealing the preceding act. The corporation had assumed banking privileges.

O.L., XXXV, 513, April 3, 1837. An act to incorporate the Cleveland Female Orphan Asylum. Lowry Willy and 11 other women incorporators.

O.L., XXXVI, 185, March 5, 1838. An act to incorporate the Columbus Female Benevolent Society. Mary Cressy and six other women.

O.L., XLI, 112, March 2, 1843. An act to incorporate the St. Aloysius Orphan Asylum of Cincinnati.

O.L., XLII, 172, March 12, 1844. An act to incorporate the Dayton Female Association for the benefit of orphans.

O.L., XLIII, 101, February 18, 1845. An act to incorporate the trustees of the New Orphans' Asylum of Colored Children of Cincinnati.

EDUCATION OF DELINQUENTS

O.L., XLI, 74, March 13, 1843. An act for the regulation of county jails. Each inmate shall be furnished with a Bible. Sheriff shall keep a record of means furnished prisoners of literary, moral and religious instruction.

O.L., XLIII, 446, March 6, 1845. Resolution. Directors of Ohio Penitentiary authorized to employ a suitable person as a religious and moral instructor.

O.L., XLIII, 393, March 12, 1845. An act to authorize the City of Cincinnati to erect a House of Correction.

ACTS CONCERNING THE EDUCATION OF TEACHERS

O.L., XXX, 232, February 13, 1832. An act to incorporate the Western Academic Institute and Board of Education. Elijah Slack and 14 others.

O.L., XXXII, 217, February 27, 1834. An act to incorporate the Teachers' Institute. For instructing professional school teachers. Lyman Beecher and eight others. Board shall report annually to the Secretary of the State of Ohio.

O.L., XXXI, 18, December 17, 1832. An act to incorporate the Marietta Collegiate Institute and Western Teachers' Seminary.

O.L., XXXI, 193, February 19, 1833. An act to incorporate the Wayne County, Ohio, Teachers' Association.

O.L., XXXV, 417, April 1, 1837. An act to incorporate The Teachers' Institute at Fair Mound, in Licking County.

O.L., XXXVIII, 192, March 23, 1840. An act to incorporate The American Lyceum of Education in the City of Cincinnati. A model school and one in which experiments may be made to be one feature.

O.L., XLV, 67, February 8, 1847. An act to incorporate Teachers' Institutes. Act in force only in the Counties of Ashtabula, Lake, Geauga, Cuyahoga, Erie, Lorain, Medina, Trumbull, Portage, Summit and Delaware.

O.L., XLVII, 261, February 15, 1849. An act to incorporate the Farmington Normal School in the County of Trumbull. Edwin Loveland and eight others. Citizens raised $2,575.00 for school. Site donated.

ACTS CONCERNING SUPPLEMENTARY EDUCATIONAL AGENCIES

Libraries:

O.L., III, 288, February 21, 1805. Dayton Library Society.

O.L., V, 62, January 26, 1806. Library society to be known as "Granville Alexandrian Society," in the town of Granville, in the County of Licking. (Repealed later for banking activities.)

O.L., VI, 127, February 10, 1808. New Town Library Company, in the County of Hamilton.

O.L., VIII, 141, February 19, 1810. Western Library Association.

O.L., VIII, 197, February 19, 1810. Poland Library Society.

O.L., VIII, 251, February 19, 1810. Washington Social Library Company.

O.L., X, 5, December 17, 1811. Wooster Library Society.

O.L., X, 14, December 23, 1811. Lebanon Library Society.

O.L., X, 178, February 20, 1812. Platonic Library Society, in the towns of Sunbury and Berkshire in Delaware County.

O L., XI, 14, January 2, 1813. Circulating Library Society of Cincinnati.

O.L., XII, 55, January 18, 1814. Boardman Library Society, in the County of Trumbull.

O.L., XII, 61, January 19, 1814. Troy Library Society.

O.L., XII, 147, February 10, 1814. Euclid Library Society, in the County of Cuyahoga.

O.L., XIII, 11, December 22, 1814. Circulating Library Society of Cincinnati.

O.L., XIII, 14, December 22, 1814. Village Library Society of Burton, in the County of Geauga.

O.L., XIII, 75, January 13, 1815. Eaton Library Society, in the County of Preble.

O.L., XIII, 285, February 16, 1815. Northern Social Library Company of Harpersfield.

O.L., XIV, 6, December 16, 1815. Waynesville Library Company.

O.L., XIV, 256, February 20, 1816. Fearing Library Society, in the County of Washington.

O.L., XIV, 263, February 21, 1816. Social Library Company of Salem, in the County of Ashtabula.

O.L., XVII, 154, February 8, 1819. Amendatory. Circulating Library Company of Cincinnati.

O.L., XX, 36, February 1, 1822. Amendatory. Social Library Company of Salem.

O.L., XXII, 36, January 20, 1824. Relating to State Library.

SEC. 1. Librarian, $200 per year.

SEC. 2. Bond of $2,000.

SEC. 3. Librarian shall give receipt for all books, etc., to the treasurer of the state.

SEC. 4. Three hundred and fifty dollars appropriated annually for purchase of "useful books" and maps.

SEC. 5. List of books needed may be submitted by members, judges, etc.

SEC. 6. Covering resignation of librarian.

SEC. 7. Provision for necessary furniture.

O.L., XXIII, 3, December 29, 1824. Elizabethtown Social Library Society, in the County of Hamilton.

O.L., XXIII, 101, January 28, 1825. Social Library of Kendal, in the County of Stark.

O.L., XXIII, 76, February 7, 1825. Windham Library Society, in the County of Portage.

O.L., XXIV, 5, December 23, 1825. Frederickstown Library Society, in the County of Knox.

O.L., XXIV, 24, January 17, 1826. Preble County Library Society.

O.L., XXIV, 35, January 24, 1826. Bloomfield Social Library Society, in the County of Trumbull.

O.L., XXIV, 81, February 4, 1826. Social Library Society, in the town of Fairfield, County of Columbiana.

O.L., XXIV, 85, February 7, 1826. Eldridge Library Association, in the County of Huron.

O.L., XXV, 8, December 15, 1826. Franklin Library Company of Little Sandy.

O.L., XXV, 3, January 9, 1827. Dayton Library.

O.L., XXV, 57, January 6, 1827. Buffalo Library Society, in the Counties of Guernsey, Morgan and Muskingum.

O.L., XXV, 56, January 23, 1827.   Columbia Library Society, in the County of Lorain.

O.L., XXV, 42, January 26, 1827.   Brookfield Social Library Society of the County of Morgan.

O.L., XXV, 55, January 26, 1827.   Harmony Library Society, in the County of Fayette.

O.L., XXVI, 3, December 14, 1827.   Newburgh Library Society, in the County of Cuyahoga.

O.L., XXVI, 4, December 18, 1827.   Liberty Library Society, in the County of Butler.

O.L., XXVI, 26, January 1, 1828.   Hubbard Library Company, in the County of Trumbull.

O.L., XXVI, 41, January 16, 1828.   Union Library Society of Lexington.

O.L., XXVI, 119, January 21, 1828.   Yellow Spring Library Society, of the County of Greene.

O.L., XXVI, 107, January 29, 1828.   Lorain County Library Society.

O.L., XXVI, 106, February 11, 1828.   The Hartford Library Society, in the County of Trumbull.

O.L., XXVI, 161, January 29, 1828.   Monroe Traveling and Circulating Library Society.

O.L., XXVII, 5, December 22, 1828.   Social Library Company of Madison, in the County of Geauga.

O.L., XXVII, 10, December 24, 1828.   Amendatory.   Frederickstown Library Society.

O.L., XXVII, 10, December 29, 1828.   Social Library of Greene, in County of Trumbull.

O.L., XXVII, 14, December 29, 1828.   The Chester Library Association, in the County of Geauga.

O.L., XXVII, 21, January 5, 1829.   Sunbury Library Association, in the County of Delaware.

O.L., XXVII, 63, January 30, 1829.   Olive Social Library Society, of the County of Morgan.

O.L., XXVII, 95, February 9, 1829.   Nelson Library Society.

O.L., XXVII, 96, February 9, 1829.   Barlow Library Society, in the County of Washington.

O.L., XXVII, 103, February 9, 1829.   Granville Library, in the County of Licking.

O.L., XXVII, February 2, 1829.   Lyme and Ridgefield Circulating Library Society, in the County of Huron.

O.L., XXVII, 127, February 11, 1829.   Madison Library Association, in the County of Hamilton.
    SEC. 2.   Milford Circulating Library Society declared a body politic.

O.L., XXVII, 139, February 11, 1829.   Vernon Library Association, in the County of Scioto.

O.L., XXVIII, 8, December 31, 1829.   Venice Library Society, in Butler County.

O.L., XXVIII, 22, January 12, 1830.   Bricksville Columbian Library Society, in the County of Cuyahoga.

O.L., XXVIII, 23, January 12, 1830.   Dresden Library Association in the County of Muskingum.

O.L., XXVIII, 46, January 21, 1830.   Windsor Library Society, in the County of Ashtabula.

O.L., XXVIII, 62, February 2, 1830.   Mesopotamia Social Library Company, in the County of Trumbull.

O.L., XXVIII, 70, February 9, 1830.   Marietta Library.

O.L., XXVIII, 164, February 22, 1830.   Newbury Social Library Society, in the County of Geauga.

O.L., XXIX, 11, December 21, 1830.   Dover Library Association, in the County of Athens.

O.L., XXIX, 18, December 27, 1830.   Ashtabula Social Library Association.

O.L., XXIX, 25, December 21, 1830.   Williamsburg Library Society, in the County of Clermont.

O.L., XXIX, 41, January 6, 1831.   Social Circulating Library Association, in village of Waverly, County of Pike.

O.L., XXIX, 49, January 17, 1831.   Hamilton and Rossville Library Society, in the County of Butler.

O.L., XXIX, 50, January 17, 1831.   Middleberry Library Company.

O.L., XXIX, 57, January 31, 1831.   Olmsted Library Company, in the County of Cuyahoga.

O.L., XXIX, 67, January 31, 1831.   Athens Library Society, in the County of Athens.

O.L., XXIX, 83, February 7, 1831.   Austinburg Social Library Association, in the County of Ashtabula.

O.L., XXIX, 119, February 11, 1831.   Wayne and Cherry Valley Union Library Association, in County of Ashtabula.

O.L., XXIX, 142, February 24, 1831.   Utica Library Society, in the County of Licking.

O.L., XXIX, 179, March 2, 1831.   Capitol Library Society of Columbus.

O.L., XXX, 4, December 19, 1831.   Harrisville Library Association, in the County of Medina.

O.L., XXX, 60, January 31, 1832.   New Paris Library Society, in County of Preble.

O.L., XXX, 87, February 2, 1832.   First Universalian Religious Library Society of Marietta.

O.L., XXX, 133, February 7, 1832.   Clarksfield Library Society, of Huron County.

O.L., XXX, 134, February 7, 1832.   Dark County Library Society, in the County of Dark.

O.L., XXX, 244, February 11, 1832.   Guernsey County Library and Reading Room.

O.L., XXX, 267, February 11, 1832.   Farmers' Library Company, in County of Seneca.

O.L., XXX, 275, February 11, 1832.   Library Society of London, in Madison County.

O.L., XXX, 276, February 11, 1832.   West Branch Library Association, in Miami County.

O.L., XXX, 277, February 11, 1832.   Farmers' and Mechanics' Library Society of Berkshire, in the County of Delaware.

O.L., XXXI, 10, December 24, 1832.   Dane Law Library.

O.L., XXXI, 31, January 15, 1833.   Milford Library Association, in the County of Union.

O.L., XXXI, 63, January 31, 1833.   Cleveland Library Company.

O.L., XXXI, 83, February 6, 1833.   Farmers' and Mechanics' Library Association, in Aurora, Portage County.

O.L., XXXI, 89, February 6, 1833.   Massillon Library Society.

O.L., XXXI, 94, February 7, 1833.   Eden Library Association, in County of Seneca.

    Sec. 1.   Incorporated name, "Eden Social Library."

O.L., XXXI, 105, February 12, 1833.   Franklin Library Association of Guilford, in the County of Medina.

O.L., XXXI, 132, February 19, 1833.   Fitchville Library Society, in Huron County.

O.L., XXXI, 159, February 19, 1833.   Wadsworth Library Society, in the County of Medina.

O.L., XXXI, 195, February 23, 1833.   Lancaster Library Association, in County of Fairfield.

O.L., XXXII, 16, December 31, 1833.   Rome Library Company, in County of Ashtabula.

O.L., XXXII, 51, February 3, 1834.   Richfield Social Library Company, in the County of Medina.

O.L., XXXII, 122, February 21, 1834.   Akron Lyceum and Library Association Company, in Akron, Portage County.

O.L., XXXII, 150, February 24, 1834.   Harmony Library Company, in Salena Township, Muskingum County.

O.L., XXXII, 177, February 25, 1834.   Gustavus Centre Library Company, in County of Trumbull.

O.L., XXXII, 191, February 25, 1834.   Lagrange Library Association, in the County of Lorain.

O.L., XXXII, 195, February 25, 1834.   Cincinnati Law Library.

O.L., XXXII, 225, February 28, 1834.   Springboro Library Company, in the County of Warren.

O.L., XXXII, 238, March 1, 1834.   Free Discussion Library of Andover, in Ashtabula County.

O.L., XXXII, 265, March 1, 1834.   Montville Social Library Company, in the County of Geauga.

O.L., XXXIII, 38, February 3, 1835.   Penfield Library Society, in Penfield Township, Lorain County.

O.L., XXXIII, 38, February 3, 1835.   New Lyme Young Men's Library Society.

O.L., XXXIII, 117, February 24, 1835.   The Milford Library Association.

O.L., XXXIII, 119, February 25, 1835.   Delaware Library Association, in the County of Delaware.

O.L., XXXIII, 149, February 26, 1835.   Roscoe Social Library Company, in the County of Coshocton.

O.L., XXXIII, 149, February 26, 1835.   Hinckley Social Library Company, in Hinckley Township, Medina County.

O.L., XXXIII, 160, March 3, 1835. Darrtown Library Company, in the County of Butler.

O.L., XXXIII, 197, March 5, 1835. Painesville Lyceum and Library Society.

O.L., XXXIII, 305, March 7, 1835. Wellington Social Library Company, in Wellington Township, Lorain County.

O.L., XXXIII, 320, March 7, 1835. Vermilion Library Company, of Huron County.

O.L., XXXIII, 330, March 7, 1835. Urbana Juvenile Library.

O.L., XXXIV, 25, January 5, 1836. Young Men's Mercantile Library Association of Cincinnati.

O.L., XXXIV, 83, January 27, 1836. Bellville Library Company, in the County of Richland.

O.L., XXXIV, 133, February 29, 1836. Highland Library Association.

O.L., XXXIV, 197, March 1, 1836. Bedford Library Company, in the County of Cuyahoga.

O.L., XXXIV, 383, March 10, 1836. Hopewell Library Company, in Muskingum County.

O.L., XXXIV, 467, March 14, 1836. Westfield Library Society, in Township of Westfield in County of Medina.

O.L., XXXIV, 468, March 14, 1836. Brooklyn Library Company, in Cuyahoga County.

O.L., XXXIV, 468, March 14, 1836. Greensville Library Association.

O.L., XXXIV, 488. March 14, 1836. Port Washington Lyceum and Library Company, in County of Tuscarawas.

O.L., XXXIV, 488, March 14, 1836. Rutland Library Association.

O.L., XXXV, 47, January 10, 1837. Paris Library Association, of Richland County.

O.L., XXXV, 53, January 23, 1837. Blendon Library Society, in the County of Franklin.

O.L., XXXV, 96, February 18, 1837. North Royalton Social Library Society, in the County of Cuyahoga.

O.L., XXXV, 104, February 27, 1837. Darby Creek Lyceum and Library Association, in the County of Union.

O.L., XXXV, 119, March 2, 1837. Braceville Library Company, in the County of Trumbull.

O.L., XXXV, 195, March 13, 1837. Monroe Lyceum of Natural History, and Library Association, in Ashtabula County.

O.L., XXXV, 196, March 13, 1837. Ruggles Library Society, of Huron County.

O.L., XXXV. 227, March 14, 1837. New Philadelphia Library Society.

O.L., XXXV, 340, March 27, 1837. Sandusky City Lyceum and Library Association, in the County of Huron.

O.L., XXXV, 346, March 29, 1837. Parma Library Association, in Cuyahoga County.

O.L., XXXV, 353, March 29, 1837. Creating an additional number of directors of the Platonic Library Society, of the County of Delaware.

O.L., XXXV, 445, April 3, 1837. Amendatory. Young Men's Mercantile Library Association of Cincinnati.

O.L., XXXV, 562, April 1, 1837. Resolution appointing a committee to select new works for State Library.

O.L., XXXVI, 106, February 23, 1838.   Granger Library Association, in County of Medina.

O.L., XXXVI, 127, February 27, 1838.   Lenox Library Association, in Ashtabula County.

O.L., XXXVI, 270, March 13, 1838.   "Young Men's Association of the City of Toledo."

SEC. 1.   Funds to be used only for supporting a Lyceum and Public Library.

O.L., XXXVI, 378, March 17, 1838.   Painesville Library Association, in County of Geauga.

O.L., XXXVII, 21, January 21, 1839.   McConnelsville Library and Reading Room Association.

O.L., XXXVII, 84, February 28, 1839.   First Universalian Religious Library Society of Harmar.

O.L., XXXVII, 126, March 7, 1839.   St. Mary's Library Association, in County of Mercer.

O.L., XXXVII, 144, March 9, 1839.   Martinsville Silliman Institute and Library Company.

O.L., XXXVII, 147, March 9, 1839.   Franklin Library Association, in the County of Mercer.

O.L., XXXVII, 217, March 12, 1839.   Elizabethtown Circulating Library Society, in the County of Licking.

O.L., XXXVII, 219, March 12, 1839.   Perrysburgh Lyceum and Library Association.

O.L., XXXVII, 257, March 16, 1839.   Worthington Literati.

SEC. 1.   To establish a library and lyceum.

O.L., XXXVII, 263, March 16, 1839.   Fredonia Social Library, in the County of Licking.

O.L., XXXVII, 295, March 16, 1839.   Fairfield Library Association, in the County of Huron.

O.L., XXXVIII, 19, January 17, 1840.   Youth's Neville Library Society.

O.L., XXXVIII, 28, January 29, 1840.   Marysville Library Institute.

O.L., XXXVIII, 29, January 29, 1840.   Oxford Library Society, in the County of Butler.

O.L., XXXVIII, 36, February 3, 1840.   Addison Library Association, of Champaign County.

O.L., XXXVIII, 37, February 3, 1840.   Athenian Library Society, in the County of Warren.

O.L., XXXVIII, 45, February 7, 1840.   Portsmouth Library Company.

O.L., XXXVIII, 71, February 18, 1840.   Kalida Lyceum and Library Association.

O.L., XXXVIII, 111, March 9, 1840.   Burlington Library Association, in the County of Lawrence.

O.L., XXXVIII, 179, March 20, 1840.   Twinsburg Library Association, in the County of Summit.

O.L., XXXVIII, 183, March 21, 1840.   Reading Mutual Improvement and Library Association, in Hamilton County.

O.L., XXXVIII, 197, March 23, 1840. Repealing charter of Washington Social Library Company.

O.L., XXXIX, 53, March 20, 1841. Franklin Library Association, of Carlisle and Elyria, in the County of Lorain.

O.L., XXXIX, 54, March 20, 1841. Orange Library Association, in County of Cuyahoga.

O.L., XXXIX, 103, March 27, 1841. Mayfield Circulating Library, in Township of Mayfield, in County of Cuyahoga.

O.L., XXXIX, 104, March 27, 1841. Franklin Library Society of Waterford, in Knox County.

O.L., XL, 5, January 5, 1842. First Moral Library Association, of Williamsfield, in the County of Ashtabula.

O.L., XL, 16, January 27, 1842. Chagrin Falls Mechanics' Library Association, in the County of Cuyahoga.

O.L., XL, 31, February 15, 1842. Union Library Association of Richmond, in the County of Ashtabula.

O.L., XL, 35, February 26, 1842. Dover Library Association, in the County of Cuyahoga.

O.L., XL, 36, February 26, 1842. Donnelsville Library Association, in the County of Clark.

O.L., XL, 85, March 5, 1842. Orwell Library and Reading Society, of Township of Orwell, Ashtabula County.

O.L., XL, 113, March 7, 1842. Repealing Granville Alexandrian Society because of banking activities.

O.L., XLI, 52, February 2, 1843. Badger Library Society, of Plain, in the County of Wood.

O.L., XLI, 85, February 17, 1843. New Orange Library Society, of Cass, in Miami County.

O.L., XLI, 91, February 28, 1843. Jefferson Library Association, of Township of Jefferson, in County of Ashtabula.

O.L., XLI, 176, March 11, 1843. Mechanics' Lyceum and Library Association, of town of Warren, in County of Trumbull.

O.L., XLII, 110, February 26, 1844. Champeon Library Association at Chagrin Falls, in the County of Cuyahoga.

O.L., XLII, 169, March 11, 1844. Cincinnati Philosophical Library Association, in County of Hamilton.

O.L., XLII, 213, March 12, 1844. Ravenna Library Association.

O.L., XLIII, 58, March 6, 1845. Regulating the State Library.

    SEC. 1. The State Library shall be under control and management of board of commissioners consisting of Governor, Secretary of State, and State Librarian.

O.L., XLIII, 61, February 3, 1845. Young Men's Book Association of West Canaan, in the County of Madison.

O.L., XLIII, 64, February 3, 1845. German Library Association of Cincinnati.

O.L., XLIII, 68, February 10, 1845. New Carlisle Social Library Company, in Clark County, and the Library Association of Harlem, Carroll County.

O.L., XLIII, 70, February 10, 1845. Tallmadge Library Association, in County of Summit.

O.L., XLIII, 274, March 6, 1845.   Miamisburg Library Association.

O.L., XLIII, 311, March 8, 1845.   Act for relief of creditors of Granville Alexandrian Society.

O.L., XLIII, 361, March 11, 1845.   Incorporating certain literary societies:

    Sec. 4.   Farmers' and Mechanics' Library Association of West Lodi, Seneca County.

    Sec. 9.   German Catholic Library Association of Cincinnati.

    Sec. 10.   Donnellsville Library Association, in Clark County.

    Sec. 13.   Hanover Social Library Association, in Butler County.

O.L., XLIII, 389, March 12, 1845.   Linton Library Association, of County of Coshocton.

O.L., XLVI, 149, February 18, 1848.   Cleveland Library Association.

O.L., XLVIII, 632, March 22, 1850.   Young Men's Catholic Association of Cincinnati.

    Sec. 1.   A library association.

O.L., XLVIII, 640, March 23, 1850.   Warren Library Association.

O.L., XLII, 250, December 30, 1843.   Resolution.   Relative to the incorporation of churches, religious societies, library associations, literary societies, etc. Bills shall be referred to the standing Committee on Corporations, of the House in which presented, which committee shall be instructed to retain the same until near the close of the session of the General Assembly, when they shall report one bill for the incorporation of all such churches, and religious societies, one for the incorporation of literary societies, library associations, etc.

O.L., XLII, 260, March 6, 1844.   Resolution.   WHEREAS, By resolution of the General Assembly of March 13, 1843, authorizing the Secretary of State to furnish each college, university and scientific and literary institution in this state, when called for at the office of the secretary, one copy each (of various reports).

    Resolved, To furnish documents in the same manner to all incorporated library associations.

O.L., XLIII, 70, March 11, 1845.   An act to regulate literary and other societies.

    Sec. 1.   That from and after the passage of this act it shall be lawful for any literary, scientific, Odd Fellows or other benevolent association within this state, to elect any number of their members, not less than three, to serve as trustees and one member as clerk, who shall hold their offices during the pleasure of the society.

    Sec. 2.   Proceedings of such election to be recorded with the county recorder.

    Sec. 3.   Trustees shall have perpetual succession and shall possess the powers and privileges, and be subject to the restrictions imposed under the act entitled "An act to regulate incorporated literary societies," etc., passed March 7, 1831.

Athenaeums, lyceums, literary societies, etc.:

O.L., XXVII, 6, December 22, 1828.   Zanesville Athenaeum.

    "Funds not to be employed for any other than literary purposes, the purchase of books, maps, charts, pamphlets and newspapers."

O.L., XXIX, 126, February 14, 1831.   Cincinnati Lyceum.
  Morgan Neville, named with 11 others, including Salmon P. Chase.
  SEC. 1.   "with their associates who have united together for the purpose
  of promoting the diffusion of useful knowledge among all classes of the
  community."
  SEC. 3.   "with power to establish such schools, classes and professor-
  ships, and appoint such professors, lecturers, and teachers therein as to
  them shall seem expedient."
O.L., XXX, 229, February 13, 1832.   Steubenville Athenaeum.
O.L., XXXI, 58, January 29, 1833.   Mount Vernon Lyceum.
O.L., XXXI, 81, January 29, 1833.   Cincinnati Literary Society.
O.L., XXXI, 92, February 6, 1833.   McConnelsville Athenaeum.
O.L., XXXI, 117, February 13, 1833.   Cleveland Lyceum.
O.L., XXXI, 227, February 25, 1833.   Urbana Athenaeum.
O.L., XXXI, 234, February 25, 1833.   Xenia Lyceum.
O.L., XXXII, 8 December 24, 1833.   Medina County Athenaeum.
O.L., XXXII, 31, February 3, 1834.   Young Men's Reading and Literary Society
  of Morgan, Ashtabula County.
O.L., XXXII, 105, February 20, 1834.   Springfield Lyceum.
O.L., XXXII, 140, February 24, 1834.   Elyria Lyceum.
O.L., XXXII, 150, February 24, 1834.   Guilford Lyceum.
O.L., XXXII, 165, February 24, 1834.   Chillicothe Lyceum and Mechanics'
  Institute.
O.L., XXXII, 217, February 27, 1834.   Zanesville Juvenile Lyceum.
O.L., XXXII, 234, February 28, 1834.   Circleville Athenaeum.
O.L., XXXIII, 77, February 17, 1835.   Sidney Lyceum.
O.L., XXXIII, 148, February 26, 1835.   Gallipolis Lyceum.
O.L., XXXIII, 396, March 9, 1835.   Cuyahoga Falls Lyceum.
O.L., XXXIII, 411, March 9, 1835.   Peru (Delaware County) Lyceum.
O.L., XXXIV, 190, February 29, 1836.   The Wellsville Literary Institute.
O.L., XXXIV, 191, March 1, 1836.   Bedford Lyceum.
O.L., XXXIV, 546, March 14, 1836.   Brooklyn Lyceum.
O.L., XXXV, 22, January 3, 1837.   Putnam Lyceum.
O.L., XXXV, 49, January 23, 1837.   New Lisbon Lyceum.
O.L., XXXV, 167, March 10, 1837.   Columbus Literary and Scientific Institute.
O.L., XXXV, 336, March 23, 1837.   Litchfield Lyceum and Society.
O.L., XXXV, 405, April 1, 1837.   Stark County Lyceum.
O.L., XXXVI, 39, January 26, 1838.   Newark Athenaeum.
O.L., XXXVI, 187, March 5, 1838.   The Literary, Historical and Philosophical
  Society of Canton, Stark County.
O.L., XXXVI, 270, March 13, 1838.   Canal Dover Lyceum.
O.L., XXXVII, 13, January 9, 1839.   Johnstown Lyceum, Licking County.
O.L., XXXVII, 18, January 11, 1839.   Rockport Lyceum, Cuyahoga County.
O.L., XXXVII, 168, March 12, 1839.   Woodsfield Lyceum.
O.L., XXXVII, 190, March 12, 1839.   Conneaut Lyceum.
O.L., XXXVII, 294, March 16, 1839.   Malta Lyceum.
O.L., XXXVIII, 6, December 23, 1839.   Airington Lyceum.
O.L., XXXVIII, 19, January 17, 1840.   Harmer Lyceum.

O.L., XXXVIII, 30, January 29, 1840.   The Literary and Philosophical Society, Smithfield, Jefferson County.

O.L., XXXVIII, 163, March 19, 1840.   Franklin Literary Society of Bellville, Richland County.

O.L., XXXIX, 7, January 26, 1841.   Ridgeville Lyceum, Lorain County.

O.L., XXXIX, 9, January 28, 1841.   Massillon Lyceum, Stark County.

O.L., XXXIX, 27, March 11, 1841.   Jamestown Literary Society.

O.L., XXXIX, 52, March 20, 1841.   Columbus Literary Lyceum.

O.L., XXXIX, 52, March 20, 1841.   Beaver Lyceum.

O.L., XXXIX, 53, March 20, 1841.   Franklin Institute, Portsmouth.

O.L., XXXIX, 53, March 20, 1841.   Lower Sandusky Literary and Scientific Institute.

O.L., XL, 121, March 8, 1842.   Findlay Literary Lyceum.

O.L., XL, 123, March 7, 1842.   Wilkesville Lyceum, Gallia County.

O.L., XLI, 9, January 10, 1843.   Berlin Union Society, Holmes County.

O.L., XLI, 14, January 10, 1843.   Young Men's Literary Association of Springfield.

O.L., XLI, 15, January 11, 1843.   Defiance Literary Lyceum.

O.L., XLI, 52, February 2, 1843.   Wayne Township Lyceum, Jefferson County.

O.L., XLI, 86, February 17, 1843.   Alexandria Literary Society.

O.L., XLI, 175, March 11, 1843.   Massillon Young Men's Polemic Society.

O.L., XLII, 102, February 24, 1844.   Erodelphian Society of Gallipolis.

O.L., XLII, 112, March 4, 1844.   Institute of Lower Sandusky.

O.L., XLIII, 361, March 11, 1845.   Newcomerstown Literary Society.   Corwin Literary Institute, Springboro, Warren County.

O.L., XLVIII, 635, March 21, 1850.   Western Liberal Institute, Marietta.

O.L., XLVIII, 640, March 23, 1850.   Mt. Pleasant Philomathean Society, Kingston Township, Ross County.

Mechanics' institutes and lyceums:

O.L., XXVII, 92, February 29, 1829.   The Ohio Mechanics' Institute.

Sec. 1.   "for advancing the best interests of the mechanics, manufacturers and artizans, by the more general diffusion of useful knowledge in these important classes of the community."

Sec. 2.   May establish professorships and appoint such professors, lecturers and teachers, etc.

O.L., XXXV, 339, March 27, 1837.   Mechanics' Institute, Lebanon, Warren County.

O.L., XXXVI, 365, March 16, 1838.   First Mechanics' Lyceum of Marietta.

O.L., XXXVII, 135, March 9, 1839.   Dayton Mechanics' Institute.

O.L., XXXVIII, 139, March 16, 1840.   Farmers' and Mechanics' Institute, Greene Township, Hamilton County.

O.L., XL, 16, January 27, 1842.   Mechanics' Institute, Urbana.

O.L., XL, 121, March 7, 1842.   Batavia Mechanics' Institute.

O.L., XL, 122, March 7, 1842.   Portsmouth Mechanics' Institute and Mechanics' Library Association.

O.L., XLI, 226, March 13, 1843.   Mechanics' Association of Fulton.

College societies, fraternities, etc.:

O.L., XXIX, 74, February 29, 1831.   Erodelphian Society of Miami University.

O.L., XXIX, 196, March 8, 1831.   Philomathesian Society of Kenyon College.

O.L., XXXI, 65, January 31, 1833.   Nu Pi Kappa Society of Kenyon College.

O.L., XXXII, 105, February 20, 1834.   Phylozetian Society of Western Reserve College.

O.L., XXXII, 193, February 25, 1834.   Philosophic Literary Society of Franklin College.

O.L., XXXIV, 289, March 7, 1836.   Jefferson Literary Society of Franklin College.

O.L., XXXIV, 381, March 10, 1836.   The Calliopean Society of the Granville Literary and Theological Institution.

O.L., XXXV, 3, December 19, 1836.   Franklin Scientific and Rhetorical Society of Western Reserve College.

O.L., XXXV, 5, December 19, 1836.   Athenian Literary Society, Ohio University.

O.L., XXXVI, 15, January 5, 1838.   Rush Medical Society of Willoughby University of Lake Erie.

O.L., XXXVI, 186, March 5, 1838.   Adelphic Society of Western Reserve College.

O.L., XXXVII, 146, March 9, 1839.   Philomathean Society of the Ohio University.

O.L., XXXVIII, 78, February 26, 1840.   Alpha Kappa Society of Marietta College.

O.L., XXXVIII, 104, March 6, 1840.   Miami Society of Miami University.

O.L., XXXVIII, 125, March 12, 1840.   Union Literary Society of Miami University.

O.L., XXXIX, 4, December 24, 1840.   Phi Delta Society of Western Reserve College.

O.L., XXXIX, 44, March 20, 1841.   Psi Gamma Society of Marietta College.

O.L., XL, 23, February 4, 1842.   Philomathean Literary Society of Monroe Academy.

O.L., XL, 122, March 7, 1842.   Amendatory.   Philozethian Society, Western Reserve College.

O.L., XLI, 30, January 19, 1843.   Young Men's Franklin Society of Granville College.

O.L., XLI, 125, March 7, 1843.   Miami Union Literary Society of Miami University.

O.L., XLI, 220, March 13, 1843.   Amendatory.   Young Men's Franklin Society, to Franklin Society of Granville College.

O.L., XLII, 102, February 24, 1844.   Amendatory.   Calliopean Society Granville Literary and Theological Institution.

O.L., XLII, 102, February 24, 1844.   Oberlin Young Men's Lyceum.

O.L., XLII, 102, February 24, 1844.   Handel Society of Western Reserve College.

O.L., XLIII, 130, February 25, 1845.   Hunterian Society, Medical Department Western Reserve College.

Miscellaneous organizations and societies:

O.L., XX, 47, February 1, 1822.   Historical Society of Ohio.

O.L., XXVI, 30, January 11, 1828. Cincinnati Academy of Fine Arts.

O.L., XXVIII, 179, February 22, 1830. Lancaster Harmonic Society.

O.L., XXIX, 122, February 11, 1831. Amendatory. Cincinnati Academy of Fine Arts.

O.L., XXIX, 122, February 11, 1831. Historical and Philosophical Society of Ohio.

O.L., XXXIII, 161, March 3, 1835. Eclectic Academy of Music, Cincinnati.

O.L., XXXIX, 50, March 20, 1841. Cincinnati Academy of Fine Arts.

O.L., XLI, 174, March 11, 1843. New Paris Musical Institute.

O.L., XXXIV, 110, February 5, 1836. The Western Academy of Natural Sciences, Cincinnati.

O.L., XXXVIII, 138, March 16, 1840. Cleveland Academy of Natural Sciences.

O.L., XLII, 122, March 4, 1844. Cincinnati Astronomical Society.

O.L., XLVII, 256, February 7, 1849. Ohio Institute of Natural Science, Cincinnati.

O.L., XLI, 114, March 2, 1843. Columbian Association of Cincinnati (for diffusion of useful knowledge).

O.L., XLVI, 228, February 22, 1848. Western Art Union.

O.L., XLVII, 267, March 8, 1849. Columbus Art Union.

O.L., XLVII, 268, March 8, 1849. Ohio Education Society of Evangelical Lutheran Church.

O.L., XXXVI, 238, March 10, 1838. Society of United Christians, Berea (literary and benevolent purposes).

O.L., XXXIII, 317, March 7, 1835. Western Baptist Education Society.

O.L., XLIII, 86, February 10, 1845. Ohio Baptist Education Society.

O.L., XLIII, 361, March 11, 1845. Lower Sandusky Phrenological Mesmeric Institute of Sandusky County.

APPENDIX B

VOLUME XXV

General:

Local:

VOLUME XXVI

VOLUME XXVII

General:

VOLUME XXVIII

Volume XXIX

VOLUME XXX

VOLUME XXX—Second Session

VOLUME XXXI

Volume XXXII

General:

ACTS INCORPORATING EDUCATIONAL AND LITERARY INSTITUTIONS

Medina County Athenaeum, 8; Medina County Medical Lyceum, 9; Rome Library Company, 16; Young Men's Reading and Literary Society in Morgan, Ashtabula County, 31; German Lutheran Seminary, 46; Richfield Social Library, 51; Baptist Convention of Ohio, 63; (amendatory) Norwalk Academy, 85; Springfield Lyceum, 105; Phylozetian Society, Western Reserve College, 105; Akron Lyceum and Library Association, Portage County, 122; Elyria Lyceum, 140; Harmony Library Company, Muskingum County, 150; Guilford Lyceum, Medina County, 150; Chillicothe Lyceum and Mechanics' Institute, 165; Ravenna Academy, 177; Gustavus Center Library Company, Trumbull County, 177; Lagrange Library Association, Lorain County, 191; Philosophic Literary Society, Franklin College, 193; Cincinnati Law Library, 195; (amendatory) Granville Literary and Theological Institution, 215; Zanesville Juvenile Lyceum, 217; The Teachers' Institute, 217; Union Academy, Wayne County, 223; Springboro Library Company, Warren County, 225; Oberlin Collegiate Institute, 226; Circleville Athenaeum, 234; Vinton Academy, Gallia County, 234; Free Discussion Library, Andover, Ashtabula County, 238; Montville Social Library Company, Geauga County, 265; Springfield High School, 270; Female Academy, Mt. Vernon, 333; Willoughby University of Lake Erie, 376; (amendatory) The Theological Seminary of the Protestant Episcopal Church, 380.

ACTS CONCERNING CHURCH AND RELIGIOUS INCORPORATIONS MENTIONING EDUCATIONAL FUNCTIONS

Presbyterian Church, Long Run, Columbiana County, 31; Free Will Baptist Church, Conneaut, Ashtabula County, 64; First Baptist Church Society, Ashtabula, Ashtabula County, 161; Mt. Zion M. E. Church, Clark County, 167; Presbyterian Church, Steubenville, 194; Baptist Church and Society, Conneaut, Ashtabula County, 329.

ACTS CONCERNING THE SELLING OR LEASING OF SCHOOL LANDS

Guernsey County, 30; Virginia Military School Lands, 42; Huron County, 43; Jefferson County, 53; Hamilton County, 88; Columbiana County, 95; Butler County, 162; Athens County, 184; Allen County, 189; Tuscarawas County, 193; Washington County, 214; Stark County, 233; Sandusky County, 325.

CITY AND TOWN ACTS CONCERNING SCHOOLS

46. (Amendatory).   Town of Chillicothe; (amendatory) town of Fulton, 116; City of Cincinnati (Sections 29 to 36), 244.

Resolutions concerning:

Trustees, Charity School of Kendal, 435; trustees, Ohio University, 436; distributing school laws, 450; public lands for education, 452; trustees, Deaf and Dumb Asylum, 453; West Point Military Academy, 456.

VOLUME XXXIII

General acts:

(Amendatory).   The method of levying taxes, 48; incorporation of townships, 49.

Local acts:

(Amendatory).   Distribution of United States Military School Funds, 15; appointing trustee of the Miami University, 33; distribution of interest of Western Reserve School Fund, 394; appropriation for the Deaf and Dumb Asylum, 435.

ACTS CONCERNING INCORPORATION OF EDUCATIONAL AND LITERARY INSTITUTIONS

Stephen Strong's Manual Labor Seminary, 5; Richmond Classical Institute, Jefferson County, 21; (amendatory) Woodward High School, Cincinnati, 23; Penfield Library Society, Lorain County, 38; New Lyme Young Men's Library Society, 38; Kingsville High School, Ashtabula County, 48; Conneaut Academy, 51; Marietta College, 53; Sidney Lyceum, 77; renaming the Ashtabula Institute of Science and Industry, Grand River Institute, 79; Windham Academy, 87; Granville Female Seminary, 87; Fellenburgh Institute, Medina County, 112; Milford Library Association, 117; (amendatory) Education Society, Painesville, 118; Delaware Library Association, 119; Gallipolis Lyceum, 148; Roscoe Social Library, Coshocton County, 149; Hinckley Social Library Company, Medina County, 149; Western Female Seminary, Mansfield, 153; Darrtown Library Company, Butler County, 160; Eclectic Academy of Music, Cincinnati, 161; Wadsworth Academy, 190; Painesville Lyceum and Library Society, 197; Academic Institution of Richfield, Medina County, 199; (amendatory) Miami University, 298; Hamilton and Rossville Female Academy, 305; Wellington Social Library Company, 305; Western Baptist Education Society, 317; Vermilion Library Company, Huron County, 320; Circleville Female Seminary, 321; Bishop's Fraternal Calvanistic [*sic*] Baptist Seminary, 328; Urbana Juvenile Library, 330; (amendatory) Springfield High School, 341; Cuyahoga Lyceum, 396; Peru Lyceum, 411.

Bellville Library Company, Richland County, 83; Western Academy of Natural Sciences, 110; Highland Library Association, 133; Wellsville Literary Institute, 190; Putnam Classical Institute, 190; Bedford Lyceum, 191; Bedford Library Company, Cuyahoga County, 197; (amendatory) Nelson Academy, 222; Seneca County Academy, 242; Madison Liberal Institute, 242; Jefferson Literary Society, Franklin College, 289; Calliopean Society, Granville Literary Institution, 381; Hopewell Library Company, 383; Wooster Academy, 386; North Union School Association, Carroll County, 402; Shaw Academy, Cuyahoga County, 408; Rome Academical Company, Ashtabula County, 411; Academy of Sylvania, 458; Granville Academy, 460; Westfield Library Society, Medina County, 467; Brooklyn Library Company, Cuyahoga County, 468; Greensville Library Association, 468; Port Washington Library and Lyceum Company, Tuscarawas County, 488; Rutland Library Association, 488; Sharon Academy, Medina County, 514; McIntire Poor School, Zanesville, 514; Medina Academy, 545; Brooklyn Lyceum, Cuyahoga County, 546; Cleves Independent School, Hamilton County, 547.

ACTS CONCERNING CHURCH AND RELIGIOUS INCORPORATIONS MENTIONING EDUCATIONAL FUNCTIONS

Associated Reform Church, Piqua, Miami County, 7; M. E. Church, Canton, Stark County, 11; First Congregational Church, Rome, Ashtabula County, 28; Presbyterian Church, Monroeville, Jefferson County, 43; German Reform Church, Dayton, Montgomery County, 45; First Methodist Society, Sandusky, Huron County, 47; Wardens and Vestrymen of Grace Church, Huron County, 51; Protestant Episcopal Church, Bellevue, Huron County, 53; First Congregational Society, Lagrange, Lorain County, 79; Lutheran and German Reform Church, New Rumley, Harrison County, 82; First Congregational Society, Concord, Geauga County, 95; Cheviot Presbyterian Church, Hamilton County, 98; German Reform Church, Greene County, 119; Presbyterian Congregation, Carrolton, 182; M. E. Church, Wellsville, Columbiana County, 193; First Presbyterian Church, Lower Sandusky, Sandusky County, 246; First Presbyterian Church, Knoxville, Jefferson County, 248; First Presbyterian Church, Norwalk, Huron County, 290; First Presbyterian Church, New Lisbon, 292; First Presbyterian Church, Olive Township, Morgan County, 293; Akron and Middlebury Baptist Church, 390; Free Will Baptist Society, Ashtabula County, 478; Presbyterian Church, Hebron, Licking County, 483; First Episcopal Church, Maumee City, Lucas County, 486; Wardens and Vestrymen, St. Paul's Church, Norwalk, 513; Second Baptist Church and Society, Geauga County, 524; First Baptist Church, Madison, Geauga County, 555; First Baptist Church, Massillon, 587.

ACTS CONCERNING THE SELLING OR LEASING OF SCHOOL LANDS

(Amendatory) Virginia Military District, 13; Carroll County, 16; Richland County, 72; Seneca County, 91; Jackson County, 118; Ohio Company's Purchase, 121; (extending the time of payment) Butler County, 128; Wayne County, 130; Butler County, 134; Seneca County, 134; Relief of Charles Steward, 144; twelve mile reserve, 152; Crawford County, 218; Guernsey County, 312; Carroll County, 313; (extending the time of payment) Richland County, 373; Crawford County, 400; (extending the time of payment) Logan County, 447; (extending the time of payment) Richland County, 447; Ohio Company's Purchase, 523; Gallia County, 589.

VOLUME XXXV

Institute, Lebanon, Warren County, 339; Sandusky City Lyceum and Library Society, Huron County, 340; Monroe Seminary, Monroe County, 342; Parma Library Association, Cuyahoga County, 346; Baptist Literary and Collegiate Institute, Huron County, 347; (amendatory) Platonic Library Society, Delaware County, 353; Wesleyan Collegiate Institute, 378; Troy Academy, Miami County, 380; Stark County Lyceum, 405; New Philadelphia Academy, 406; Teachers' Institute, Licking County, 417; Massillon Academy, 425; (amendatory) Young Men's Library Association, Cincinnati, 445; Cleveland Female Seminary, 511; Cleveland Female Orphan Asylum, 513.

ACTS CONCERNING THE SELLING AND LEASING OF SCHOOL LANDS

(Extending time of payment) Virginia Military school lands, 10; Ohio Company's Purchase, 14; relief of John Feller, Fairfield County, 58; Muskingum County, 170; (repealing) relief of John Feller, 175; Monroe County, 184; Putnam County, 207; Crawford County, 221; Hamilton County, 224; Miami County, 229; (extending time of payment) Logan County, 230; (extending time of payment) Butler County, 242; Carroll County, 243; Wood County, 247; Monroe County, 261; Darke County, 265; Washington, Meigs and Gallia Counties, 267; Crawford County, 275; Jefferson County, 290; Wood County, 297; Crawford County, 319; Wood County, 321; Ohio Company's Purchase, 352; Hardin County, 437; (amendatory) selling of Section 16, 446.

CITY AND TOWN ACTS CONCERNING SCHOOLS

City of Toledo, Section 29, 32.

Resolutions concerning:

Athens College (requiring reports), 543; trustees, Deaf and Dumb Asylum, 558; Dr. Howe's Report, education of the blind, 559; appropriation, State Superintendent of Common Schools, 560; State Library, 562; trustees, Ohio Institution for the Blind, 566.

VOLUME XXXVI

General:

For the support of Common Schools, 21; for the relief of the Medical College of Ohio, 37; making further provision for the Institution of the Blind, 49; amending the act for the sale of Section 16, 63; an act relating to information in the nature of Quo Warranto (fines for schools), 68; authorizing County Auditors to permit certain school districts to receive their portion of school funds, 73; (amendatory) distribution of the surplus revenue, 79; levying a tax for state and school purposes, 85; regulating office of County Auditors (school duties), 90; appropriations, State Library, Deaf and Dumb Asylum, Professor Stowe's Report, and Superintendent of Common Schools, 92.

Local:

Authorizing certain school districts to borrow money for schoolhouses, Stark County, 164; authorizing the sale of public square, Winchester, Adams County(to erect school-house), 198; authorizing a loan to Ohio University, 204; for the relief of the town of Dover, Tuscarawas County, 211; authorizing a school district in Stark County to borrow money (building), 227; appointing trustees Miami University, 269.

Rush Medical Society of Willoughby University of Lake Erie, 15; (amendatory) Lane Seminary, 22; Theological Seminary of the Associated Reform Synod of the West, 34; Newark Athenaeum, 39; Akron High School, Portage County, 52; Cambridge Academy, Guernsey County, 98; Massillon Female Seminary, Stark County, 98; Granger Library Association, Medina County, 106; High Falls Primary Institute, Chagrin Falls, Cuyahoga and Geauga Counties, 107; Lenox Library Association, 127; Western Reserve Wesleyan Seminary, 157; Edinburgh Academy, 159; Columbus Female Benevolent Society, 185; Adelphic Society, Western Reserve College, 186; Literary, Historical and Philosophical Society, Canton, Stark County, 187; Wayne Academy, 190; Logan College, 203; Emigrants' Friends Society, Section 2, Cincinnati, 208; Norwalk Female Seminary, 210; Chester Academy, Geauga County, 223; Eaton Academy, Preble County, 231; Sandusky Academy, Huron County, 235; Canal Dover Lyceum, Tuscarawas County, 270; Young Men's Association, Toledo, 270; Union Academy, Union County, 287; Dover Academy, Tuscarawas County, 317; Lebanon Medical Society, 347; Marion Academy, Marion County, 362; First Mechanics Lyceum, Marietta, Washington County, 365; Newark Association for the Promotion of Education, 371; Painesville Library Association, Geauga County, 378.

Society of United Christians, Berea, Cuyahoga County, 238.

Monroe County, 38; (extending time of payment) Warren County, 49; Richland County, 50.

(Amendatory) town of Fulton (Section 2), 199; (amendatory) City of Cincinnati (Section 6), 241; City of Chillicothe (Section 30), 274; (amendatory) Town of Portsmouth (Sections 14 to 23), 329.

Resolutions concerning:
State Superintendent of Common Schools, 399; Trustees, Medical College of Ohio, 402; Professor Stowe's Report (Elementary Public Education in Europe), 402; Members of the Geological Corps, 403; Geological Survey, 404; Professor Stowe's Report, 404; appropriating five hundred dollars, Professor Stowe, 404; trustees, Charity School of Kendal, 404; trustees, Ohio Institution for the Blind, 408; trustees, Deaf and Dumb Asylum, 409; Common School Reports and C. E. Stowe's Report, 410; appointing Superintendent of Common Schools, 411; school tax on colored people, 412; school lands in land acquired from Indians, 413; Report of Superintendent of Common Schools, 415; concerning a state University for teachers, 418.

VOLUME XXXVII

General:

To regulate incorporated literary societies, 49; (amendatory) for the regulation of Common Schools, 61; authorizing the Canal Fund Commissioners to borrow money, 68; making appropriations of various items concerning education, 71; for the relief of holders of leases of Section 16, 78.

Local:

Authorizing school trustees to borrow money, Gallipolis, 20; (amendatory) trustees of Windham School Fund, 50; organizing Hamilton, Butler County, into two school districts, 51; authorizing Chillicothe to borrow money (school purposes), 64; concerning medical and surgical supervision of the Commercial Hospital of Ohio, 71; authorizing Troy and Miami Counties to borrow money, school building, 136; to remit a building tax, Ashtabula County, 224; to levy a school tax, 235; appointing trustees, Ohio University, 277; authorizing Wooster to borrow money (school purposes), 283; dividing Akron into two school districts, 385.

ACTS CONCERNING INCORPORATION OF EDUCATIONAL AND LITERARY
INSTITUTIONS

Bigelow High School, Xenia, 6; Johnstown Lyceum, Licking County, 13; Rockport Lyceum, Cuyahoga County, 18; McConnelsville Library and Reading Room Association, 21; Martinsburg Academy, Knox County, 30; Blendon Young Men's Seminary, 43; Ashland Academy, Richland County, 44; Western Reserve Teachers' Seminary, 79; Oxford Female Academy, 80; First Universalian Religious Library Society, Harmar, 84; Asbury Seminary, Chagrin Falls, 109; St. Mary's Library Association, 126; Dayton Mechanics' Institute, 135; Worthington Female Seminary, 141; Martinsville Silliman Institute and Library Company, 144; Philomathean Society, Ohio University, 146; Franklin Library Association, 147; Universalist Institute, Ohio City, 155; Parkman Academy, Geauga County, 156; Monroe Academical Association, Monroe County, 166; Woodsfield Lyceum, 168; Harveysburg High School Company, Warren County, 169; Barnesville Male Academy, 172; Conneaut Lyceum, 190; Literary and Botanico Medical College of the State of Ohio, 208; Elizabethtown Circulating Library Company, Licking County, 217; Perrysburgh Lyceum and Library Association, 219; Brooklyn Centre Academy, 222; Auglaize Seminary, 254; Lithopolis Academy, 255; Worthington Literati, 257; Meigs County High School and Teachers' Institute, 257; Mt. Pleasant Boarding School, 262; Fredonia Social Library, Licking County, 263; Cuyahoga Falls Institute, 282; Ravenna Female Seminary, 291; Malta Lyceum, 294; Fairfield Library Association, Huron County, 295; Philomathean Literary Institute changed to Madison College, Guernsey County, 308; New Hagerstown Female Seminary, 344; (supplementary) Theological Seminary Protestant Episcopal Church, 353.

ACTS CONCERNING THE SELLING AND LEASING OF SCHOOL LANDS

(Extending time of payment) Butler County, 10; Columbiana County, 39; Jefferson County, 88; (relief of John Wolfe) Montgomery County, 130; Hocking County, 140; Greene County, 170; Jackson County, 198; (extending time of payment) Holmes County, 260; (relief of two lessees) Clark County, 315; Jefferson County, 387.

Support and better regulation of public schools, Zanesville, 194; (amendatory) City of Cincinnati, Section 6, 297.

Resolutions concerning:

Report of the Superintendent of Common Schools, 394; trustees, College of Ripley, 395; trustees, Blind Asylum, 403; Miami University, 403; register, Virginia Military District School Lands, 404; (exemption from tuition) two deaf and dumb students, 405; trustees, Deaf and Dumb Asylum, 414.

VOLUME XXXVIII

General:

Levying taxes, Section 1, 3; an act concerning inclosures (fines for schools), 4; inspection of salt (fines for schools), 23; (amendatory) an act for the punishment of certain offences, 57; (amendatory) incorporating townships, 58; (amendatory) sale of Section 16, 61; (amendatory) sale of school lands, United States Military School District, 62; (amendatory) levying taxes, Section 1, 81; (extending time of payment) purchasers of school lands, 83; abolishing the office of Superintendent of Common Schools, 130; making appropriations (various educational items), 144.

Local:

Appointing trustees, Miami University, 96; (amendatory) regulating the fur trade (fees for schools), 129; to establish a school district, Warren County, 145; (amendatory) to establish a school fund in Warren County, 149.

ACTS CONCERNING INCORPORATION OF EDUCATIONAL AND LITERARY INSTITUTIONS

Airington Lyceum, 6; Harmer Lyceum, 19; Youth's Neville Library Society, 19; Marysville Library Institute, 28; Oxford Library Society, Butler County, 29; Bascom Seminary of Waynesburg, Stark County, 29; Literary and Philosophical Society, Smithfield, Jefferson County, 30; Addison Library Association, Champaign County, 36; Athenian Library Society, Warren County, 37; Portsmouth Library Company, 45; Kalida Lyceum, 71; Alpha Kappa Society, Marietta College, 78; (repealing) Stark County Orphans' Institute, 87; Miami Society, 104; Burlington Library Association, Lawrence County, 111; Union Literary Society, Miami University, 125; Greenfield Institute, Huron County, 127; Streetsborough High School, 127; Cleveland Academy of Natural Sciences, 138; Farmers' and Mechanics' Institute, Hamilton County, 139; Willoughby Female Academy, 155; Protestant Methodist Academy of Brighton, 155; Franklin Literary Society, Bellville, Richland County, 163; (amendatory) establishing a college in Worthington, 174; Twinsburg Library Association, 179; Reading Mutual Improvement and Library Association, Hamilton County, 183; American Lyceum of Education, Cincinnati, 192; (repealing) Washington Social Library Company, 197.

ACTS CONCERNING THE SELLING AND LEASING OF SCHOOL LANDS

Steubenville land district, 14; Lawrence County, 42; relief of lessee, Harrison County, 62; Preble County, 66; Washington County, 77; Knox County, 81; Greene County, 96; Lucas County, 97; (relief of Timothy Evarts) Richland

County, 107; Williams County, 109; Allen County, 125; Columbiana County, 131; Scioto County, 132; Delaware County 133; Athens County, 143; Shelby County, 144; Akron School District, 145; (relief of two lessees) Washington County, 160; Tuscarawas County (Moravian school lands), 164; Lucas County, 177; (relief of lessees) Stark County, 178; Columbiana and Carroll Counties, 180; (amendatory) Ohio University lands, 183; (relief of David Holbrook) Morgan County, 195; Meigs County, 211.

CITY AND TOWN ACTS CONCERNING SCHOOLS

City of Cincinnati, Sections 9 to 12, 157.

Resolutions concerning:

Use of State Library, 217; deaf and dumb student, 217; interest on school funds, 220; report of Deaf and Dumb Asylum, 224; admission of certain indigent students to Deaf and Dumb Asylum, 233; trustees, Deaf and Dumb Asylum, 243; trustees, Ohio University, 244; trustee, Ohio Institution for Instruction of Blind, 246.

VOLUME XXXIX

General:

Extending time for payment to purchasers of school lands in this state, 25; making appropriations (various educational items), 29; (amendatory) for the prevention of certain immoral practices, 33; (amendatory) providing for the distribution of this state's proportion of the surplus revenue, 41; an act declaratory of the law in certain cases, and to prohibit the appraisers of land from purchasing same, 42; (amendatory) an act for the support and better regulation of Common Schools, 44.

Local:

Appointing trustees of the Miami University, 122; authorizing the trustees of Zanesville Township to lay off in school districts the part of the township not included in the limits of Zanesville, 128; to form a new school district, Franklin County, 177; to form a new school district, Troy Township, Richland County, 178.

ACTS CONCERNING INCORPORATION OF EDUCATIONAL AND LITERARY
INSTITUTIONS

The Phi Delta Society of Western Reserve College, 4; The Ridgeville Lyceum, Lorain County, 7; Massillon Lyceum, Stark County, 9; The Cincinnati New Jerusalem Church School Association, 11; Jamestown Literary Society, Greene County, 27; Psi Gamma Society, Marietta College, 44; Cincinnati Academy of Fine Arts, 50; Edinburgh Academy, Wayne County, 51; Columbus Literary Lyceum, 52; Beaver Lyceum, 52; Franklin Institute of the Town of Portsmouth, 52; Lower Sandusky Literary and Scientific Institute, 53; Franklin Library Association of Carlisle and Elyria, Lorain County, 53; Orange Library Association, Cuyahoga County, 54; Burlington Academy, Lawrence County, 62; Athens Female Academy, 65; Berkshire Education Society, Delaware County, 103; Mayfield Circulating Library, Cuyahoga County, 103; Franklin Library Society, Waterford, Knox County, 104; (amendatory) Berea Seminary, Cuyahoga County, 104; Canton Male Seminary, Stark County, 125; Middletown Academy, Butler County, 134; Gustavus Academy, Trumbull County, 134; Kinsman Academy, Trumbull County, 134; Literary and Botanico Medical College, 161.

hoga County, 59; Trustees of the Central College of Ohio, 77; Eaton Medical Society, 83; St. Xavier College, 84; Orwell Library and Reading Society, Ashtabula County, 85; Pine Grove Academy, Porter, Gallia County, 86; (amendatory) Urbana Academy, 88; (amendatory) Wesleyan University, 111; (repealing) Granville Alexandria Society, 113; Ohio Conference High School, Springfield, Clark County, 114; Canaan Union Academy, 116; Tallmadge Academical Institute, 117; Bath High School, Bath, Summit County, 119; Lafayette University, New Carlisle, Clark County, 119; Findlay Literary Lyceum, Hancock County, 121; Batavia Mechanics Institute, 121; Portsmouth Mechanics Institute and Mechanics Library Association, 122; (amendatory) Philozethian Society of the Western Reserve College, 122; Wilksville Lyceum, Gallia County, 123; (amendatory) Miami University, 123; (amendatory) Barnesville Male Academy, 128.

ACTS CONCERNING THE SALE AND LEASING OF SCHOOL LANDS

Athens County, 3; Seneca County, 36; Sandusky County, 66; Crawford County, 81; Marion County, 86; Crawford County, 89; Muskingum County, 101; Lucas County, 108; Perry County, 124; Lucas County, 128; Jackson County, 135; Meigs County, 137; Miami Purchase, 138; Sandusky County, 141; Williams County, 144; Putnam County, 150; Tuscarawas County, 173; Sandusky County, 198.

CITY AND TOWN ACTS CONCERNING SCHOOLS

(Amendatory) City of Cincinnati, Section 2, 143.

Resolutions concerning:

An indigent blind student, 205; trustees, Charity School of Kendal, 206; a certain blind student, 211; register of the Virginia Military District School Lands, 212; trustees, Charity School of Kendal, 212; a certain deaf and dumb student, 215; a certain blind student, 215; a certain deaf and dumb student, 216; a blind student, 217; a deaf and dumb student, 217; Ohio University lands, 218; trustees, Deaf and Dumb Asylum, 228; trustee, Ohio Institute for the Blind, 230.

VOLUME XL—Second Session

ACTS CONCERNING THE SELLING AND LEASING OF SCHOOL LANDS

Lucas County, 2.

Resolutions concerning:

A certain deaf and dumb student, 7, use of State Library, 7.

VOLUME XLI

General:

An act to extend the time of payment of purchasers of school lands in this state, 4; regulating the sale of ministerial and school lands and the surrender of permanent leases thereto, 20; (amendatory) making further provision for the instruction of the blind, 57; (amendatory) for the support and better regulation of Common Schools, etc., 59; for the regulation of county jails, 74; making appropriations (various educational items), 95.

Local:

(Repealing) Incorporating the town of Mount Eaton, 49; authorizing the trustees of Milton Township, Trumbull County, to lay off the township into school districts, 60; authorizing the trustees of Painesville Township, Licking County, to divide the town into school districts, 62; appointing trustee of Miami University, 87; an act to erect the Risdon Common School District, 125; Morgan County Medical Society, 145; trustees of the Methodist Female Collegiate Institute of Cincinnati, 146; Oakland Female Seminary, Hillsborough, 148; making a special appropriation to Champaign County for school purposes, 155; New Paris Musical Institute, Preble County, 174; Massillon Young Men's Polemic Society, Stark County, 175; Mechanics Lyceum and Library Association of Warren, Trumbull County, 176; to divide the town of Lancaster into school districts, 216; to divide School District No. 1, Warren Township, Trumbull County, 219; to change the name of the Franklin Society of Granville College, 220; Bellefontaine Ohio College, 220; Mechanics Association of Fulton, Hamilton County, 226.

ACTS CONCERNING THE INCORPORATION OF EDUCATIONAL AND LITERARY
INSTITUTIONS

Berlin Union Society, Holmes County, 9; amending the charter of Ohio Wesleyan University, 12; trustees of the Germania College, 12; Young Men's Literary Association of Springfield, 14; New Lisbon Academy, Columbiana County, 14; Defiance Literary Lyceum, Williams County, 15; (amendatory) trustees of the Windham School Fund, 26; The Young Men's Franklin Society of Granville College, 30; St. Mary's Female Institute, Cincinnati, 46; Wayne Township Lyceum, Jefferson County, 52; Badger Library Society of Plain, Wood County, 52; Maumee City Academy, Lucas County, 62; Providence College, Harrison County, 63; New Orange Library Society of Cass, Miami County, 85; Western Reserve Free Will Baptist Academical Society, 85; Alexandria Literary Society, Licking County, 86; Jefferson Library Association, Jefferson Township, Ashtabula County, 91; Beverly College at Beverly, 92; Aloysius Orphan Society of Cincinnati, 112; Cambrian Association of Cincinnati for the Diffusion of Useful Knowledge, 114; The Miami Union Literary Society, Miami University, 125; Lebanon Academy, Warren County, 127; (amendatory) the German Lutheran Seminary of the German Lutheran Synod of Ohio, 129; (declaratory) the Ohio University, 144.

ACTS CONCERNING THE SALE AND LEASING OF SCHOOL LANDS

Hamilton County, 61; Wood County, 90; Richland County, 90; Washington County, 110; Putnam County, 111; Hancock County, 111; United States Reserve, Lucas County, 112; Hancock County, 126; Monroe County, 141; Athens County, 141; Wood County, 142; Seneca County, 142; Athens County, 143; Tuscarawas County, 143; Columbiana County, 144; Williams County, 175; Darke County, 176; Paulding County, 177; Williams County, 217; Williams County, 218.

CITY AND TOWN ACTS CONCERNING SCHOOLS

(Amendatory) The City of Cleveland, 130.

Resolutions concerning:

Remission of taxes on certain university lands, 241; the instruction of a certain blind Chinese child, 245; reports from state instruction, 248; a deaf and dumb student, 248; a deaf and dumb student, 249; trustees, Asylum for Deaf and Dumb, 253; a deaf and dumb student, 253; compensation of Ephraim Cutler as Commissioner of Schools, 256; Deaf and Dumb Asylum, 261.

VOLUME XLII

General:

An act in relation to the Deaf and Dumb Asylum, 8; reducing the compensation of members of the General Assembly and certain other state and county officers, 21; an act in addition to an act to provide for the inspection of salt (fines for schools), 33; preventing the introduction and spread of the Canada Thistle (fines for schools), 37; increasing the revenue of the state Common School Fund and making permanent the transfer thereto, 38; an act to amend an act entitled, "An act to extend the time of payment of purchasers of School Lands in this state," 39; an act to amend the act to regulate the sale of school and ministerial lands and the surrender of permanent leases thereto, 43; an act to amend the act entitled, "An act for the support and better regulation of Common Schools, etc.," 48; an act making appropriations for the year 1844 (various educational items), 78.

Local:

To erect a school district in Portage Township, Summit County, 3; to divide School District No. 1, Warren Township, Trumbull County, 19; authorizing School Districts 10 and 11, Painesville Township, Lake County, to levy a special tax, etc., 126; vesting the property belonging to the Knoxville School Company in the Knoxville School District in Jefferson County, 212.

ACTS CONCERNING THE INCORPORATION OF EDUCATIONAL AND LITERARY INSTITUTIONS

Sylvania High School Company, Lucas County, 60; Lebanon Academy, 80; (amendatory) Western Reserve College, 95; (amendatory) Calliopean Society of the Granville Literary and Theological Institution, 102; Acts to incorporate certain societies therein named, 102:

1. The Oberlin Young Men's Lyceum,
2. Erodelphian Society, Gallipolis,
3. The Handel Society of Western Reserve College;

West Lodi Academy, Seneca County, 107; Champeon Library Association, Chagrin Falls, Cuyahoga County, 110; Institute of Lower Sandusky, Sandusky County, 112; Franklin Academy, Portage County, 115; Cincinnati Astronomical Society, 122; (amendatory) Beverly College, 160; Western Reserve Free Will Baptist Educational Society, 163; Cincinnati Philosophical Library Association, Hamilton County, 169; Dayton Female Association for the Benefit of Orphans, 172; Salem Academy, Buckskin Township, Ross County, 178; Dudley Medical University of Wadsworth, 179; Summit County Medical Society, 183; Laurain Institute, 184; The Board of Directors of the English Lutheran Theological and Collegiate Institute at Wooster, Wayne County, 189; Waynesville Academy,

Warren County, 191; Keene Academy, Coshocton County, 210; Ravenna Library Association, 213; (amendatory) North Union School Association of Carroll County, 221.

ACTS CONCERNING THE SALE AND LEASING OF SCHOOL LANDS

Hancock County, 6; Sandusky County, 29; Carroll County, 66; Gallia County, 67; Columbiana County, 83; Twelve Mile Square Reserve, 99; Morgan County, 111; Putnam County, 121; Williams County, 131; Meigs County, 132; Sandusky County, 132; Monroe County, 133; Crawford County, 146; Hocking County, 149; Hocking County, 155; Williams County, 156; Ottawa County, 156; Williams County, 157; Seneca County, 158; Monroe County, 161; Mercer County, 161; Meigs County, 178; Scioto County, 190; Delaware County, 194; Butler County, 206; Williams County, 206.

Resolutions concerning:

Incorporation of churches, religious societies, towns, literary societies, library associations, etc., 250; report of the Deaf and Dumb Asylum, 251; report of the Asylum for the Blind, 252; an oculist for the Asylum for the Blind, 253; clothing for certain blind, and deaf and dumb students, 256; trustees, Neville Institute, 256; trustees, Deaf and Dumb Asylum, 258; documents for library associations, 260; apparatus, etc., for the Blind Asylum, 270; trustees, Institution of the Blind, 270; trustees, Ohio Medical College, 271; trustees, Ohio University, 273.

VOLUME XLIII

General:

An act to prevent the firing of cannons upon public streets and highways (fines for the use of schools), 17; fixing the minimum price for school lands, 58; regulating the State Library, 58; regulating literary and other societies, 70; (amendatory) for the support and better regulation of Common Schools, etc., 98; making appropriations (various educational items), 129; (amendatory) for the support and better regulation of Common Schools, 132.

Local:

Authorizing certain investments of a fund bequeathed by Mrs. Eunice Buckingham for the purposes of Female Education, 42; to regulate the fur trade, etc., (fines for the use of schools), 140; for the relief of Johnathan D. Schultz, 255.

To regulate Common Schools in the Township of Portland, Erie County, 285; for the relief of creditors of the Granville Alexandrian Society, 311; for the relief of School District No. 10 in Sugar Creek township, Greene County, 334; for the relief of the township of Hocking, Fairfield County, 353; to divide the town of Hudson, Summit County, into two school districts, 368; authorizing the trustees of Cincinnati College to borrow money to erect college buildings, 376; authorizing the towns of Painesville and Norwalk to levy a tax for the benefit of Common Schools therein, 379; authorizing the City of Cincinnati to erect a house of correction, 393; for the relief of the Mount Pleasant Boarding School, 398; to attach certain territory to the City of Columbus for school purposes, 404; supplementary to an act increasing the number of trustees and visitors of Common Schools, Cincinnati, 413.

ACTS CONCERNING THE INCORPORATION OF EDUCATIONAL AND LITERARY
INSTITUTIONS

(Amendatory) Marietta College, 4; Tallmadge Academical Institute, Summit County, 12; Calvinistic Book Concern, 15; Bedford Seminary, Cuyahoga County, 16; College of Dental Surgery, Cincinnati, 32; Cincinnati Classical Academy, 39, 42; (amendatory) Granville Literary and Theological Institution, 54; Ohio Baptist Book and Tract Society, 56; The Young Men's Book Association, West Canaan, Madison County, 61; German Library Association, Cincinnati, 64; Trustees of the Columbus Academical and Collegiate Institute, 65; New Carlisle Social Library Company, Clark County, and the Library Association of Harlem, Carroll County, 68; Tallmadge Library Association, Summit County, 70; Aurora Academical Institute, Portage County, 75; Fort Meigs University, 80; Ohio Baptist Education Society, 86; Cooper Female Academy in Dayton, 87; Akron Institute, 89; New Orphans' Asylum of Colored Children of Cincinnati, 101; Rocky River Seminary, 121; Hunterian Society of the Medical Department of Western Reserve College, 130; (amendatory) the Summit College Medical Society, 141; Findlay Academical Institute, Hancock County, 203; Putnam Union Sunday School Depository, Muskingum County, 205; (amendatory) North Union School Association of Carroll County, 213; Vermillion Institute, 229; Miamisburg Library Association, 274; Cottage Hill Academy in Trumbull County, 289; Normal High School, Carroll County, 292; The Trustees of the Protestant University of the United States, 338; trustees of the Medical Institute of Cincinnati, 357; to incorporate certain literary societies, 361; Sec. 3. Newcomerstown Literary Society, Tuscarawas County; Sec. 4. Farmers and Mechanics Library Association, West Lodi, Seneca County; Sec. 7. Corwin Literary Institute, Springboro, Warren County; Sec. 8. Middletown Academy in Butler County; Sec. 9. German Catholic Library Association of Cincinnati; Sec. 10. Donnelsville Library Association, Clark County; Sec. 11. Union Society of Oberlin Collegiate Institute, Lorain County; Sec. 12. Trustees and subscribers of the School Fund Society, Ross County; Sec. 13. Hanover Social Library Association in Butler County; Sec. 14. Erie County Antiquarian Society; Sec. 15. Lower Sandusky Phrenological Mesmeric Institute, Sandusky County; Board of Directors of Wittenberg College, 375; London Academy, Madison County, 384; Linton Library Association in Washington County, 389; West Jefferson Academical Institute, Madison County, 409.

ACTS CONCERNING SELLING AND LEASING SCHOOL LANDS

Putnam County, 9; Seneca County, 12; Mercer County, 18; Putnam County, 22; Fairfield County and Licking County, 30; Athens and Meigs County, 38; Lucas County, 39; Lucas County, 41; Marion County, 48; Twelve Mile Square Reserve, 66; Williams County, 92; Sandusky County, 115; Washington County, 120; Allen County, 124; Sandusky County, 125; Sandusky County, 126; Richland County and Knox County, 128; Williams County, 140; Hamilton County, 143; Sandusky County, 146; Putnam County, 169; Lucas County, 170; Lucas County, 176; Perry, Morgan and Muskingum Counties, 205; Holmes County, 221; Stark County, 224; Fairfield and Licking Counties, 236; Williams County, 256; Athens County, 270; Holmes County, 325; Monroe County, 343; Meigs County, 344; Marion County, 357; Monroe County, 364; Gallia County, 367; Fairfield County, 372; Belmont County, 397; Crawford County, 407.

CITY AND TOWN ACTS CONCERNING SCHOOLS
Columbus, 57; Mt. Vernon, 150.

Resolutions concerning:

Ohio Historical and Philosophical Society, 432; a certain blind student, 432; Government grants for aid of instruction of the deaf and dumb and blind, 434; a certain blind student, 435; sending school laws to certain counties, 438; distributing court decisions to library institutions, 438; furnishing documents to the New York Historical Society, 441; trustees, Miami University, 442; copies of school laws to Summit County, 443; religious and moral instructor for the Ohio Penitentiary, 446; forwarding certain documents to Alexander Vattemare, Paris, France, 448; register of Virginia Military school lands, 450; reports from the Deaf and Dumb and Blind Asylums, 451; oculist for the Institution of the Blind, 451; admission of teachers into state asylums and the state library, 463; trustee, Ohio Institution for Blind, 464; trustees, Asylum for the Deaf and Dumb, 465.

VOLUME XLIV

General:

An act more effectually to prevent gambling (fines for the use of schools), 10; an act for the more effectual protection of enclosures, (fines for the use of schools) 76; an act in relation to religious, literary and other incorporated societies, 79; an act authorizing school districts to establish libraries for the use of Common Schools, 81; an act for levying taxes on all property in this state, etc., 85; an act to amend such acts in relation to the Asylums for the Deaf and Dumb and for the Blind, 111; (amendatory) for the support and better regulation of Common Schools, 114; an act making appropriations (various educational items), 130.

Local:

For the relief of School District 5, Eaton Township, Lorain County, and School District 5, Caesar's Creek Township, Greene County, 3; an act for the relief of John N. Ingalls and Wesley Johnson, Muskingum County, 29; authorizing the town of Putnam, Muskingum County, to divide School District No. 1, in said town, 33; authorizing the city council of Cleveland to levy an additional tax for Common School purposes, 55; (amendatory) an act dividing the town of Lancaster into school districts, 89; authorizing Findlay Township, Hancock County, to divide District No. 1, 108; authorizing the directors of School District No. 1, Napoleon Township, Henry County, to exchange certain lots, 121; relief of trustees, Saybrook township, Ashtabula County, 121; authorizing the president of Chillicothe Academy to convey certain property, 123; an act for the relief of the sureties of Hamilton Robb, 200; authorizing the trustees of the several townships in Mercer County to select a section of land for school purposes in lieu of Section 16, 226; for the relief of School District No. 4, in Bath Township, Greene County, 238; to enlarge school house, Delhi Township, Hamilton County, 244; an act for the relief of School District 14, Fairfield County, 268.

ACTS CONCERNING THE INCORPORATION OF EDUCATIONAL AND LITERARY INSTITUTIONS

Baldwin Institute, Middleburg, Cuyahoga County, 4; (amendatory) Vermillion Institute at Haysville, Ohio, 65; Loudonville Academy, Richland County, 107; Norwalk Institute, 122; (amendatory) Cincinnati College, 157; Madison

Education Society, Lake County, 161; Farmers' College of Hamilton County, 163; trustees of the Wesleyan Female College of Cincinnati, 171; the Liverpool Seminary, Columbiana County, 236.

ACTS CONCERNING THE SELLING AND LEASING OF SCHOOL LANDS

Crawford County, 11; Columbiana County, 13; Fairfield County, 25; Jefferson County, 35; Lucas County, 77; Gallia County, 78; Jefferson County, 80; Seneca County, 92; Connecticut Western Reserve School Land, 104; Seneca County, 124; Butler County, 126; Meigs County, 166; Monroe County, 244; Scioto County, 253.

TOWN AND CITY ACTS CONCERNING SCHOOLS

(Amendatory) City of Cincinnati, 7; an act for the better classification of Schools of Cincinnati and Dayton, and for other purposes, 91; (amendatory) City of Toledo, 208; an act to regulate Common Schools in Maumee City, in the County of Lucas, and Elyria, in the County of Lorain, 261.

Resolutions concerning:

Trustees, Charity School of Kendal, 293; copies of the school law for Washington County, 293; McIntire School Fund, 294; Reports of the Institution for the Blind, 295; reports for the Institution for the Deaf and Dumb Asylum, 296; printing report of the Deaf and Dumb Asylum, 296; the title to certain school lands, 298; copies of the school laws to Lorain County, 299; trustee, Miami University, 302; copies of the school law, 315; trustees, Ohio University, 317; trustees, Institution for the Deaf and Dumb, 324; trustees, Institution for the Blind, 325.

VOLUME XLV

General:

Amending the act to extend the time of payment to purchasers of school lands, etc., 21; repealing the act providing for the inspection of salt, etc., 22; amending the act for the support and better regulation of Common Schools, etc., 26; an act to provide for the appointment of county superintendents of Common Schools, and defining their duties in certain counties therein named, 32; an act regulating the sale of intoxicating liquors (fines for schools), 39; an act making appropriations (various educational items), 56; an act to amend the act for levying taxes on all property, etc., 60; an act to incorporate teachers' institutes, 67.

Local:

Authorizing the sale of certain lots in the town of Jefferson, Fairfield County, and the application of the proceeds to the erection of a school-house, 73; authorizing the president and trustees of Miami University to relinquish certain rents, 85; (amendatory) authorizing the city council of Cincinnati to erect a house of correction, 112; an act to prevent Intemperance in Medina, Huron and Erie Counties, 131; for the relief of School District No. 2, German Township, Harrison County, and School District No. 10, Washington Township, Clermont County, 139; an act to quiet the title of certain lands in Paulding County, 149; an act to enable the town of Bellville to convey a lot of land, 166; an act to provide for the funding of debts for the Ohio University, 176.

ACTS CONCERNING THE INCORPORATION OF EDUCATIONAL AND LITERARY
INSTITUTIONS

(Amendatory) Willoughby University of Lake Erie, 7; authorizing the establishment of professorships in the Farmers' College, Hamilton County, 67; (amendatory) Baldwin Institute, 89; Mansfield Academical Institute, and amending the act to incorporate the Ohio Mechanics' Institute, 99; Marietta Female College, 140.

ACTS CONCERNING SELLING AND LEASING SCHOOL LANDS

Wyandot County, 4; Belmont County, 5; Belmont County, 8; Stark County, 10; Washington County, 14; Carroll County, 53; Gallia County, 54; Fairfield County, 54; Van Wert County, 66; Williams County, 71; Richland County, 103; Seneca and Wyandot Counties, 104; Greene County, 116; Meigs County, 121; Hamilton County, 158; Seneca County, 167; Perry County, 173; Morgan County, 174; Delaware County, 174; Hamilton County, 176; Stark County, 191; Defiance County, 192.

CITY AND TOWN ACTS CONCERNING SCHOOLS

An act for the support and better regulation of Common Schools in School District No. 1 in Ravenna, 121; (amendatory) City of Cleveland, Section 1, 135; Town of Marion, Marion County, Section 9, 161. For the support and better regulation of Common Schools in the town of Akron, 187; authorizing the city council of Cincinnati to levy taxes for school purposes, 193.

Resolutions concerning:

Reports of the Deaf and Dumb Asylum, 196; Institution for the Blind, 199; the collection of natural curiosities for the State Library, 200; forwarding school laws to Sandusky County, 201; trustees Charity School of Kendall, 204; report of the Superintendent of Common Schools, 207; furnishing the Superintendents of the Asylums with copies of the revised laws, 208; trustees, Medical College of Ohio, 208; trustee, Ohio University, 212; trustee, Deaf and Dumb Asylum, and Blind Asylum, 223; employment of James Russell by Smithsonian Institute, 224.

VOLUME XLVI

General:

An act to secure the returns of the statistics of Common Schools, 28; an act amending the act granting licenses to peddlers, etc. (fines for Common Schools), 36; an act to enable the inhabitants of the Connecticut Reserve to give their consent to the sale of their school lands, 38; an act to provide for extending the provisions of an act entitled "an act for the support and better regulation of Common Schools in the town of Akron," and the amendatory acts thereto, to the cities and incorporated towns of this state, 48; an act to amend the 18th Section of the School Law of March 7, 1838, 51; an act further to amend the act for levying taxes, 69; an act to provide for the education of black and mulatto persons and to amend the act entitled, "an act for the support and better regulation of Common Schools, etc.," 81; an act to amend the act for the support and better regulation of Common Schools, etc., 83; an act to amend the act to encourage teachers' institutes and to extend the provisions of the acts providing for teachers' institutes and county superintendents in the several counties of this state, 86; an act making appropriations (various educational items), 103.

Local:

An act to levy a tax on the Town of Lancaster, 5; authorizing the president and town council of Portsmouth to levy a tax for school and other purposes, 37; an act to provide for the erection of school-houses in Springfield, Clark County, 85; an act for the relief of School District No. 1, Pickaway County and District No. 4, Ashland County, 139; authorizing the directors of School District No. 3, Moorefield Township, Harrison County, to sell a school lot, 150; authorizing the directors of School District No. 6, Jefferson Township, Madison County, to sell a certain school lot, 157; authorizing the directors of School District No. 2, Gratis Township, Preble County, to sell a school lot, 176; authorizing the directors of School District No. 3, Montgomery Township, Ashland County, to sell the school-house and lot, 190; an act to incorporate School District No. 1 in Perry Township, Stark County, 223; amending an act to dispose of two escheated lots in Mansfield, Richland County, 232; an act for the support and better regulation of Common Schools in the Lebanon District in Warren County, 237; to regulate the sale of intoxicating liquors in the town of Cuyahoga Falls, 269.

ACTS CONCERNING THE INCORPORATION OF EDUCATIONAL AND LITERARY SOCIETIES

Changing the name of the Richmond Classical Institute of Jefferson County, 7; the R. M. Bartlett's Commercial College, Cincinnati, 12; Board of Directors of Muhlenberg College in Jefferson, Harrison County, 19; the Gundry-Bacon Cincinnati Mercantile College, 21; Starling Medical College in Columbus, 31; (amendatory) Cincinnati Classical Academy, 46; the Medical and Surgical Society of the County of Ashland, 76; (amendatory) Miami University, 88; (amendatory) to enable the Knoxville School Company to close its concerns, 107; Xenia Academy, 114; Richland Academic Institute, Logan County, 126; The Felicity Female Seminary, Clermont County, 135; Cleveland Library Association, 149; Medina Academy, 188; Newton College, Hamilton County, 211; Edinburgh College, 220; The Western Art Union, 228; The State Medical Society of Ohio, 231.

ACTS CONCERNING THE SALE AND LEASING OF SCHOOL LANDS

Greene County and Pike County, 8; Wyandot County, 24; Wyandot County, 27; Muskingum County, 33; Scioto County, 35; Meigs County, 37; Allen County, 38; Paulding County, 48; Mercer County, 49; Montgomery County, 80; Williams County, 85; Richland County, 91; Montgomery County, 91; Seneca County, 92; Crawford and Wyandot County, 92; Sandusky County, 102; Muskingum County, 134; Morgan County, 137; Stark County, 139; Shelby County, 140; Montgomery County, 141; Defiance County, 144; Ashland County, 145; Ottawa County, 162; Carroll County, 188; Paulding County, 207; Lucas County, 219; Hamilton County, 241; Paulding County, 265; Mercer County, 274.

CITY AND TOWN ACTS CONCERNING SCHOOLS

(Amendatory) An act for the support and better regulation of Common Schools in the town of Akron, 40; (repealing) an act for the support and better regulation of Common Schools in School District No. 1, Ravenna, 51; (amenda-

tory) an act for the support and better regulation of Common Schools in Zanesville, 54; for the better regulation and support of schools in the City of Cleveland,
150; for the support and better regulation of Common Schools in the town of
Lithopolis, Fairfield County, 185; for the support and better regulation of Common Schools in Lancaster, 199; (amendatory) an act for the support and better
regulation of Common Schools in the City of Columbus, 259.

Resolutions concerning:
    Virginia Military District School Lands, 282; report on medical societies
and colleges, 286; report of the Superintendent of Schools, 286; trustees, Ohio
University, 288; trustees, Miami University, 291; directing the printing of the
Akron Law for Common Schools with the General Laws, 295; report of the
Institution for the Deaf and Dumb, 296; correcting an error in the school funds
in Troy and Sullivan Townships, Ashland County, 300; appointing a director of
the Blind Asylum, 303; trustees, Deaf and Dumb Asylum, 307; furnishing Wyandot County with School Laws, 309; asking the Governor to examine and report
upon the Deaf and Dumb.and Blind Asylums, 317.

VOLUME XLVII

General:
    An act to authorize the establishment of separate schools for the education
of colored children, and for other purposes, 17; amending an act to incorporate
teachers' institutes, 19; an act for the better regulation of the public schools in
cities, towns, etc., 22; (amendatory) an act for the support, etc., of Common
Schools, 39; (amendatory) an act for the support, etc., of Common Schools, 43;
(amendatory) an act for the support and better regulation of Common Schools in
the Town of Akron, 45; an act making appropriations (various educational items)
45; (amendatory) an act for the support, etc., of Common Schools, 52.

Local:
    An act in relation to taxes, schools and sewers in the City of Toledo, 205;
an act to regulate a certain school district in Orwell Township, Ashtabula County,
224; an act for the support and better regulation of Common Schools in
District No. 4, Washington Township, Preble County, 224; to organize School
District No. 7, Liberty Township, Clinton County, 229; (amendatory) for the
support and better regulation of Common Schools in Columbus, 230; to divide the
town of St. Clairsville, Belmont County, into two school districts, 240; granting
to the trustees, etc., of Greenfield Seminary authority to confer degrees and testi-
monials, 240; authorizing the directors of School District No. 13, Jefferson Township, Fayette County, to sell a school lot, 246; authorizing the trustees of Clay Township, Knox County, to redistrict said township, 250; authorizing the county
Auditor of Holmes County to levy an additional tax on a school district for school-
house purposes, 252; amending an act to repeal the act for the support, etc., of
Common Schools in School District No. 1, Ravenna Township, 253; (repealing)
the provisions of the Akron Act for the town of New Lisbon, Columbiana County,
253; to amend the charter of the City of Ohio, 278; an act for the relief of John D.
Burrill, 342.

VOLUME XLVIII

of Springfield and Beaver," Mahoning County, 642; to authorize the directors of School District No. 4, Delhi Township, Hamilton County, to appropriate certain funds for building purposes, 643; extending the provisions of the act for the better regulation of public schools in cities, towns, etc., to Union School District No. 7, Springfield and Suffield Townships, Summit and Portage Counties, 648; an act amending and reviving the act to create permanently the office of Treasurer, Township No. 1, Range 1, Whitewater Township, Hamilton County, 663; authorizing the trustees of Monroe Township, Knox County, to redistrict said township, 668; an act to amend the act to create permanently the office of Treasurer, Township No. 1, Range 1, Hamilton County, and to give additional powers to the trustees of School Section No. 16, Greene Township, Hamilton County, 670.

ACTS CONCERNING THE INCORPORATION OF EDUCATIONAL AND LITERARY INSTITUTIONS

Elliott Female Seminary of Monroe County, 614; Vinton High School, Gallia County, 617; Miller Academy, Washington, Guernsey County, 618; Capital University, 619; Cambridge College, 621; Geneva Hall, Winfield, Logan County, 622; Urbana University, 624; (amendatory) the Charity School of Kendal, 625; Defiance Female Seminary, Defiance County, 625; Western Reserve Eclectic Institute, Portage County, 627; Western College of Homeopathic Medicine, 629; Tiffin Academy, Seneca County, 630; (amendatory) Oberlin Collegiate Institute, 632; Young Men's Catholic Association of Cincinnati, 632; Cincinnati College of Pharmacy, 634; Western Liberal Institute, 635; Ripley Library Association, 636; Thompson Library Association, 636; Xenia Female Academy, 637; Hartford High School, 638; Soeurs de Notre Dame Female Educational Institute of Chillicothe, Ross County, 639; Mt. Pleasant Philomathean Society, Kingston, Ross County, 640; Warren Library Association, 640.

ACTS CONCERNING THE SALE AND LEASING OF SCHOOL LANDS

Lucas County, 643; Jefferson County, 644; Hardin County, 644; Columbiana County, 644; Allen County, 645; Fairfield County, 646; Meigs County, 646; Ottawa County, 647; Belmont County, 648; Hardin County, 649; Lucas County, 649; Jefferson County, 650; Ohio Company's Purchase, 650; Lawrence County, 653; Defiance County, 653; Seneca County, 653; Lucas County, 654; Lawrence County, 654; Hancock County, 655; Paulding County, 655; Athens County, 656; Williams County, 656; Belmont County, 657; Lucas County, 657; Gallia County, 658; Harrison County, 658; Monroe County, 659; Gallia County, 659; Williams County, 659; Gallia County, 660; Putnam County, 661; Mercer County, 661; Town of Athens, 664; Crawford County, 665; Lawrence County, 665; Shelby County, 666; Darke County, 666; Hardin County, 666; Tuscarawas County, 668; Richland and Huron Counties, 669; Jefferson County, 669; Shelby County, 669; Sandusky County, 676.

CITY AND TOWN ACTS CONCERNING SCHOOLS

(Amendatory) An act to incorporate the town of Fulton (Sections 10 and 11), 373; an act to incorporate the town of Fremont, Sandusky County (Section 5), 404; an act to incorporate the city of Piqua (Sections 25 to 30), 421; an act to incorporate the City of Springfield (Sections 29 to 32), 446; an act to incorporate the City of Zanesville, Muskingum County (Sections 26 to 38), 473; (amendatory) for the support and better regulation of Common Schools in the town of Lancaster, 647; (repealing) the provisions of the act for the better regulation of schools in cities, towns, etc., for the town of Hanover, Columbiana County, 648; amending an act for the support and better regulation of Common Schools in the town of Akron, 650; authorizing the citizens of Wooster to vote for or against adopting the Akron Act, 651; exempting the town of Mt. Vernon from the provisions of the Akron School Law, 662; authorizing the appointment of a Superintendent of Common Schools in the City of Cincinnati, and for other purposes, 662; extending the powers of the Board of Education of the town of Putnam, Muskingum County, 667; authorizing the Board of Education in the town of Cambridge, Guernsey County, to levy a school building tax, 695.

Resolutions concerning:

Certain school lands in Lucas and Williams Counties, 728; appointing a committee to examine and report on the school system of this state, 728; trustees, Charity School of Kendal, 729; trustees, Miami University, 729; trustees, Neville Institute, 730; trustees, Medical College of Ohio, 730; two deaf and dumb students, 742; a certain blind student, 742; forwarding school laws to Greene County, 743; forwarding school laws to Ashland County, 746.

BIBLIOGRAPHY

SOURCES

Acts of the State of Ohio, First Session of the General Assembly, Vol. I, Chillicothe, printed by N. Willis, printer to the state, 1803.

Acts of the State of Ohio, Second Session, Vol. II, Chillicothe, printed by N. Willis, printer to the state, 1804.

Acts of the State of Ohio, passed and revised, Vol. III, Chillicothe, printed by N. Willis, printer to the state, 1805.

Acts of the State of Ohio, Vol. IV, Chillicothe, T. G. Bradford and Joseph S. Collins & Company, printers for the state.

Acts passed at the First Session of the Fifth General Assembly of the State of Ohio, Vol. V, Chillicothe, Joseph S. Collins & Co., printer to the state of Ohio, 1807.

Acts of the Sixth General Assembly of the State of Ohio, Vol. VI, Chillicothe, R. D. Richardson, printer to the state of Ohio, 1808.

Acts passed at the First Session of the Seventh General Assembly, Vol. VII. Chillicothe, J. S. Collins, 1809.

Acts passed at the First Session of the Eighth General Assembly, Vol. VIII, Chillicothe, J. S. Collins & Company, 1810.

Acts passed at the First Session of the Ninth General Assembly, Vol. IX, Zanesville, White, Sawyer and Chambers, 1811.

Acts passed at the First Session of the Tenth General Assembly, Vol. X, Zanesville, Sawyer and Chambers, 1812.

Acts passed at the First Session of the Eleventh General Assembly, Vol. XI, Chillicothe, Nashee and Denny, 1812.

Acts passed at the First Session of the Twelfth General Assembly, Vol. XII, Chillicothe, John Bailhache, 1814.

Acts passed at the First Session of the Thirteenth General Assembly, Vol. XIII, Chillicothe, Nashee and Denny, 1814.

Acts passed at the First Session of the Fourteenth General Assembly, Vol. XIV, printed by Nashee and Denny for Bailhache, 1816.

Acts passed at the First Session of the Fifteenth General Assembly, Vol. XV, Columbus, P. H. Olmsted, 1817.

Acts passed at the First Session of the Sixteenth General Assembly, Vol. XVI, Columbus, P. H. Olmsted, state printer, 1818.

Acts passed at the First Session of the Seventeenth General Assembly, Vol. XVII, Chillicothe, George Nashee, 1819.

Acts of a general nature enacted, revised and ordered to be reprinted at the First Session of the Eighteenth General Assembly, Vol. XVIII, Columbus, P. H. Olmsted, 1820.

Acts of a local nature passed by the First Session of the Eighteenth General Assembly, Vol. XVIII, Columbus, P. H. Olmsted, 1820.

Acts passed at the First Session of the Nineteenth General Assembly, Vol. XIX, Columbus, David Smith, 1821.

Acts of a general nature passed at the First Session of the Twentieth General Assembly, Vol. XX, P. H. Olmsted, 1822.

Acts of a local nature passed at the First Session of the Twentieth General Assembly, Vol. XX, P. H. Olmsted, 1822.

Acts passed at the Second Session of the Twentieth General Assembly, Columbus, P. H. Olmsted, 1822.

Acts of a general nature passed at the Twenty-first General Assembly, Vol. XXI, P. H. Olmsted, 1823.

Acts of a local nature passed at the Twenty-first General Assembly, Vol. XXI, P. H. Olmsted, 1823.

Acts of a general nature enacted, revised and ordered to be reprinted at the First Session of the Twenty-second General Assembly, Vol. XXII, Columbus, P. H. Olmsted, 1824.

Acts of a local nature passed at the First Session of the Twenty-second General Assembly, Vol. XXII, Columbus, P. H. Olmsted, 1824.

Acts of a general nature passed at the First Session of the Twenty-third General Assembly, Vol. XXIII, Columbus, P. H. Olmsted, 1825.

Acts of a local nature passed at the First Session of the Twenty-third General Assembly, Vol. XXIII, Columbus, P. H. Olmsted, 1825.

Acts of a general nature passed at the Twenty-fourth General Assembly, Vol. XXIV, Columbus, George Nashee, state printer, 1826.

Acts of a local nature passed at the Twenty-fourth General Assembly, Vol. XXIV, Columbus, George Nashee, state printer, 1826.

Acts of a general nature passed at the Twenty-fifth General Assembly, Vol. XXV, Columbus, George Nashee, state printer, 1827.

Acts of a local nature passed at the Twenty-fifth General Assembly, Vol. XXV, Columbus, George Nashee, state printer, 1827.

Acts of a general nature passed at the Twenty-sixth General Assembly, Vol. XXVI, Columbus, P. H. Olmsted, state printer, 1828.

Acts of a local nature passed at the Twenty-sixth General Assembly, Vol. XXVI, Columbus, P. H. Olmsted, state printer, 1828.

Acts of a general nature passed at the Twenty-seventh General Assembly, Vol. XXVII, Columbus, Olmsted, Bailhache and Cameron, state printers, 1829.

Acts of a local nature passed at the Twenty-seventh General Assembly, Vol. XXVII, Columbus, Olmsted, Bailhache and Cameron, state printers, 1829.

Acts of a general nature passed at the Twenty-eighth General Assembly, Vol. XXVIII, Columbus, Olmsted and Bailhache, 1830.

Acts of a local nature passed at the Twenty-eighth General Assembly, Vol.   ·
XXVIII, Columbus, Olmsted and Bailhache, 1830.

Acts of a general nature enacted, revised and ordered to be reprinted, passed by the First Session of the Twenty-ninth General Assembly, Vol. XXIX, Columbus, Olmsted and Bailhache, 1831.

Acts of a local nature passed by the First Session of the Twenty-ninth General Assembly, Vol. XXIX, Columbus, Olmsted and Bailhache, 1831.

Acts of a general nature passed at the First Session of the Thirtieth General Assembly, Vol. XXX, Columbus, David Smith, state printer, 1832.

Acts of a local nature passed at the First Session of the Thirtieth General Assembly, Vol. XXX, Columbus, David Smith, state printer, 1832.

Acts of a general nature passed at the Second Session of the Thirtieth General Assembly, Columbus, David Smith, state printer, 1832.

Acts of a local nature passed at the Second Session of the Thirtieth General Assembly, Columbus, David Smith, state printer, 1832.

Acts of a general nature passed by the Thirty-first General Assembly, Vol. XXXI, Columbus, David Smith, state printer, 1833.

Acts of a local nature passed by the Thirty-first General Assembly, Vol. XXXI, Columbus, David Smith, state printer, 1833.

Acts of a general nature passed by the Thirty-second General Assembly, Vol. XXXII, Columbus, David Smith, state printer, 1834.

Acts of a local nature passed by the Thirty-second General Assembly, Vol. XXXII, Columbus, David Smith, state printer, 1834.

Acts of a general nature, passed by the Thirty-third General Assembly of the State of Ohio, Vol. XXXIII, Columbus, James B. Gardiner, printer to the state, 1835.

Acts of a local nature passed by the Thirty-third General Assembly, Vol. XXXIII, Columbus, James B. Gardiner, printer to the state, 1835.

Acts passed at the Second Session of the Thirty-third General Assembly, Vol. XXXIII, Columbus, J. B. Gardiner, 1835.

Acts of a general nature passed at the First Session of the Thirty-fourth General Assembly, Vol. XXXIV, James B. Gardiner, printer to the state, 1836.

Acts of a local nature passed at the First Session of the Thirty-fourth General Assembly, Vol. XXXIV, James B. Gardiner, printer to the state, 1836.

Acts of a general nature passed at the First Session of the Thirty-fifth General Assembly, Vol. XXXV, S. R. Dolbee, printer to the state, 1837.

Acts of a local nature passed by the First Session of the Thirty-fifth General Assembly, Vol. XXXV, James B. Gardiner, printer to the state, 1837.

Acts of a general nature passed by the Thirty-sixth General Assembly, Vol. XXXVI, Samuel Medary, printer to the state, 1838.

Acts of a local nature passed by the Thirty-sixth General Assembly, Vol. XXXVI, Samuel Medary, printer to the state, 1838.

Acts of a general nature passed by the Thirty-seventh General Assembly, Vol. XXXVII, Samuel Medary, printer to the state, 1839.

Acts of a local nature passed by the Thirty-seventh General Assembly, Vol. XXXVII, Samuel Medary, printer to the state, 1839.

Acts of a general nature passed by the Thirty-eighth General Assembly, Vol. XXXVIII, Samuel Medary, printer to the state, 1840.

Acts of a local nature passed by the Thirty-eighth General Assembly, Vol. XXXVIII, Samuel Medary, printer to the state, 1840.

Acts of a general nature passed by the Thirty-ninth General Assembly, Vol. XXXIX, Samuel Medary, printer to the state, 1841.

Acts of a local nature passed by the Thirty-ninth General Assembly, Vol. XXXIX, Samuel Medary, printer to the state, 1841.

Acts of a general nature passed by the Fortieth General Assembly, Vol. XL, Samuel Medary, state printer, 1842.

Acts of a local nature passed by the Fortieth General Assembly, Vol. XL, Samuel Medary, state printer, 1842.

Acts of a local nature passed at the Adjourned Session of the Fortieth General Assembly, Vol. XL, Samuel Medary, state printer, 1842.

Acts of a general nature passed by the Forty-first General Assembly, Vol. XLI, Columbus, Samuel Medary, 1843.

Acts of a local nature passed by the Forty-first General Assembly, Vol. XLI, Columbus, Samuel Medary, 1843.

Acts of a general nature passed by the Forty-second General Assembly, Vol. XLII, Columbus, Samuel Medary, 1844.

Acts of a local nature passed by the Forty-second General Assembly, Vol. XLII, Columbus, Samuel Medary, 1844.

Acts of a general nature passed by the Forty-third General Assembly, Vol. XLIII, Columbus, Samuel Medary, 1845.

Acts of a local nature passed by the Forty-third General Assembly, Vol. XLIII, Columbus, Samuel Medary, 1845.

Acts of a general nature passed by the Forty-fourth General Assembly, Vol. XLIV, C. Scott & Company, printers, Columbus, 1846.

Acts of a local nature passed by the Forty-fourth General Assembly, Vol. XLIV, C. Scott & Company, printers, Columbus, 1846.

Acts of a general nature passed by the Forty-fifth General Assembly, Vol. XLV, Columbus, C. Scott's Steam Press, 1847.

Acts of a local nature passed by the Forty-fifth General Assembly, Columbus, Vol. XLV, C. Scott's Steam Press, 1847.

Acts of a general nature passed by the Forty-sixth General Assembly, Columbus, Vol. XLVI, Chas. Scott's Steam Press, 1848.

Acts of a local nature passed by the Forty-sixth General Assembly, Columbus, Vol. XLVI, Chas. Scott's Steam Press, 1848.

Acts of a general nature passed by the Forty-seventh General Assembly, Columbus, Vol. XLVII, Chas. Scott, state printer, 1849.

Acts of a local nature passed by the Forty-seventh General Assembly, Vol. XLVII, Columbus, Chas. Scott, state printer, 1849.

Acts of a general nature passed by the Forty-eighth General Assembly, Vol. XLVIII, Columbus, Scott and Bascom, 1850.

Acts of a local nature passed by the Forty-eighth General Assembly, Vol. XLVIII, Columbus, Scott and Bascom, 1850.

Third Annual Report of the Superintendent of the Common Schools, made to the Thirty-eighth General Assembly of the State of Ohio, by Samuel Lewis, Columbus, Samuel Medary, printer to the state, 1839.

Ohio Documents, 35th General Assembly, J. B. Gardiner, state printer, Columbus, 1836.

Ohio Documents, 36th General Assembly, Samuel Medary, state printer, Columbus, 1837.

Ohio Documents, 37th General Assembly, Samuel Medary, state printer, Columbus, 1838.

Ohio Documents, 38th General Assembly, Samuel Medary, state printer, Columbus, 1840.

United States Census Reports.

United States Statutes at Large.

Statistical Abstract of United States, 1911.

Annual Report of the Secretary of State to the Governor of the State of Ohio for the Year 1885. Columbus, The Westbote Company, state printers, 1885.

A Compilation of Laws, Treaties and Ordinances Which Relate to Lands in the State of Ohio, George Nashee, Columbus, 1825.

Journals of the American Congress. Reprint, Way and Gideon, Washington, 1823, 4 vols.

SECONDARY SOURCES

Atwater, Caleb. *A History of the State of Ohio, Natural and Civil.* Cincinnati: Glezen & Shepherd, 1838.

Blackmar, Frank Wilson. *The History of Federal and State Aid to Higher Education in the United States.* Washington: Government Printing Office, 1890.

Brownell, F. C. *Barnard's American Journal of Education*, Vol. V. Hartford, Conn., 1858.

Burns, J. J. *Educational History of Ohio.* Columbus, 1905.

Chaddock, Robert E. *Ohio Before 1850. A Study of the Early Influence of Pennsylvania and Southern Populations in Ohio.* Columbia University, New York, 1908.

Cist, Charles. *Cincinnati in 1841—Its Early Annals and Future Prospects.* Cincinnati, 1841.

Cutler, Julia Perkins. *Life and Times of Ephraim Cutler.* Cincinnati: Robert Clarke & Co., 1890.

Donaldson, T. *The Public Domain.* Washington: Government Printing Office, 1881.

Graham, A. A. "The Land and Township System of Ohio," *Annual Report of the Secretary of State to the Governor of the State of Ohio for the Year 1885*, pp. 22–29.

Hinsdale, Ann. "History of the Ohio School System," *Report of the Commissioner of Education.* Washington, 1901, Vol. I.

Hinsdale, B. A. "Documents Illustrative of American Educational History," *Report of the Commissioner of Education.* Washington, 1892–93, Vol. II, 1225–1414.

Hinsdale, B. A. *The Old Northwest*, Vols. I, II. New York: Townsend Mac Coun, 1891.

Howe. *Howe's Historical Collections of Ohio.* Cincinnati: C. J. Krehbiel & Co., 1907.

Jernegan, Marcus W. "The Beginnings of Public Education in New England," *School Review*, XXIII. Chicago, 1915.

King, Rufus. *Ohio, First Fruits of the Ordinance of 1787.* American Commonwealth Series. Boston and New York, 1888.

Knight, G. W. "History and Management of Land Grants for Education in the

Northwest Territory," *Papers of the American Historical Association*, 1884, Vol. I, 1–175.

Lewis, William G. W. *Biography of Samuel Lewis*. Cincinnati: Methodist Book Concern, 1857.

Martin, *The Evolution of the Massachusetts School System: A Historical Sketch*. New York: D. Appleton & Co., 1902.

Orth, Samuel P. *The Centralization of Administration in Ohio*. Columbia Studies in History, Economics and Public Law, Vol. XVI, No. 3.   New York, 1903.

Randall and Ryan. *History of Ohio*. New York: Century History Co., 1912.

Rice, V. M. *Special Report on the Present State of Education in the United States*, etc.   Washington, 1867.

Ryan, Daniel J. *A History of Ohio*. Columbus, 1888.

Slocum, Charles E. *The Ohio Country*, etc., 1783–1815.   New York: G. P. Putnam's Sons, 1910.

Swift, Fletcher Harper. *A History of Public Permanent Common School Funds in the United States, 1795–1905*.   New York: Henry H. Holt & Co., 1911.

Taylor, James B. *A Manual of the Ohio School System*. Cincinnati: H. W. Derby, 1857.

Venable, W. H. *Beginnings of Literary Culture in the Ohio Valley, Historical and Biographical Sketches*.   Cincinnati: Robert Clarke & Co., 1891.

Whittlesey, Charles. *Ohio Surveys*. Western Reserve Historical Society Tracts, Vol. II, Tracts 37–72.   Tract 59.   Cleveland, 1888.

Whittlesey, Charles. *Surveys of the Public Land in Ohio*. *Ibid*.   Tract 61.

Historical Sketches of the Ohio Educational Institutions and also of Benevolent and Reformatory Institutions of Ohio, 1876.   (Centennial Volume.)

Historical Sketches of Public Schools in Cities, Villages, and Townships of the State of Ohio, 1876.   (Centennial Volume.)

The Freeman's Almanack, "Maxims and Advice of Solomon Thrifty."   Cincinnati: Oliver Farnsworth & Co., 1824.

The Western Academician and Journal of Education and Science. Edited by John W. Pickett.   Cincinnati: James R. Allbach, 1837–38.

Transactions of the Western Literary Institute and College of Professional Teachers, Vols. IV, V, VI, VII, VIII.   Cincinnati, 1835–36–37–38–39.

County histories of Ohio.

INDEX

A

Academical Institution of Richfield, 79, 133.
Academic Pioneer, 107.
Academy of Alma, 79, 130.
Academy of Perry County, 79, 130.
Academy of Sylvania, 79, 134.
Adams, 1.
Addison Library Association, 172.
Adelphic Society of Western Reserve College, 177.
Agricultural Schools, 93.
Airington Lyceum, 175.
Akron, 30, 115, 170, schools of, 50–53.
Akron Act, 16, 46, 121, 124, 125.
Akron High School, 81, 136.
Akron Institute, 82, 141.
Akron Lyceum and Library Association Company, 170.
Alexander, John E., 142.
Alexandria Literary Society, 176.
Alpha Kappa Society of Marietta College, 177.
Allan, Nehemiah, 153.
American Lyceum of Education, 108, 166.
American Revolution, 59.
American Western University, 87, 88, 146. See also Ohio University.
Ames, 110.
Anderson, Joseph, 130.
Andover, 170.
Andrews, Ebenezer, 131.
Andrews, John, 139.
Antrim, 85, 135.
Apprentices, 165.
Armstrong, Harrison, 141.
Asbury Seminary, 81, 137.
Ashland Academy, 81, 137.
Ashland County, 162.
Ashtabula Academy, 79, 131.

Ashtabula County, 131, 133, 166, 167, 169, 170, 171, 172, 173, 175.
Ashtabula Institution of Science and Industry, 79, 85, 131.
Ashtabula Social Library Association, 169.
Associated Reform Synod of the West, 154.
Athenaeums, 111–112, 174-176.
Athenian Library Society, 172.
Athenian Literary Society of Ohio University, 177.
Athens, 88, 146, 151, 169.
Athens County, 169.
Athens Female Academy, 82, 139.
Athens Library Society, 169.
Atwater, Caleb, 7, 8, 9, 66–67, 111.
Atwood, Jonathan, 152.
Auglaize Seminary, 81, 138.
Aurora, 170.
Aurora Academical Institute, 82, 141.
Austinburg Social Library Association, 169.

B

Badger Library Society, 173.
Baker, Timothy, 130.
Baldwin Institute, 82, 141-142.
Baptist Church, 84, 154.
Baptist Literary and Collegiate Institute of Huron County, 96, 154.
Barber, Josiah, 8, 9.
Barger, Jacob, 159.
Barlow Library Society, 168.
Barnard, Henry D., 26.
Barnesville Male Academy, 81, 138.
Bartley, Mordecai, 109, 142.
Bartholomew, Moses, 158.
Bascom Seminary of Waynesburg, 82, 138.
Batavia Mechanics' Institute, 176.

231

Calvinistic denomination, 133.
Cambridge Academy, 81, 136.
Cambridge College, 97, 159.
Campbell, Alexander, 149.
Canaan Union Academy, 82, 139.
Canada thistles, 123.
Canal Dover Lyceum, 175.
Canal Fund, 90, 148, 175.
Canton, 12, 131, 144; population of, 45.
Canton Academy, 79, 131.
Canton Male Seminary, 82, 139.
Capitol Library Society, 169.
Capital University, 87, 97, 159
Carey, John, 140.
Carlisle, 173.
Carpenter, E. G., 139.
Carr, Henry, 133.
Carroll County, 135, 141, 144, 173.
Cass, 173.
Catholic Church, 84.
Catholics, 105.
Central College of Ohio, 97, 154–155.
Chagrin Falls, 137, 144, 173.
Chagrin Falls Mechanics' Library Association, 173.
Chalfert, Robert, 142.
Champeon Library Association, 173.
Champaign County, 172.
Charity School of Kendal, 105, 125.
Chase, Philander, 92, 150.
Chase, Salmon P., 175.
Cheney, Charles, 157.
Chester, 146.
Chester Academy, 81, 136.
Chester Library Association, 168.
Childs, Jonas, 139.
Chillicothe, 38, 46, 78, 143.
Chillicothe Academy, 78, 129.
Chillicothe Female Seminary, 79, 132.
Chillicothe Lyceum and Mechanics' Institute, 173.
Christmas, William, 131.
Cincinnati, 3, 10, 11, 45, 46, 47, 53, 66, 94, 95, 105, 106, 112, 113, 115, 123, 124, 131, 139, 144, 148, 149, 151, 155, 156, 157, 160, 161, 162, 165,

166, 169, 171, 173, 174, 178; schools of, 47–48; population of, 45.
Cincinnati Academy of Fine Arts, 112, 178.
Cincinnati Astronomical Society, 113, 178.
Cincinnati Classical Academy, 82, 141. See also St. John's College.
Cincinnati College, 96, 150, 163.
Cincinnati College of Pharmacy, 162.
Cincinnati Lancaster Academy, 78, 129.
Cincinnati Law Library, 170.
Cincinnati Literary Society, 175.
Cincinnati Lyceum, 175.
Cincinnati Medical Academy, 95, 161.
Cincinnati Medical Institute, 162.
Cincinnati New Jerusalem Church School Association, 83, 145.
Cincinnati Orphan Asylum, 165.
Cincinnati Philosophical Library Association, 173.
Cincinnati plan, 48, 49.
Cincinnati University, 87, 96, 149.
Cincinnati, Woodward High School of. See Woodward High School.
City of Ohio, Schools of, 48.
City schools, Laws concerning, 123, 125.
Circleville Academy, 79, 130.
Circleville Athenaeum, 175.
Circleville Female Seminary, 79, 133.
Circulating Library Company of Cincinnati, 166, 167.
Clark County, 132, 142, 155, 173, 174.
Clarksfield Library Society, 169.
Clermont County, 125, 142, 143, 169.
Cleveland, 3, 12, 45, 46, 48, 105, 113, 115, 124, 151; population of, 45; schools of, 48.
Cleveland Academy of Natural Sciences, 113, 178.
Cleveland Female Orphan Asylum, 165.
Cleveland Female Seminary, 81, 136.
Cleveland Library Company, 170, 174.
Cleveland Lyceum, 175.

Cleves, 134.

Cleves Independent School, 81, 134.

Cochran, Robert, 140, 141.

Cock fighting, 122.

College fraternities, 177.

College of Alma, 96, 151. See also Franklin College.

College of Dental Surgery, 162.

College of Ripley, 92, 96, 151, 152.

College of Teachers, 71.

College societies, 112, 177.

College townships, 88, 91.

Collins, Rev. John, 8, 9.

Colored children, orphan asylums for, 165; schools for, 44–45, 121.

Columbia Library Society, 167.

Columbian Association of Cincinnati, 178.

Columbiana County, 135, 139, 142, 167.

Columbus, 12, 26, 45, 46, 49, 100, 102, 103, 105, 111, 124, 142, 153, 162, 163, 164, 169; population of, 45, 46; schools of, 49.

Columbus Academical and Collegiate Institute, 82, 141.

Columbus Art Union, 113, 178.

Columbus Female Academy, 79, 131.

Columbus Female Benevolent Society, 165.

Columbus Literary and Scientific Institute, 175.

Columbus Literary Lyceum, 176.

Columbus Presbytery, 144; trustees of, 83.

Commercial Hospital and Lunatic Asylum, 160.

Committee on Corporations, 174.

Common Council, Duties of, 51.

Common School Fund, 157.

Congress, 60, 61, 67, 68, 70, 91, 92, 100, 101, 104, 148, 150, 163, 164.

Congress Lands, 9, 54, 58, 59.

Conneaut Academy, 79, 133.

Conneaut Lyceum, 175.

Connecticut, 60.

Connecticut Western Reserve, 9, 60, 126, 127. See also Western Reserve.

Converse, J. P., 138.

Coon-skin Library, 110.

Cooper Female Academy, 82, 141.

Corwin, Thomas, 140.

Corwin Literary Institute, 176.

Coshocton County, 140, 170, 174.

Cottage Hill Academy, 82, 141.

County auditor, the county superintendent, 12, 24.

County superintendent, 38.

County commissioners, 65.

Court of Common Pleas, 22, 41, 42, 65, 68, 99, 129, 163.

Cowles, Giles, 131.

Cressy, Mary, 165.

Cumberland Presbyterian Church, 156.

Curtis, Hosmer, 132.

Cutler, Ephraim, 7, 8, 9, 10, 15.

Cutler, Manasseh, 6, 7, 110.

Cuyahoga County, 134, 135, 140, 144, 145, 166, 167, 168, 169, 171, 173, 175.

Cuyahoga Falls, 38.

Cuyahoga Falls Institute, 81, 138.

Cuyahoga Falls Lyceum, 175.

D

Dane Law Library, 170.

Darby Creek Lyceum and Library Association, 171.

Darke County, 169.

Darke County Library Society, 169.

Darke County Medical Society, 162.

Darrotown Library Company, 171.

Dart, Ashbel, 133.

Davis, Louis, 159.

Dayton, 45, 46, 49, 78, 105, 124, 141; population of, 45, 46; schools of, 49.

Dayton Academy, 78, 128.

Dayton Female Association, 165.

Dayton Library, 167.

Dayton Library Association, 166.

Dayton Library Society, 110.

Dayton Mechanics' Institute, 176.

Parma Library Association, 171.
Paw, George, 143.
Pay school, 13–15.
Pease, John P., 145.
Peddling, 123.
Peak, U. H., 134.
Penfield Library Society, 170.
Penfield Township, 170.
Pennsylvania, 60.
Pennsylvania Synod, 156.
Perkins, Samuel, 141.
Perkins, Simon, 136.
Permanent funds, 31–32.
Perry County, 130, 144.
Perrysburgh, 157.
Perrysburgh Lyceum and Library Association, 172.
Peru Lyceum, 175.
Pestalozzi, 85.
Phi Delta Society of Western Reserve, 177.
Philbrick, S. B., 145.
Philomathean Literary Institute, 81, 135.
Philomathean Society of Ohio University, 81, 177.
Philomathesian Society of Kenyon College, 112, 177.
Philosophic Literary Society of Franklin College, 177.
Philomathean Literary Society of Monroe Academy, 177.
Phouts, David, 164.
Phylozethian Society of Western Reserve College, 177.
Physic, 93, 160.
Piatt, Benjamin, 161.
Picket, Robert, 107.
Pike County, 169.
Pine Grove Academy, 82, 139.
Piqua, 125.
Pittsburg, Pa., 63.
Plain, 173.
Platonic Library Society, 166, 171.
Poland Library Society, 166.
Pomeroy, Charles R., 142.
Pomeroy Academy, 83, 142.

Poor children, schools for, 105, 125.
Poor Richard, 8.
Portage County, 125, 129, 135, 136, 140, 141, 151, 166, 167, 170.
Porter, 139.
Portsmouth, 46, 48, 124, 176; schools of, 48–49.
Portsmouth Library Company, 172.
Portsmouth Mechanics' Institute and Mechanics' Library Association, 176.
Port Washington Lyceum and Library Company, 171.
Potter, Lyman, 129.
Preble County, 136, 167, 169.
Preble County Library Society, 167.
Presbyterian Church, 84, 142, 151.
Primary Schools, 51.
Prince, David, 145.
Profanity, 122.
Professional education, Acts concerning, 191–194.
Protestant Episcopal Church, 150, 165.
Protestant Methodist Academy of Brighton, 82, 139.
Protestant University of the United States, 97, 157.
Providence College, 97, 156.
Psi Gamma Society of Marietta College, 177.
Public Schools, 121.
Public School system, Methods of common school support, 28–38; organization of, 17–28.
Putnam, Rufus, 88, 146.
Putnam Classical Institute, 79, 134.
Putnam Family Library, 110.
Putnam Lyceum, 178.

Q

Quakers, 84. See also Friends.

R

Ravenna, 124.
Ravenna Academy, 79, 132.
Ravenna Female Seminary, 81, 138.
Ravenna Library Association, 173.
Rawson, Secretary, 133.